5 —

The New York Times
World of New York

Other Books Edited by
A. M. Rosenthal and Arthur Gelb

The New York Times

World of New York

An Uncommon Guide
to the City of Fantasies

EDITED BY **A. M. Rosenthal and Arthur Gelb**
IN ASSOCIATION WITH **Marvin Siegel**

Library of Congress Cataloging-in-Publication Data
Main entry under title:

World of New York.

"These articles originally appeared in the New York times"—T.p. verso.
  1. New York (N.Y.)—Addresses, essays, lectures.
2. New York (N.Y.)—Description—1981-   —Guidebooks.
I. Rosenthal, A. M. (Abraham Michael).
1922-   . II. Gelb, Arthur, 1924-   . III. Siegel,
Marvin.
F128.35.W67 1985   917.47'10443   85-24687
ISBN 0-8129-1262-4

Designed by Janis Capone
Illustrations by Rosanne Percivalle

Manufactured in the United States of America

9 8 7 6 5 4 3 2

First Edition

Owing to limitations of space, this copyright page is continued on pages 497–98.

Contents

PART I. Metropolis of the Mind

....

PART 2. 9 P.M. to 5 A.M.

....

PART 3. The City Romantic

....

PART 6. Feasting

···

PART 7. The Other Boroughs

···

Introduction

Of course, it must be understood that this particular travel book is a fantasy. It is a poem written in the late hours of the night, a great collage thrown together by a hundred mad artists, a young woman's dream on a spring evening, a traveler's alabaster mirage, a pauper's vision of golden hills, a violin in the memories of the ear, trumpets of the mind.

In this book of fantasy, a long white limousine has a name and is allowed out only at night to drive palely through broken-down streets to vast spaces where people dance in abandon and walk about in strange costumes and say, "Look at me, look at me."

People go to great museums and see the masterpieces of the ages and then rush down to step out to feed on delicacies from Indonesia and China and Greece, to choose dishes from Rome and Athens and Moscow.

Others in the dream city play chess in the hot streets, a few feet from erotic billboards and pimps and prostitutes. Young men make huge fortunes in a few days—and do not lose them, but build gardens in the sky or palaces on the beach. Men and women come from all over the world to visit this most visited of cities and from everywhere young people come to stay and become actors and writers and financiers. Many, indeed, do, and then ride the white limousine. Others fail, but know they will succeed eventually, and, of course, they will, they will, perhaps.

"New York is the city of rampant creativity, of abundant imagination, whether you are in advertising or the theater or the stock market. They are all fields built on imagination, the spinning of ideas and creations, of fantasy becoming reality. It is everything."

An explorer said that, an explorer of the mind, a psychiatrist, and he is quoted in these pages. So are actors and cooks and stockbrokers and poets and lovers and priests, and most of them say the same thing as they talk about what they do—I am here because this is my dream of life, my fantasy of all the world rolled together, and I am in the center.

In this book another group of dreamers—journalists and critics and essayists—have set down what they know of a part of the fantasy of New York. One writes about the bookstores of New York, another of dancing until three A.M. and then, inevitably, riding the ferryboat.

There are pieces about the past of New York and the future, but mostly of the present—walking the sidewalks, discovering the treasures of sculpture and painting and music, finding romance in a department store, hunting for chic clothes and chic celebrities, discovering the hidden places of the dream city.

There are wise little pieces and lists telling the reader how and where to discover the foods of the city, the music, the paintings, the dancing. There is caviar in this book and bagels, lox and champagne, and often in the city they are eaten together.

This book originated in a magazine published by *The New*

York Times—The World of New York—a semiannual. The magazine was fattened, enriched, until it grew into a nice, plump, dreamy but quite useful book.

There are terrible problems in New York City, but most of them are not reflected here. This is the rest of the city, but at least as much a part of the city as crime and an elbow in the ribs.

This book is a celebration of our city and written for two kinds of people—New Yorkers and the sophisticated traveler to our city of fantasies.

A. M. R. & A. G.

PART I

Metropolis of the Mind

CHAPTER I

....

Metropolis of the Mind

BY SAMUEL G. FREEDMAN

A beggar staggers up the aisle of the Broadway local subway and into the next car. In his wake sits a woman reading *One Hundred Years of Solitude,* by Gabriel García Márquez, the Colombian Nobel laureate. On a sidewalk off Times Square, near a souvlaki stand and a pornographic bookstore, ten men bend over five chessboards. A window is thrown open on a warm night and the sound of someone playing the English horn wafts in. It is impossible to know its source—lights burn in dozens of nearby apartment windows. And in a sense, that sound has no single origin; it is born out of New York itself.

These are scenes—snapshots, if you will—of the intellectual life of a city, New York City. This life of the mind is not a graft on the metropolitan body; it is something organically, naturally, often anonymously part of the constitution of New York. It is the contrast, or perhaps the coexistence, between life ascendant and life descendant: chess next to pornography, a book and a beggar. It is that English horn music, moving on the air like a transparent streamer, as much a part of the urban atmosphere as oxygen.

Certainly, there is a public face to intellectual accomplishment in this city. The intellectual life here has its rituals, like museum openings, and its venues, like Elio's Restaurant. There are professional philosophers and critics who by their presence give definition to the proper noun New York Intellectual. But those people, places, and events represent only the surface stratum of something deeper. Intellectual life in New York is not some sort of private club, a cerebral speakeasy where a panel slides open in a door and you whisper, "Kierkegaard sent me."

Rather, it is a range of mental endeavor—sinology and sculpture, poetry and particle physics—and it is a rich and polyglot marketplace of lectures, galleries, museums, plays, concerts, libraries, films, and, of course, dinner parties. It is the casual way great minds have always moved through the landscape: Thomas Wolfe stalking the streets of Brooklyn, Sonny Rollins practicing his saxophone on the Williamsburg Bridge. It is a painter named Mizue Sawano, who has gone to the Brooklyn Botanic Garden once a week for several years to sit with her easel beside the Lily Pools. The lily pads there remind her of Monet's lily pads, she says, and they inspire her own art. All this amounts to a kind of aura. Stephen Tim, director of scientific affairs at the Brooklyn Botanic Garden, has found an analogy in his studies. "The process is osmosis," he explains. "You absorb the intellectual life, the culture. Without even consciously learning from it, you are stimulated by it. It is almost a passive thing that happens. You cannot stop it."

Culture and intellect not only transform the individual,

they give identity to the mass, to the city as a whole. In his book *The Art of the City: Views and Versions of New York,* Peter Conrad writes, "Every city requires its own myth to justify its presumption of centrality," and he goes on to cite artistic annotators of New York, from the songwriter George M. Cohan to the painter Saul Steinberg, whose famous cover for *The New Yorker* suggests an earth largely occupied by Manhattan. Alexander Alland, Jr., the chairman of the anthropology department at Columbia University, puts the myth into words: "The intellectual life is why I am a New Yorker. It's why I stay here. I spend my summers in Europe, and when they ask me if I'm an American, I say, 'No, I'm a New Yorker.' I don't know about everyone else, but for me that's a positive statement."

New York began its rise to intellectual primacy in the 1850s. It is easy now to forget that throughout the Colonial era and the early nineteenth century, New York was at best the third city of the nation, behind Boston and Philadelphia. What shifted the gravity was the migration of the publishing industry to New York from Boston. Initially, the publishers were simply seeking more customers—New York had the largest population—but their relocation set off a chain reaction that deeply altered the city. With publishing houses came writers and editors and illustrators. Meanwhile, the city had begun to change in other ways. At the top of the New York economic scale, the captains of commerce and industry began to endow museums and to support individual artists; at the bottom, each wave of immigrants enriched and diversified the intellectual community. City College, established in 1849, acted as the great pedagogue for those without wealth and came to be known as "the poor man's Harvard." As more creative people lived in New York, even more were drawn to it. Scale is the key word: The number of college graduates living in New York City today—777,000—collectively would constitute the eleventh-largest city in the United States. With size comes sustenance for all sorts of specialized intellectual communities. Greenwich Village became an urban version of the artists' colony, a home to creators of all stripes, the neighborhood that gave Eugene O'Neill a stage in the 1920s (at the Provincetown Playhouse) and Bob Dylan a bandstand in the 1960s (at Folk City). Miles uptown, Harlem has been home in this century to a black intelligentsia that has included the writers Langston Hughes, James Weldon Johnson, James Baldwin, and Ralph Ellison, the political theorist W. E. B. Du Bois, and the photographer James Van Der Zee, whose record of his era appeared decades later in the striking album *Harlem on My Mind*. New York supports a museum of holography and a museum of dogs; it supports Yiddish theater and a Haitian newspaper. The Cathedral of St. John the Divine maintains a poet's corner, and the staff of Montefiore Hospital Medical Center includes a philosopher in residence. The whole notion of pop culture versus high culture is rendered almost meaningless, because the esoteric can enjoy a mass audience: Such demanding playwrights and composers as Tom Stoppard and Stephen Sondheim can have hit plays on Broadway, while a gospel-music version of *Oedipus at Colonus*—could anything seem more unlikely?—can become a sold-out sensation at the Brooklyn Academy of Music.

Intellectual life also commingles with political life. From A. Okey Hall, the hack figurehead for Boss Tweed, to Edward I. Koch, New York's mayors have often doubled as authors. Governor Mario Cuomo, a native of Queens, has written two books, and he spices his speeches with knowing references to Thomas More and Teilhard de Chardin. Before Senator Daniel Patrick Moynihan was a politician he was a respected and provocative academic. A debate on a thirty-year-old issue—whether or not Julius and Ethel Rosenberg were Soviet spies—still fills Town Hall and is argued with ferocity.

Like politics, religion in New York is a matter not only of passion or rote, but also of intellectual rigor. There are eleven Roman Catholic colleges in the city; there is an Islamic seminary on Queens Boulevard. And in the *shtibels*—the houses of study—of Crown Heights and Flatbush and the Upper West Side, Hasidim gather to carry on theological debates that are centuries old. The Society of Ethical Culture and Fieldston, its affiliated school in Riverdale, similarly provide education, advocacy, and a sense of community for nonbelievers. The intellectual force of New York sends ripples far beyond the city. The principal network news in the United States originates not from the nation's capital but from New York. The Associated Press news service is based here. Two major news magazines, *Time* and *Newsweek*, and two national newspapers, *The New York Times* and *The Wall Street Journal*, are published here. Most of the leading critics of theater, film, art, dance, and music make their pronouncements from Manhattan. And from the time Walt Whitman published *Leaves of Grass* in 1855, artists have been bards of New York. Whitman is the common ancestor in an artistic family that includes novelist Theodore Dreiser and photographer Alfred Stieglitz, painter Ben Shahn and poet Delmore Schwartz, composer Duke Ellington and film maker Woody Allen, Diane Arbus, photographer of the bizarre, and Martin Scorsese, director of *Mean Streets, Taxi Driver,* and *New York, New York.* These artists have drawn on New York for subject matter, and their work, in turn, has informed the world's impression of the city.

But the point here is not name-dropping. Without any of those figures, important as they are, intellectual life in New York would proceed with just as much vigor. It is, remember, largely a private and a personal affair. Manifested in individual taste and style, at its heart it has very little to do with either celebrity or vogue.

"When I see a movie like *Manhattan,*" says Mr. Alland of Columbia University, "that's not my world. I don't know if such people really exist, and if they do I'm not interested in them except as some curious sort of aborigines." For Mr. Alland, intellectual life means spending every Friday at the Metropolitan Museum of Art. For his wife, Sonia, it means playing flute in an amateur orchestra that performs every other Sunday in the couple's Chelsea loft. There is a difference, Mr. Alland points out, between a scholar and an intellectual. One is a brilliant specialist, sealed inside a single discipline; the other is eclectic, a searcher.

The intellectual sweep of New York allows almost unparalleled opportunities for eclecticism, for search and discovery. Flora Roberts, for instance, is a literary agent. Her clients include Stephen Sondheim, Maya Angelou, and Tina Howe, and her work situates her at high levels of the literary and theatrical worlds. But her passions lie elsewhere. "For me, there are two great thrills," she says. "One is going to Carnegie Hall to hear Marilyn Horne doing Rossini. The other is looking at a Goya. I grew up in New York, and I remember when I first heard Laurence Olivier scream in *Oedipus.* I think of that audience at *Death of a Salesman* leaping up out of their seats to try to keep Lee J. Cobb from killing himself. In New York, there's this marriage of feeling."

There is also a marriage of ideas. A thinker need not remain in solitude; there are circles and networks to challenge assumptions and hypotheses while supporting the act of inquiry. Dr. Bruce Yaffe's is a characteristic story. In 1981, Dr. Yaffe realized that he never got to talk about politics with knowledgeable people the same way he could talk about, oh, ulcer disease with his fellow digestive-tract specialists. So he placed a want ad in the *New York Review of Books*, looking for partners in a regular discussion group. And from that time on, Dr. Yaffe and his wife, Karen, have held a seminar every other Monday in their Upper East Side apartment. The topics have ranged from Sino-Soviet relations to evaluating public education, and in the course of collecting ammunition for the debates, the Yaffes have taken subscriptions to 150 magazines. "The mailman came up to our apartment once," Dr. Yaffe says. "He said he wanted to see who we were."

In the Yaffe apartment the going often gets, let us say, spirited. The couple had forty-three people—a record for their living room—for a discussion of the Falkland Islands war. They brought Soviet diplomats and exiled Soviet dissidents to the same symposium on internal problems in Russia, which predictably raised the decibel level. At a session on United States policy in Central America, a writer from a conservative magazine opined that Fidel Castro sought to export revolution throughout the region. "And then," Dr. Yaffe recalls, "some sixty-year-old Cuban businessman in the corner said, 'My dear, that's wrong. When Fidel and I were considering our plans in the hills of Cuba, that was the farthest thing from our minds.' "

A more public hub of intellectual activity is a great bookstore, and in New York the Strand is arguably the best. Occupying a former clothing store at Broadway and East 12th Street in Manhattan, the Strand carries some two million volumes, of such vast variety that on a single table the tomes range from *The Sonata Since Beethoven* to *Civil Aircraft of the World*. Over the years, the Strand has counted among its regular customers writers Anaïs Nin and Saul Bellow; Senator Mark Hatfield; David Hockney, the painter; and William J. Casey, Director of Central Intelligence. Zero Mostel, the comedian, once extemporized in the rare-book department on the relative artistic merits of the Mexican painters Diego Rivera and David Siqueiros. Fred Bass, the Strand's owner, recalls eavesdropping on an argument between two customers about whether Douglas R. Hofstadter's *Gödel, Escher, Bach* or Martin Heidegger's *Being and Time* was more difficult to read. His employees, typically writers or musicians, have included poet Tom Weatherly (Americana aisle) and poet/rock singer Patti Smith (typist). "I always consider that after graduating from Columbia," says Craig Anderson, a supervisor in the rare-book department, "the Strand is where I really got my education."

Nancy Graves pursued her education at Vassar and Yale and her studies in painting in Paris and Florence. For all that, her move to New York in 1966 was to affect her art profoundly. "I couldn't sleep for my first two weeks here," she recalls. "I remember the energy and the hostility. The chaos. I enjoy it. The anonymity, even. You may have a career and be somewhat visible in your field and yet have the sense of a private life."

Certainly few of the vendors in the flower district along the Avenue of the Americas recognize Miss Graves as an artist who has had several national exhibitions when she comes to buy dried vegetables. Nor do the shopkeepers in China-

town, her source for lotus root and fans, or the cashiers at
Balducci's, where she gets brussels sprouts. These are not
the makings of dinner or some sort of talisman; they are
among the organic bits of New York that Miss Graves uses
in the direct casting for her sculptures. She has also drawn
on the industrial resources of the city—the foundry that
casts her work—and on its academic sector. When she made
a film about the moon as a personal art project, she conducted research at Columbia University; when she did a
series of sculptures on a fossil theme, she studied the fossil
collections at the American Museum of Natural History.
And, again, there are the circles: Miss Graves numbers
many dancers among her friends; she serves on the board of
the Mabou Mines theater troupe. "The fact of being in New
York allows people to contact you," she says. "It's not just
artists reaching out, but others reaching in."

In fact, artists tend, to an enormous degree, to define the re-
surgent neighborhoods of the city. When Miss Graves first
moved to SoHo a decade ago, "it was hard to get cabs to go
there." Now the neighborhood is established and expensive,
so much so that she often longs for some place a little more
"ethnic and sociological." Younger artists already are advanc-
ing on a new set of frontiers. They are moving downtown, to
an area variously referred to as Alphabetland. Alphabetville,
or Alphabet City (Avenue A, B, C, and so forth on the Lower
East Side of Manhattan), across the Hudson to Hoboken and
Jersey City, across the East River to Greenpoint and Williamsburg, and to a part of Brooklyn they simply call DUMBO, for
Down Under Manhattan Bridge Overpass. Its first Häagen-
Dazs store cannot be far off.

If artists define much of the New York landscape, geographically and intellectually, then so, emphatically, do im-

migrants and refugees. The German influx of 1848, the Irish flight from famine, migrations of Jews, Italians, Greeks, Chinese, Koreans, and Vietnamese—all have brought knowledge and culture from abroad to New York, making an American city cosmopolitan. In 1933, the New School for Social Research acknowledged that rich resource by founding the University in Exile (now the Graduate Faculty of Political and Social Science) as a graduate school to be staffed by European scholars who escaped the Nazi regime. The international dynamic continues today, with the Soviet Jews of Brighton Beach, with the West Indians of Jamaica, with the Southeast Asians of Elmhurst, with Iranians like Bahman Maghsoudlou.

Until 1979, when he went into self-exile from the theocracy of the Ayatollah Ruhollah Khomeini, Mr. Maghsoudlou was a leading film scholar in Iran. Now he is one of perhaps four thousand Iranians living in New York; Mr. Maghsoudlou's own estimate is that 90 percent of Iran's artists have fled the nation since the Iranian revolution. His words are a reminder of what America and New York still mean. "It is a country of dreams, a city of dreams, to everybody all over the world," Mr. Maghsoudlou says. "Whatever happens anywhere in the world—if it is violent revolution, if it is radical change, if it is disaster— intellectuals of those countries rush to America. In our own countries, we cannot paint, write, put on a play—whatever. Here you have freedom of expression. You can lecture. You can say what you want."

Predictably, life for the Iranian intelligentsia has not been entirely easy here. Mr. Maghsoudlou has done fairly well for himself, operating a film-distribution company, studying at Columbia, writing a book on Iranian cinema. However, he also knows a film director who is driving a cab and other intellectuals who are working as doormen. But on Thursday nights, this community in exile convenes in midtown Manhattan at the Bombay Cinema (normally an Indian theater, as its name suggests), where Mr. Maghsoudlou shows Iranian films.

"The films provide the only regular Iranian gathering in a public place," Mr. Maghsoudlou says. "It is the only place Iranian intellectuals can meet, can talk. It is our rendezvous place."

The same process is slowly occurring, too, with the Polish intellectuals who have clustered in New York since martial law was declared in their homeland in December 1981. Janusz Glowacki is a journalist, novelist, and playwright whose Kafkaesque tragicomedy, *Cinders*, was mounted by the New York Shakespeare Festival. Like Mr. Maghsoudlou, Mr. Glowacki is grappling with the mix of freedom and foreignness that New York connotes. No longer does he write with the fear of censorship; but on the other hand, New York's world of agents and grant applications is strange. And crime, particularly a murder in his apartment building, has been shocking.

But Mr. Glowacki has his circle of expatriate Polish writers and professors. And his apartment building in Washington Heights is home to other Poles, too—an actress, a stage designer, various Solidarity sympathizers. Mr. Glowacki calls the building an *akademia*, the Polish word for an academy. "The first task of a man when he is in exile," he says, "is to survive. I am starting from the beginning again. I worry, will my book sell, will I make any money. Different world. All of it. But maybe this *akademia* will replace some of what we had in Poland."

That Broadway local subway; the one with the beggar and the woman reading *One Hundred Years of Solitude*, ran to South Ferry in lower Manhattan. Not far from there, wedged in amid the towers of Wall Street, sits Our Lady of Victory Church, where Father George Rutler is a priest. Although he ministers to the men and women of the financial district, he himself rejected the consumer society they serve when he chose the collar. He is, moreover, someone who might have good reason to abhor New York. A man of faith and of ideas, who reads Greek and Hebrew, who speaks French and Italian and Latin, who talks knowingly of the writings of C. S. Lewis and G. K. Chesterton, he is surrounded by sin. He has gazed out the window of his study to see cocaine sales transpiring in the alley below; if some New Yorkers can pooh-pooh such commerce, it deeply disturbs Father Rutler. New York, he says, has put a tangible face on the theological idea of Satan.

But as much as Janusz Glowacki or Nancy Graves, Father Rutler finds intellectual stimulation in the city, finds his circles: in the conservative Roman Catholic theological body Opus Dei or in conversation with a fellow Dartmouth graduate who stops in occasionally to discuss St. Augustine—in French.

And there are times, in the evenings and on weekends when Wall Street is deserted, when Father Rutler takes his daily hour of meditation in the form of a solitary run. And in the silence, paradoxically, the city becomes a stimulating and catalytic place. "When you see all the misery of this city," Father Rutler says, "it makes the grandeur of it stand out in greater relief. When you see the skyline of New York at night, it's the closest thing we've invented to the medieval depictions of the heavenly Jerusalem."

CHAPTER 2

·····································

The New York Syndrome

BY DANIEL GOLEMAN

Why do they come to New York anyway, those talented, ambitious, single-minded achievers who could have it so much easier back home? What psychological needs compel them to put up with the tigerish competition, the insatiable demands, the push and shove of the city? What inner forces drive them to risk everything in the one place where they can really become—as the swaggering song that has virtually become an anthem of New York says—"king of the hill, top of the heap"?

The questions are psychological ones; the answers, complex and subtle. But they are hardly questions of minor consequence. The city of New York, after all, has flourished by appealing to the psychological needs of those who have come here in the hope of remaking themselves on some grander scale. Indeed, the stream of talented people drawn to New York has been the city's ongoing strength, and it is essential to the prosperity of New York that it continue to tap that stream. Thus, to understand the psychodynamics of this attraction is to understand the true heart of the city itself. No psychiatrist as yet has labeled the constellation of needs that propels talented people to New York a "syndrome," but the term seems apt. We are investigating, after all, an observable condition with an identifiable set of psychological causes and signs.

Many of the city's leading psychotherapists have become authorities on this syndrome because they see aspects of it every day in their offices. In reflecting on the psychodynamics of this syndrome, these therapists are, to some degree, analyzing their own lives, since they themselves have chosen to be part of the most competitive and stimulating psychoanalytic arena in the world today. In this way, New York's therapists may be doubly qualified to offer insights into the motivations that lead people to take on New York.

The assumption is widespread that such competitive drives must be neurotic. Certainly, the syndrome can be an expression of a neurotic push toward a fraudulent "success" that is all semblance and no substance. But New York's therapists are convinced that the condition can be a decidedly healthy one as well, reflecting strengths of the ego in the sense that Freud meant the term: the part of the psyche that comes to terms with reality by transforming raw impulse into creativity and a wholesome drive for fulfillment.

New Yorkers differ from one another in a multitude of ways, but so many share the same autobiographical tale that it has become almost mythic. With countless variations and nuances, The Story goes something like this:

An able young man (or woman, of course) feels the need to leave home. Perhaps he feels misunderstood and unappreciated, surrounded by what Eugene O'Neill called "spiritual middle-classers." He yearns to escape these small-town minds and to be among people with broader vision. Perhaps he simply wants to reinvent himself by shedding the identities and labels of his childhood and youth. Or perhaps he has a dream, an aspiration too great to be realized at home. He feels imprisoned, be it in Sioux City or the Bronx. He believes that only in a great urban center like Manhattan will he find people who can understand his strivings and applaud who he is and what he has to offer. So he goes there, and whether or not his dreams are realized even partially, he eventually feels the city has spoiled him for any other place. Despite the pressure, the pace, and the grime of New York, he has the sense there of being alive. In his heart he has come to agree with the unabashed sentiment of Jimmy Walker: "I'd rather be a lamppost in New York than the Mayor of Chicago."

In reality, of course, it is possible in some degree to find in other places what New York City offers. Certainly, excellence in medicine, art, the law, entertainment, business, and education can be found elsewhere. But the New York striver has come to believe that nowhere else in the world is there a city with such a profusion of excellence and genius, such an abundance of alternatives and possibilities. And so for him success in New York symbolizes the success of successes— "If you can make it there, you can make it anywhere."

In *From Death to Morning,* the writer Thomas Wolfe tried to capture the magic of this quest: "The great vision of the city is burning in your heart in all its enchanted colors just as it did when you were twelve years old and thought about it. You think that some glorious happiness of fortune, fame and triumph will be yours at any minute, that you are about to take your place among great men and lovely women in a life more fortunate and happy than any you have ever known—that it is all here, somehow, waiting for you. . . ."

Many New Yorkers harbor the memory of a single, vivid episode that stands out as the epitome of just what is in the city, somehow, waiting for them. To the psychoanalyst, such special moments from the past are known as "screen memories," episodes in life that are striking because they carry a special psychological meaning.

Take, for example, the episode recalled by Dr. Gerald Fogel, a training and supervising analyst at the Columbia University Psychoanalytic Center. "I grew up in Detroit and came to New York the summer just after I graduated from high school," he says. "I remember the first weekend I spent in New York as a sixteen-year-old, with my friends. We arrived on a Sunday evening, checked into a midtown hotel, and then went walking around town. And there, a few blocks away at a jazz club, was Dave Brubeck, playing on a Sunday night. And I could walk in off the street and see him at midnight on a Sunday. Sunday at midnight! I couldn't conceive of such a thing—it was like heaven.

"When I look at myself now, I realize my interest in jazz as an adolescent stood for other kinds of aspirations. The idea of jazz, James Dean, Marlon Brando, and all that signified a freedom, social and sexual, from the kinds of inhibitions a shy adolescent feels.

"New York meant all that. It was the place where the action was. It had all of it: the sophistication and freedom, the underside of life, the vitality. It had all the seductive allure of a place you could do things you could not do anywhere else."

It is that allure, in one form or another, that draws people to the city in what is typically a radical break from home and past.

Psychiatrists say that the move away from home is a key step in psychological development. It marks the break between the person one has been as a child and the person one will become as an adult. "The classic psychoanalytic notion is that to express your autonomy, to become your own person, you have to leave home, if only psychologically," Dr. Fogel says. "Home, in this sense, stands for that part of the self that keeps you inhibited and limited. Some people have to go far away to make the break. To become someone else, they seek out people unlike members of their own family. That is why some people marry out of their religion or social class—they feel they can be sexually freer with someone who does not belong to their own group. For a person from a small town or another part of the country, New York may have that same exotic attraction."

Dr. Ethel Person is director of the Columbia University Psychoanalytic Center, one of New York's principal institutes for training psychoanalysts. When she was a twelve-year-old in Kentucky, she decided that she was meant to live in New York City even though she had never been there. "Leaving home lets you reinvent yourself," Dr. Person says. "For me, the quintessential New Yorker is someone who came to Manhattan—or stays here—by choice, to do just that.

"I like to be with people who don't know who I was when I was seventeen years old. In New York you have that lovely double thing: the anonymity to experiment with new identities and the chance to tie in to people who share those interests. Those people are your truer family. New York is the city par excellence of invented families.

"A lot of people leave for New York because their particular gifts or way of being in the world make them misfits where they are," Dr. Person explains. "In my generation, which grew up in the 1950s, it was the woman who didn't want to follow the traditional role of just being a wife and homemaker, who wanted a career of her own. A more contemporary equivalent might be a woman who wants to be a mother, but who does not want to be married. That would be no picnic among people with small-town attitudes, but there would be more support for it here in the city."

But why, of all cities, should someone be drawn to New York in particular?

"Every city has its personality, its unique style that will attract its own to it," says Dr. James Hillman, a well-known Jungian analyst who for many years was director of training at the C. G. Jung Institute in Zurich. In keeping with Jungian thought, which deals freely in archetypes and myth, Dr. Hillman sees the pull of the city in terms of a larger psychological dimension.

"Dallas, where I lived for a while, is for people in the fast lane, people concerned with consuming," Dr. Hillman says. "It pulls to it those who are already Dallas types. Whether they be in Illinois or Pennsylvania, they are meant for Dallas.

"Likewise, New York draws the cosmopolite, the person who wants to be challenged the most, who needs the most varied and rich stimulation. It is the person who is full of possibilities, but who needs New York to draw them out of him. You come to New York to find the ambience that will evoke your best. You do not necessarily know precisely what that might be, but you come to New York to discover it.

"If there were a god of New York, it would be the Greek's

Hermes, the Roman's Mercury," suggests Dr. Hillman. "He embodies New York qualities: the quick exchange, the fastness of language and style, craftiness, the mixing of people and crossing of borders, imagination.

"New York is the city of rampant creativity, of abundant imagination, whether you are in advertising or the theater or the stock market. They are all fields built on imagination, the spinning of ideas and creations, of fantasy becoming reality. It is everything. Any syndrome that might characterize another city is found in New York: manic energy, depression and hopelessness, the extreme excitement of the hysteric, the anger of the paranoid. Psychologically, New York is the complete city." There are many—too many—who are drawn to the city only to end up depressed by it, hating it, even destroyed by it. But the person who fits the syndrome is, archetypally, someone who is exhilarated by the intensity of the city's challenges, who is invigorated rather than defeated by them.

"New York is a city that loves what has been called the 'Type A' personality: always feeling the press of time, aggressive and competitive, a workaholic, dedicated to achievement," says Dr. Anthony Zito, a psychiatrist who numbers among his patients many artists and performers. Dr. Zito, who also is engaged in research on the mechanisms of stress, adds, "This is the Type A's town. There is a common breed here who prefer that intense level of stimulation, who seek the greater challenge. For them, it's not stressful—it's the level of action they prefer. They are unhappy without it. That need is a defining quality of the New Yorker." The Type A pattern was first identified as an indicator of susceptibility to heart disease. The original research suggested that while it might make people highly successful, it could also kill them. Subsequent studies, however, have focused on determining what makes some people with this hard-driving pattern more hardy, and thus able to thrive under pressure that might make others more prone to coronary disease. It is important, Dr. Zito observes, that people match their preferred level of activity with their environment.

"Because of its pace, this city offers more of a challenge to the person who dares take it on," Dr. Zito says. "He knows that if he fails, he will get plowed under. That kind of risky challenge appeals particularly to the person who seeks to define himself through his achievements."

Why come to compete in New York City rather than settle for success in a smaller venue? In the view of those psychotherapists who are familiar with the syndrome, the intense drive to compete and succeed on the grandest scale is of primary psychological importance. From the clinical perspective, that kind of person falls in the category of "narcissist." The negative connotations the term holds in lay understanding are unfortunate, psychologists say, because to some degree a streak of narcissism is essential for mental well-being and is particularly necessary for success.

"The concept of narcissism, to put it simply, refers to self-love, or self-esteem," says Dr. Robert Michels, chairman of the department of psychiatry at Cornell University Medical College and psychiatrist-in-chief at the Payne Whitney Clinic. "One of the key psychological themes of human life is the need to feel proud of yourself. A great many achievements are motivated by that desire. In that way, narcissism can be one of the things that leads a person to success.

"Its origins are linked in early development with parental

regard and approval, the desire to be the kind of person you believe your parents like and approve of. As you grow up, that becomes an internal psychological reality rather than an interpersonal one: You desire to be the kind of person you yourself hold in high regard. In its healthy form, that can lead you to many accomplishments. Take the case of someone in a small town who recognizes he has great talents. The person with a healthy dose of narcissism would seek the environment that would allow him to maximize his potential, and so may leave for a city like New York.

"The boundary between normal and pathologic depends on whether one's pursuit of success actually leads to enhanced performance or simply is in the service of a psychological hunger that can never be gratified," Dr. Michels says. "People who are hungry for applause are never satisfied with the reality of their feats. They feel an ever-present yearning; the praise is never enough to appease what is, unconsciously, a craving for the total approval from the infant's mother. But the infant's mother is never there, in reality. That moment is past, and there never was such a thing as total approval, by definition. They are left seeking something they can never find.

"Still, you have got to have a bit of narcissism to succeed. To some extent healthy narcissism is one of the key motives in achievement. In order to achieve, one has to work, one has to pride oneself, to put off gratifications. All those things require a strong, healthy narcissistic pleasure in the rewards of success, and a willingness to pay the multiple prices to get that success."

As Dr. Michels suggests, a related ingredient for success is the capacity to work, and to work hard. Lionel Trilling once noted how, in past centuries, people were thought to be driven by pleasure, while in modern times people seem to be more driven by a sense of self-worth, for which they will forgo all kinds of pleasures. If any city epitomizes that ethic, it is New York.

From the psychoanalytic perspective, this drive for a higher satisfaction entails some degree of masochism, not in the sexual sense, but in the psychological meaning of the term: the taking of pleasure from painful sacrifice and intense work.

"This need for mastery requires great pain and sacrifice, but it offers another order of satisfaction, not what we ordinarily think of as pleasure," says Dr. Arnold Cooper, a psychoanalyst who has written about the psychodynamics of this variety of masochism and how it interacts with narcissism. "It is like a person who runs a marathon and feels great pleasure in the achievement afterward, while putting up with great pain during it.

"Bertrand Russell said toward the end of his life that the writing of his great treatise, the *Principia Mathematica*, had permanently damaged his brain. Whether apocryphal or not, the point is that he was not at all sorry he had done it. The process was painful and excruciating, but one he and the world would say was worth it."

Dr. Cooper adds, "The urge to be great is within the spectrum of healthy narcissism. That spectrum includes those who simply do their thing well and live productive lives. They don't dream they will write the Great American Novel; they are satisfied just doing their work. There is another group with higher aspirations. They work harder, push themselves a bit more, take fewer vacations. And finally there are the narcissists who really aspire to be great. Some of them really have talent, and it makes sense for them to aim that high. But some of them actually just want people to declare them great. They have no intention of doing the hard work that greatness takes. That is where pathological narcissism begins.''

Thus, the New York striver is usually the kind of person who is drawn to the city because it gives him the opportunity to make himself over in terms of excellence. At its best, the psychological drives involved are narcissistic in the healthy sense. In this case, the striver desires to assert his worth by displaying his talents, and he is willing to test himself through arduous efforts in order to find a place on the grand stage that the city offers.

And then there is the school of thought that holds that city life may be good for the soul.

''The city, in its mythic aspect, has traditionally been maligned as crushing the soul, while nature nourishes it,'' says Dr. Hillman, the Jungian analyst. ''I don't agree. I believe the city is good for the soul. In fact, it is as if there were a human need to have cities to manifest the richness, including the darkness, of human nature. In nature there is no human past, no trace of man's unique stamp, of his creativity. But the city, as Lewis Mumford put it, is a living work of art. It manifests the human imagination. The alive, pulsing city is the greatest artistic achievement of humankind.''

CHAPTER 3

Somewhere in New York, You Can Buy a Good Book

BY JAMES ATLAS

London has Charing Cross Road, Paris has its quays, and New York used to have Fourth Avenue, but those days are gone. Except for the Strand and one or two unpromising secondhand shops, the bookstores that once lined both sides of the avenue have disappeared, leaving the city without a geographic center for bibliophiles. If it's diamonds you want, go to West 47th Street; antiques are on Hudson Street, flowers on the Avenue of the Americas in the Twenties. But if you're looking for a copy of Ford Madox Ford's *Great Trade Route* or Frank Budgen's memoir of James Joyce, you can expect to spend the greater part of a day wandering up and down Manhattan.

This isn't necessarily such a bad thing. Bookstores tend to be in attractive parts of town (no doubt because their proprietors tend to have esthetic sensibilities), and one can do worse than spend a day going from the Upper West Side to Greenwich Village, down to SoHo, and over to St. Mark's

Place, then back up Madison Avenue by way of the Strand on Fourth Avenue. You still might not find what you were looking for, but you're unlikely to come home empty-handed. I never have—which is why books are piled up under chairs and couches all over my apartment.

New York is famous for its indifference to tradition. "One story is good only till another is told," Henry James complained in *The American Scene.* In no other world capital, he noted, does the new so pitilessly erase the old. Dauber & Pine on Lower Fifth Avenue is gone, as are those less ancient but venerable institutions, the Eighth Street Bookshop and the New Yorker on West 89th. The only "old" bookstores I know of in town are the Strand and the Gotham Book Mart, on West 47th Street. It's possible to waste a whole day in the Strand, so reminiscent of the bookshop in Orwell's *Keep the Aspidistra Flying,* where "novels lined the room on three sides ceiling-high, row upon row of gaudy oblong backs, as though the walls had been built of many-coloured bricks laid upright." Over eight miles of books, claims their ad, and I believe it. The shelves on the walls rise two stories, and the metal stacks in the back contain more novels, maybe, than have ever been written. (I was reassured once to find nine copies of *Herzog.* You couldn't have too many.) The Strand's high ceiling and dim light give it a cathedral gloom. Furtive patrons—why aren't they at work in the middle of the day?—browse in the devotional hush. Behind the dusty glass of locked mahogany shelves are rows of first editions; there are no "finds" at the Strand. People go there to paw among the remainder tables, where review copies peddled by indigent critics are half off. (Writers who can't resist looking for their own books are likely to find them, often copies lovingly inscribed to friends.) There is some pretense of organization, but the Strand invariably puts me in mind of Walter Benjamin's description in his essay, "Unpacking My Library" of that transitional moment when one's books are out of their boxes and piled up on the floor, "not yet touched by the mild boredom of order."

The Gotham, a crowded shop in the midst of the diamond district, has been around for decades. A blowup of the famous "Gotham Book Mart photograph" that appeared in *Life* in 1948 and has since been reproduced in so many biographies (the occasion was a party for Edith Sitwell) hangs in the back room; the keen literary eye can discern, among distinguished others, an unwrinkled Auden, a youngish Tennessee Williams, and a boyish Gore Vidal. Beneath it are tables of little magazines you won't find in B. Dalton—*Blue Pig, Bomb, Slow Loris Reader.* In the busy front room are old books, new books, a whole section devoted to works by and about Joyce, and the largest selection of contemporary poetry in New York.

But the Gotham's appeal to serious collectors is the serendipitous find. On my first visit there, when I was in college, I snapped up (if that's the right verb for such a recondite possession) a collection of English tributes to Proust brought out by Thomas Seltzer in 1923. "OP $7.50" was penciled in on the title page. A bargain? I couldn't say. But I went up to the cash register expecting it to be confiscated and locked away in the rare-editions cabinet.

There are a handful of other stores that carry modern first editions and old books worth owning, notably the Phoenix, at 22 Jones Street in the Village, which carries a good assortment of hard-to-find periodicals like *Furioso* and *Hound & Horn;* and the Gryphon, at 2246 Broadway, between 80th and 81st streets. But the trade is largely carried on through dealers these days; the books one used to chance upon—a first edition of *The Naked and the Dead*, a signed copy of Wyndham Lewis's *Apes of God*—are squirreled away in offices, under the vigilant eyes of men who know their worth.

Bibliophiles by their very natures have a perhaps excessive reverence for old books just because they're old, preferring an aura of dilapidation to the suspect authority of the new. But there are new bookstores in the city that manage to emulate a quaint old-fashioned shop even though they purvey only recent titles and paperbacks. The Endicott, on Columbus Avenue between 81st and 82nd streets, is only five years old, but its carpeted rooms and wood-paneled decor give it a dowdy comfort, and there's a couch in the back where no one minds if you loiter for a whole afternoon. Books & Company, on Madison Avenue just down from the Whitney Museum, has the air of a London bookshop; displayed in its small-paned window are signed copies of newly published books, and there's a gallery upstairs where readings and parties are held. Three Lives, on the corner of Waverly and 10th in the West Village, has only been in its new location for a few years, but it feels as if it's been there forever. Its stamped-tin ceiling, green-shaded lamps, and Persian rugs make it the coziest bookshop in New York.

But it's not decor that distinguishes these stores; it's what they stock. Both Three Lives and the Endicott have impressive selections of modern literature, and Books & Company boasts what is known as "The Wall," a long shelf of books by contemporary authors that contains just about every title in print (and quite a few that aren't). The buyers for these stores have clearly scoured publishers' catalogues to find out what's on their "backlist"—that is, what books they've reissued or kept in print. It's a pleasure to walk in and find, say, Boswell's *London Journal* or Leslie Marchand's biography of Byron—not exactly hot titles, I know, but there are people who get a sudden craving for them late at night.

The other things a good bookstore needs are a lot of magazines and a regular clientele. Spring Street Books and the St. Mark's Bookshop have both. The walls of these casual establishments are papered with notices of concerts and local readings, ads from psychics, apartments for rent, and furniture sales—a vestige of the '60s. Making my way through *The London Review of Books* in the St. Mark's one night, I had a sudden nostalgia for "the trough," as the magazine section of Reading International in Harvard Square was known; I'd whiled away a good decade in front of it. Then Allen Ginsberg walked in, and I remembered why I'd come to New York.

CHAPTER 4

....

Specialty Bookshops: A Browser's Guide

BY JAMES BARRON

New York is a city of readers, a place where people demand more than the best sellers. That is why New York, perhaps more than any other major American city, can support bookstores that concentrate on only one or two subjects. From mysteries to military affairs, these specialty bookshops cater to people who enjoy hunting down a good book almost as much as they enjoy reading it—customers who love to spend long weekend tours browsing for rarities, remainders, and those impossible-to-find titles.

Some of the city's specialty bookstores are new, some are musty, and some are out of the way—but not so far from the big, general-interest bookstores on Fifth Avenue between 48th and 57th streets.

More often than not, a booklover can walk in and talk to a clerk who knows all the titles in the store, and who knows precisely where each one has been shelved. Unlike some of the larger stores, specialty bookstores tend to order titles that do not sell in huge quantities—books that bigger shops never stock. At the specialty shops, customers snap up every copy.

Specialty shops set their prices according to their own formulas; some charge full cover prices, some far less. The owners say their profits tend to be slimmer than average in an industry known for the slimness of its profits; most specialty bookshops worry about increases in rent and postage (since most do a substantial part of their business by mail).

From paperback to hard-cover, remainders to rare edition, here is a look at some of the city's specialty bookshops.

STAGE, MOVIES, DANCE

Three bookshops are within easy walking distance of Manhattan's theater district: **Drama Bookshop,** on the second floor of 723 Seventh Avenue, at 48th Street (212-944-0595); **Theater Books,** on the third floor of 1576 Broadway, near 47th Street (212-757-2834); and **Theater Arts Bookshop,** 405 West 42nd Street (212-564-0402). The Drama Bookshop, with its uncluttered ultramodern design, and Theater Arts concentrate on new and in-print material, while the collection at Theater Books is more eclectic.

Drama Bookshop: Monday, Tuesday, Thursday, and Friday, 9:30 A.M. to 6 P.M.; Wednesday, 9:30 A.M. to 8 P.M.; Saturday, 10:30 A.M. to 5 P.M.; Sunday, closed. **Theater Books:** Monday through Friday, 10:30 A.M. to 6 P.M.; Saturday, noon to 5 P.M.; Sunday, closed. **Theater Arts Bookshop:** Monday through Saturday, 10 A.M. to 8 P.M.; Sunday, noon to 7 P.M.

Remember Archie Leach? **Richard Stoddard Performing**

Arts, at 90 East 10th Street (212-982-9440), does, and theater-trivia buffs will be delighted. For $10, this shop was selling a forty-page *Playbill* from Archie Leach's 1929 Broadway debut (in *A Wonderful Night* at the Majestic). Soon after, Archie Leach changed his name to Cary Grant.

In addition to its playbill inventory—more than four thousand Broadway bills and a huge off-Broadway file—the shop specializes in rare theater books, with emphasis on scenic and costume designs. There are also plays for a dollar, as well as shelves on circuses, vaudeville, and classical music. One out-of-print book, priced at $17, is *People and Pianos*, the history of Steinway & Sons.

Wednesday through Saturday, 11 A.M. to 6 P.M.; Sunday, 1 to 6.

Applause, 100 West 67th Street, between Broadway and Columbus Avenue (212-496-7511), stocks anthologies of plays about the California gold rush, twentieth-century American melodramas, and Russian satiric comedies. But the emphasis is on British drama. This shop's four thousand titles include out-of-print plays by Shaw and off-the-wall Monty Pythonesque collections. Of course, there is always the *Annotated Shakespeare,* edited by A. L. Rowse ($75).

"I haven't been to London myself," the manager, Beck Lee, said, "but customers say this shop has much more British theater in one place than any of the shops there."

Monday through Saturday, 10 A.M. to 7 P.M.; Sunday, noon to 6.

Books about movies get top billing at **Cinemabilia,** 611 Broadway (212-533-6686), but books are not all the store sells. For $3.50, there's a picture of Paul Muni as he ap-

peared in the original *Scarface* or, for $4.50, a shot of Alan
Alda in the film *Jenny*, in which he appears next to a life-size
shredded-wheat biscuit. Cinemabilia also sells old movie
posters and hard-to-find film magazines.

Monday through Saturday, 11 A.M. to 7 P.M.; closed
Sunday.

The Ballet Shop, 1887 Broadway, in the Empire Hotel,
at 63rd Street (212-581-7990), began when Norman Crider,
a champion juggler in the late 1960s, decided to open a
bookstore in the tradition of the English bookseller Cyril
Beaumont. "I started by specializing in ballet history," he
said. But his inventory quickly became much broader, and
more modern. Now he has more than two hundred dance
titles in stock, plus out-of-print and rare books on dance,
opera, and music.

Monday through Saturday, 11 A.M. to 7:30 P.M.; Sunday,
noon to 7 during the ballet season.

FOR CHILDREN

Remember a magic rabbit? Or a land of monsters? Or the
little girl who lives in a hotel? They are all alive and well at
Books of Wonder, 464 Hudson Street, at Barrow Street
(212-989-3270). And the clerks know the stock well enough
to find the books you read when you were young, even if you
have forgotten the titles—*Masquerades* and *Eloise,* for example.

The shop's hottest sellers are L. Frank Baum's Oz
books—one whole wall is devoted to editions of them—and
Books of Wonder has twenty versions of *Alice's Adventures
in Wonderland* by Lewis Carroll. "These days," Peter Glass-

man, one of the owners, said, "parents understand that buying old or rare books for children is not like buying breakable toys. They can be wonderful to share." Weekdays are the best time for browsing.

Monday through Thursday, 11 A.M. to 7 P.M.; Friday and Saturday, noon to 9; Sunday, noon to 5.

Perhaps the best-known children's bookstore in town is **Eeyore's.** For $15 or $25, its two well-stocked bookstores will send packages to readers at summer camp and choose the titles if the campers' parents don't.

Eeyore's sells only new children's books; on many weekends story hours are scheduled, often with well-known writers of children's books. Call ahead for details.

The West Side Eeyore's, at 2252 Broadway, at 81st Street (212-362-0634), is open Monday through Saturday from 10 A.M. to 6 P.M.; Sunday, 10:30 to 5. The store at 1066 Madison Avenue, also at 81st Street (212-988-3404), keeps the same hours except for Sunday, when it opens at noon.

COOKING

Kitchen Arts & Letters, 1435 Lexington Avenue, at 94th Street (212-876-5550), bills itself as a food bookstore, not a cookbook store. Perhaps, then, it is no surprise that the shop's best-selling author is M. F. K. Fisher, who writes about food, but has never written a cookbook per se.

"I have no trouble keeping Julia Child or Craig Claiborne in stock," the owner, Nahum J. Waxman, said, "but when people come here, they want things like *Traditional Recipes of Laos.*" It costs $19.95 in trade paperback, $25 in hardcover.

Mr. Waxman, himself a former publishing executive, says his main challenge is to stock up on unusual cookbooks before they go out of print. An amateur chef (Indian dishes and "big soups"), Mr. Waxman has only one complaint: "Since opening the store, I don't get as much chance to cook as I used to."

Monday through Friday, 10 A.M. to 6 P.M.; Saturday, 11 to 6.

MYSTERIES

Whodunit? The clues are at **The Mysterious Bookstore,** 129 West 56th Street (212-765-0900). The shop specializes in rare books (a first edition of *The Return of Sherlock Holmes* sells for $750), but that should not deter readers who just want good paperback page-turners. The first floor of the shop is filled with them; rarer items are upstairs.

Monday through Saturday, 11 A.M. to 7 P.M.

Murder Ink, 271 West 87th Street, between Broadway and West End Avenue (212-362-8905), is smaller but boasts its own Inspector Clouseau—a mostly black cat who shadows customers through the well-stocked shop. And the site is appropriate—in the early Ellery Queen books, the detective's home was on 87th Street, according to one of the shop's owners, Carol Brener. Miss Brener's own tastes run to classic mysteries—she dislikes "gratuitous gore."

Monday through Saturday (except Thursday), 1 to 7 P.M.; Thursday, 1 to 10. Closed Sunday.

Another mystery bookshop is **Foul Play,** 10 Eighth Avenue, at West 12th Street (212-675-5115). Its laquered shelves carry nothing but paperbacks, and it also has a secret door (hint: it's well camouflaged along the back wall). There is also an uptown store at 1465B Second Avenue, at 76th Street (212-517-3222).

What may be most notable about Foul Play is what lurks behind the front counter—such titles as *The Cannibal Who Overate* ($2.95) and Edward Gorey's *Epiplectic Bicycle* ($6.95). The shop also stocks tapes of old radio thrillers and T-shirts inscribed with such sayings as "I Haven't a Clue" ($8).

Monday through Saturday, noon to 10 P.M.; Sunday, noon to 6.

MILITARY

Harris Colt used to be an investment banker who spent weekends searching for World War II histories. "Wherever I went," he said, "I found the same tired titles over and over again." So he opened his own shop—the **Military Book-man,** at 29 East 93rd Street (212-348-1280), between Fifth and Madison avenues.

Mr. Colt avoids best sellers and current events; there are no titles on the Falklands or Grenada, and not many on Vietnam. Instead, browsers will find *The Confederate Infantry Tactics Manual* and *Intercepted Letters of Napoleon from Egypt*.

Tuesday through Saturday, 10:30 A.M. to 5:30 P.M.

By contrast, **Sky Books International** spotlights modern military affairs, aviation, and weapons. The shop, on the second floor of 48 East 50th Street (212-688-5086), has titles on the Navy's Blue Angels, the German Luftwaffe, and the "secret squadrons" of the British Royal Air Force in World War II.

The Reagan administration's push to increase the defense budget has helped business, according to the manager, Daniel David. So have recent world events. "The Falklands might have done a lot for Mrs. Thatcher," he said, "but we made out even better."

Monday through Saturday, 10 A.M. to 7 P.M.

The Soldier Shop, 1222 Madison Avenue, at East 88th Street (212-535-6788), puts less emphasis on the political side of military history. "We stay away from opinionated authors," the owner, Peter Blum, said. It is a strategy that apparently serves the shop well. "Even in the antiwar periods," he said, "younger readers always came in here because this is basically history." The row of toy soldiers in the window and the helmets and swords in the shop are also a visual treat.

Monday through Friday, 10 A.M. to 6 P.M.; Saturday, 10 to 5.

ASTROLOGY AND THE OCCULT

The shelves at **Samuel Weiser,** 740 Broadway, near Astor Place (212-777-6363), are divided into more than thirty categories—parapsychology, the "demedicalization" of childbirth, even crystal balls. But perhaps the most unusual section of the store—which began as a general-interest bookstore in the 1920s but gradually came to focus on the supernatural—is a case containing rare books. On its shelves are a 1653 French volume on demonology, an 1881 *Technology of*

Soap and Candles, and, for $400, a book of card tricks edited by Harry Houdini.

Daily except Thursday, 9 A.M. to 6 P.M.; Thursday, 10 to 7; Saturday, 9:30 to 5.

SCIENCE FICTION

The **Science Fiction Shop,** 56 Eighth Avenue, at Horatio Street (212-741-0270), carries only books, no comics or toys. The shop emphasizes British paperbacks and hard-covers, as well as first editions, such as *The Moon Is a Harsh Mistress* by Robert A. Heinlein ($750). An autographed edition of Frank Herbert's novel, *Heretics of Dune,* is on sale for $75.

No science-fiction shop would be complete without *Star Trek* books, and they are here, along with *Di Fate's Catalogue of Science Fiction Hardware* ($8.95). It lists the bizarre battle machines and spaceships that regular science-fiction readers encounter all the time.

Monday through Friday, 11:30 A.M. to 7:30 P.M.; Saturday, 11 to 6; Sunday, noon to 6.

COMICS

Bam! Pow! Zoom! The forces of good and evil slug it out in full color in three Manhattan shops: **Funny Business Comics,** 666 Amsterdam Avenue, at 92nd Street (212-799-9477); **Back Date Magazines,** 228 West 23rd Street, next to the Chelsea Hotel (212-243-9349); and **West Side Comics,** 107 West 86th Street near Columbus Avenue (212-724-0432).

The owner of the eight-year-old West Side shop, David Toplitz, saved comic books as a child but says that his mother discarded them. Now he presides over an extensive collection. Some are sold at collectors' prices—$75 for a 1945 Walt Disney comic book with Donald Duck on the cover.

"A lot of our clientele is adults," Mr. Toplitz said. "Most are just keeping up with the new stuff that's coming out." Mr. Toplitz will not say which characters are his favorites. "These days," he said, "I'm more into reading mysteries."

Funny Business Comics: Monday through Thursday, 1 P.M. to 8 P.M.; Friday 1 P.M. to 6 P.M.; Saturday and Sunday, noon to 5 P.M. **Back Date Magazines:** Monday through Saturday, 9:30 A.M. to 6:30 P.M.; Sunday, 11 A.M. to 5 P.M. **West Side Comics:** Monday through Thursday, noon to 6 P.M.; Friday, noon to 7 P.M.; Saturday, 11:30 A.M. to 6 P.M.; Sunday, 1 P.M. to 5 P.M.

FOREIGN LANGUAGES

Perhaps because so many United Nations diplomats live in New York, the city can support foreign-language bookstores. **Adler's Foreign Books,** 28 West 25th Street, between Broadway and the Avenue of the Americas (212-691-5151), has one of the broadest collections of books in German and French. Francophiles can browse in **Le Bookstore** at the Alliance Française, 22 East 60th Street, east of Fifth Avenue (212-355-6100), and **La Librairie de France,** 610 Fifth Avenue in the Rockefeller Center Promenade (212-581-8810).

When it was recently faced with a 500 percent rent increase, the **French and Spanish Book Corporation,** Fifth Avenue and 19th Street (212-673-7400), reduced the size of its shop by 70 percent. The rent still doubled, but the inventory has not shrunk. The shop features foreign-language dictionaries and novels, and not just in French and Spanish. There are dictionaries for Indian dialects and Serbo-Croatian.

Adler's Foreign Books: Monday through Thursday, 9 A.M. to 6 P.M.; Friday, 9 A.M. to 5 P.M.; Saturday and Sunday, closed. **Le Bookstore:** Monday through Friday, 10 A.M. to 6 P.M.; Saturday and Sunday, closed. **La Librairie de France:** Monday through Saturday, 10 A.M. to 6 P.M.; Sunday, closed.

Mary Rosenberg was sixteen years old when she began helping out in her father's bookstore in Germany, where she sold schoolbooks to Henry A. Kissinger. The Nazis seized the inventory; in 1939 she fled to New York and started her own bookselling business. It has grown into one of the country's largest collections of German and French texts, at 17 West 60th Street, a few steps west of Broadway (212-362-4873).

Over the years, her customers have included Albert Einstein, the pianist Rudolf Serkin, and the conductors Bruno Walter and Erich Leinsdorf. In addition to an extensive stock of Thomas Mann (a former customer), Bertolt Brecht, and Martin Buber, the hundred thousand volumes in her shop include some first editions by Sigmund Freud.

Monday through Friday, 9 A.M. to 5:30 P.M.; Saturday, 9 to 2:30.

Kerekes Brothers began sixty years ago, when German was still spoken regularly on the streets of Yorkville. It is a general-interest bookstore at 177 East 87th Street, between Lexington and Third avenues (212-289-2020), with a sprinkling of Hungarian titles among the hundred thousand neatly arranged German books and magazines, cheery, not

academic. This is the place to go for the German translation
of the latest Robert Ludlum or Harold Robbins novel.

Monday through Friday, 10 A.M. to 5 P.M.; Saturday, 10
to 2:30.

For readers of things Oriental, there are **China Books,**
125 Fifth Avenue, at 19th Street (212-677-2650); the **Zen
Oriental** bookstores at 115 West 57th Street, near the Avenue of the Americas (212-582-4622), and 521 Fifth Avenue,
near 43rd Street (212-697-0840); and the **Paragon Book
Gallery,** at 2130 Broadway, at 74th Street (212-496-2378).
Rachel Faerber started what became the Paragon shop in
1942 in Shanghai. Paragon's inventory has grown, but she
says the only ones from China itself are on art.

"Things are a little easier than they used to be," Mrs.
Faerber said, "but Communists don't write many books."

For that reason, she has reprinted some. In the 1960s, she
reprinted *Chinese Jews* in conjunction with the University of
Toronto, an account of Jewish traders in China in the eleventh century who married and gradually came to be considered Chinese ($30). Japanese history and literature are also
Paragon specialties, along with books on Iran and Egypt.

China Books: Monday through Saturday, 10 A.M. to 6
P.M.; Sunday, noon to 5 P.M. **Zen Oriental bookstores:**
Monday through Saturday, 10 A.M. to 8 P.M.; Sunday, noon
to 7 P.M. **Paragon:** Monday through Friday, 10 A.M. to 5:45
P.M.; Saturday, noon to 4:30 P.M.

IRISH

When he collected two books of Irish folklore nearly a century ago, William Butler Yeats wrote of trooping fairies, leprechauns, and clurichauns. In New York, a new $7.95 paperback edition of Yeats's work can be found amid the Irish books and records at **Facsimile,** a quiet shop at 16 West 55th Street, near Fifth Avenue (212-581-2672). **Keshcarrigan,** 90 West Broadway, near Chambers Street (212-962-4237), also deals in Irish culture, and **Rivendell,** 109 St. Mark's Place (212-533-2501), specializes in Celtic folklore and mythology.

Facsimile: Monday through Friday, 10 A.M. to 6:30 P.M.; Saturday, 11 A.M. to 6 P.M.; Sunday, closed. **Keshcarrigan:** Monday through Friday, 11 A.M. to 5 P.M.; Saturday, noon to 5 P.M.; Sunday, closed. **Rivendell:** Monday through Saturday, noon to 8 P.M.; Sunday, closed.

NEW YORK

East Side, West Side, **Urban Center Books** in the Villard Houses on Madison Avenue at 50th Street (212-935-3595), has books from all around the town. The Urban Center specializes in what the manager, John Frazier, calls "the built world" of architecture, landscape architecture, and historic preservation.

The shop, which carries four thousand titles, is operated by the Municipal Art Society, with financial backing from the J. M. Kaplan Fund.

Monday through Saturday, 10 A.M. to 6 P.M.

New York Bound, 43 West 54th Street (212-245-8503), specializes in out-of-print books, such as the six-volume

Phelps Stokes *Iconography of Manhattan Island* in its original edition ($5,000), a work that reproduces all major maps of the city from the days of Dutch settlers to the early twentieth century. Or, for $5, there is *A True History of Riverside Drive.*

Tuesday through Friday, 10 A.M. to 5:30 P.M.; Saturday, noon to 5.

TRAVEL

Travel books, says Edward Feeley of the **Complete Traveler,** 199 Madison Avenue, at 35th Street (212-679-4339), are perhaps the fastest growing segment of the publishing industry. "We're no longer innocents abroad," he said. "Europe is no longer a once-in-a-lifetime experience, and people want more information and more details to make intelligent choices."

One of the shop's most popular guides is Georgina Masson's *Companion Guide to Rome* ($8.95). Mr. Feeley also stocks Nagel's encyclopedic guides on everywhere from Ireland ($22) to China ($55 for 1,600 pages).

Monday through Friday, 9 A.M. to 6 P.M.; Saturday, 10 to 6; Sunday, noon to 5.

WOMEN'S STUDIES

Womanbooks, 201 West 92nd Street, at Amsterdam Avenue (212-873-4121), stocks six thousand titles by, for, and about women—from *The Collected Stories of Collette* ($19.95) to Rosalind Rosenberg's *Beyond Separate Spheres: Intellectual Roots of Modern Feminism* ($9.95). The shop also sells what it describes as nonsexist, nonracist children's books, and there is a corner where young readers can sit while their parents browse through the rest of the bright, well-organized shop. Also, there is a sizable collection of recordings of music composed by women.

The store tries to carry the complete works of female writers. "If we don't have it, the publisher doesn't," the owner, Karyn Landon, said. Womanbooks regularly finds books from feminist publishing houses that never make it to general-interest shops.

Tuesday through Saturday, 10 A.M. to 7 P.M.; Sunday, noon to 6.

AUTOMOBILES

From *A* (for Alfa Romeo) to *V* (for Volvo), **Albion Scott Motobooks** is crammed with titles about racing, rallying, runabouts, and roadsters—everything but the Beach Boys' "Little Deuce Coupe." The shop, at 48 East 50th Street (212-980-1928), has volumes on Porsches, Maseratis, and even Matchbox toys. It also has a $15 calendar with pictures of foreign fire engines.

The shop stocks dozens of repair manuals (including one for the ill-fated Chevrolet Corvair) which are certain to delight mechanics—a category that does not include the shop's general manager, Michael Hespen. "I live in Manhattan," he said. "I wouldn't dare have a car—any car—here."

Monday through Friday, 10 A.M. to 7 P.M.; Saturday, 10 to 6.

WHERE TO BIND YOUR BOOK

Whether it's a beloved first edition that is falling apart in your hands or your favorite graduate's just-completed doctoral dissertation, there is a bookbinding service that can make a cover worth judging the book by.

While the art of bookbinding is becoming increasingly rare, there are still more than fifty bookbinders in New York City. They will bind, rebind, or restore books for as little as $15 a volume. Here is a partial list of binders who accept small-quantity orders:

Distinctive Bookbinding, Inc., Suite 8-B, 382 Third Avenue, between 26th and 27th streets (212-685-4004). Prices: $35 an hour for a buckram or leatherette binding, with five lines of gold stamping on the spine; $85 an hour for real leather or other materials, such as Nigerian goatskin. Binding an average book here takes an hour.

Eudaldo Ginesta, 47 West 27th Street, between Broadway and Avenue of the Americas (212-689-3866). Minimum price: $30 a book.

Froelich Leather Craft Company, 63–20 Austin Street, Rego Park, Queens (718-897-7000). Typical prices: cloth cover, $65; leather, $85–$90.

National Edition, 244 West 49th Street, between Broadway and Eighth Avenue (212-246-4392). Minimum price: $15 a book.

CHAPTER 5

....

The Berg Collection: Salon for the Silent Life of the Mind

BY McCANDLISH PHILLIPS

Mere yards from the honk and growl of city traffic, the swirl and haste of morning and evening pedestrian tides, where 42nd Street splits West/East at Fifth Avenue, Room 320 of the New York Public Library seems as remote, as detached and serene, as the private library in some great English manor.

Room 320 is the grand foyer to that irreplaceable, and consequently priceless, throng of first editions and original manuscripts called the Berg Collection of English and American Literature.

The great aristocrats of the written English language are here—many in autograph and inscription, letters and manuscripts in their own hand (often showing some of their labor, a fascinating aspect that today's computer manuscripts blip into limbo). Authors of the foremost rank address their lovers tenderly or self-mockingly or with playful wit.

The roll of names here is stunning: Byron and Kipling and Shelley, Wordsworth, Hawthorne, Keats, Poe, the

47

Brownings, Tennyson, Thoreau, Galsworthy, Carlyle, Emerson, Melville, Whitman, Conrad, Crane, Eliot, O'Casey, Woolf, Shaw, and hundreds of others whose fame has survived the ravening of time.

Playful spirits wink from the catalog, among them Twain and Tarkington and Lardner and that supremely protean parodist, Sir Max Beerbohm.

The Beaux-Arts structure in which this monarch's treasure is found is more than a mansion for Everyman. It is a palace; yet more than a palace, a place of amplitude and grandeur. Beyond the Fifth Avenue terrace and steps rising to this building's main entrance, through the bronze doors, the sky-reaching vault of Astor Hall looks as if it had been carved from a mountain of white marble. The enduring wonder of the place is that it is free and open to all. Yet within this most deliberately accessible and public of places, those who wander through its marble halls learn that there are some reference areas from which the general public is locked out.

Room 320 is one of these. Few pass through its double set of doors—the outer set is windowed, the inner paneled—into one of the city's choicest sanctuaries. Calling 320 a room is like calling a symphony a tune.

It is a salon for the silent life of the mind.

When he took up his pen on Christmas Eve, 1919, in his Hotel Belmont suite on Park Avenue at 42nd Street, what exactly did Edward John Moreton Drax Plunkett, Lord Dunsany, write to the more moderately named Clayton Meeker Hamilton?

What pair of moral-reformist American sisters of a hundred years ago mounted a lengthy and spirited attack on "that unpardonable enormity, strong butter!" and meant every word of it?

Where may the last will and testament of a sweet-natured and uncommonly articulate dog—conceivably influenced by association with a family in which artistic genius gleamed among the shadows of psychic desperation—be read in its unsigned original?

Why did that impeccably proper Englishman, Robert Smythe Hichens, writing to a rising young man about New York, repeatedly implore him to cast into the fire some earlier letters in which Hichens had lifted a curtain on the window of his soul?

The Berg Collection yields the answers to these questions. A long finger-march through its card catalog leads to letters, diaries, essays, broadcasts, photographs, autographs, holographs, plays, poems, biographies, novels, telegrams, cables, caricatures, reviews, sketches, broadsides, offprints, speeches, clippings, galleys, drafts, manuscripts, author's corrections, marginal entries, fragments, inscriptions, notes, notebooks, royalty statements, little magazines and journals, engravings, drawings, presentation copies, phonograph records, bookplates, publishing contracts, and a thicket of literary miscellany carefully tucked among the many major holdings. In short, everything to inebriate the bibliophile.

In one typical afternoon the only violation of the Room's reverent hush was a "humph" let out by a scholar—not a *humph* in the lower register of scholarly disdain, but a *humph* in the upper register of recognition and discovery. That chunky little exclamation was packed, bratwurst-tight, with satisfaction. It stood out as a distinct event.

That does not mean that the Room is not also a place of laughter. Serenity here is often butted into head-on by hilarity.

The voice of Dylan Thomas thunders out of the collection in a gust of boisterous satire about the rounds European writers often make of American reading circles, starting out fresh in New York and returning to the city mind-spent and needing its neon succor.

"There they go, every spring, from New York to Los Angeles," the impudent Welsh cherub said in one of a series of radio talks published in *Quite Early One Morning* in 1954, the year after his death at thirty-nine, "exhibitionists, polemicists, histrionic publicists, theological rhetoricians, historical hoddy-doddies, balletomanes, ulterior decorators, windbags, and bigwigs, and humbugs . . . men with elephantiasis of the reputation . . . myself among them booming with the worst."

They thrash in "boiling hotel bedroom ovens," visit "the great State University factories," are toasted with "washing sherry."

Having wheeled through "a list of engagements long as a New York menu or a half hour with a book by Charles Morgan," a breathless poet comes "bedraggedly back to New York which struck him all of a sheepish never-sleeping heap at first but which seems to him now, after the rigours of a lecturer's spring, a haven cosy as toast, cool as an icebox, and safe as skyscrapers."

Perhaps the mystery and the glory of a collection like the Berg is that its leaves lie in darkness, powerless to exert any effect until they are requested—some not more than once in thirty years. Yet the moment the light strikes them, they leap to life. Words, so long inert, rise to dance upon the comprehension.

The Berg Collection occupies a spacious third-floor suite in the Central Research Library, as the 1911 structure on Fifth Avenue is formally known.

A user cannot get in until let in by a staff member using a key or an electric buzzer. Once in, one is locked in—the door has no inside handle—and can get out only with the same assistance.

The door to the Room is opened to certified scholars and published authors for specifically stated purposes and periods, but you may go in right now on my twenty-two-day card of admission.

The Room, quietly opulent and utterly formal, is nearly forty feet long and twenty-five feet wide, with a ceiling two stories high. The floor is marble. Nearly all the rest is richly paneled in Austrian oak. The wood absorbs the lamp glow of the windowless reading room and mutes it to a soft and welcoming gloss.

Just inside, over the entrance, is an unclad torso of Moses—here so corrugatedly muscular as to suggest that he spent a good deal of time lifting weights and chewing protein wafers—holding the tablet of the Law. It is the work of the Renaissance artist Giovanni Della Robbia.

The torso and a small flat figure of James Joyce wrought in silver that catches Joyce unmistakably, seem slightly, delightfully, almost slyly assertive in a space that otherwise has a somewhat mortuarylike aspect.

Everything is set in rigid relationship to everything else, creating an atmosphere of static perfection. Two carved-oak Corinthian columns flanking the portals seem fixed in a perpetual salute to two more at the far end of the room. Five huge bookcases on one side, filled with the works of Dickens, are balanced by five on the other side devoted to Thackeray.

At a pair of identical tables, nearly ten feet long and fifty-four inches wide—each with four comfortable chairs, two on either side—scholars bend in pursuit of the collection's secrets.

For practical and comfortable accommodation, this handsome, stilted chamber, with its more than ten square feet of table space for each user, is nobility defined.

Among the great aristocrats of the written English language here, Longfellow lifts his pen to Whitman, complying with an 1881 request for an autograph. If one has acquired sufficient literary fame even bodily symptoms, and the poultices applied thereto, may find a niche in literary history.

In a long letter to Oliver Wendell Holmes—the author and physician, not the jurist—Washington Irving's doctor accuses his ailing patient of an act of murder, not of a person but of his own sleep.

In a nine-page letter, written from 19 East 15th Street, on January 5 or 6, 1859, Dr. John C. Peters informed Holmes that Irving was "suffering from nervous nip" as well as sleep peculiarities of a willful nature. He details the latter at great length and perhaps with mounting exasperation, informing Holmes that Irving "enjoys this gipsey and catlike way of murdering good christian sleep."

The New York doctor reports that he has "tried all reasonable homeopathic treatment"—five grains of this, two grains of that, three of another, twelve of yet one more—with scant result, having treated him "with faithfulness—with freedom from prejudice—with a most earnest desire to benefit a man whom I love inexpressibly."

Irving died that year on November 28. Peters collected reams of newspaper coverage of the death and funeral. They are in quite good condition in a box more than two inches high, tied, like a gift, in red ribbon.

On opening the four folds of the box, one finds a thick volume, in painted-on marble, marked in gold letters HER-BARIUM. It is an apt title, for there are, indeed, some exotic prose flowerings in it, in need of severe pruning. One quite typical New York press account of Irving's death begins:

> Full of years and honors, in the mellow evening of a well-spent, honorable life, and in the mellow evening, too, of the year, ere the frosts of age had found power to chill his genial heart and brain, or the frosts of winter robbed the landscape that he loved of Autumn's solemn, soothing charms, WASH-INGTON IRVING, the patriarch of American letters, and the last link that remained to us between the age of Scott and Campbell and Southey and Byron, and our own, has passed away, as calmly as he lived.

Possibly nine words of that bulletin, not more than one of them an adjective, would survive in any newsroom of this century.

Under the heading MR. IRVING'S CELIBACY, one paper ran a stout defense of that state of omission, after another newspaper had given out that the "one defect" in Irving's life was his never having married.

"At the present time," the answering volley ran, "so extravagant are the habits of women, so precarious the resources of men . . . that those who hesitate in the matrimonial path . . . are the conscientious; and whoever has shared the family troubles incident to the contrary

course, when rashly adopted, will never thoughtfully re-
proach a celibate."

The Berg Collection is more than a club of the very emi-
nent dead. Its holdings reach from 1480 down to the lip of
the present decade. Most of the five centuries of works that
crowd its shelves are out of sight, but all are scrupulously
kept, nothing is jumbled here.

Request any item in the collection and it is fetched in
thin-sliced minutes by a four-member staff that could not
be more attentive or courteous or prompt if its members
were in your own employ and sustained on your private
payroll.

Such efficiency seems wondrous in a place where 150,000
original manuscripts and 300,000 printed items, by rough
measure, are hoarded, the bulk of them in cool, dark rooms
maintained at nearly constant temperature (62 degrees) and
humidity (50 to 55 percent) in the ultimately losing race
against decay, a race in which delay or prolongation is the
custodian's only prize.

Of the ceaseless low thrumm of the air-conditioning ducts
in the stacks, a librarian said, "Sometimes I wonder if the
noise bothers them," nearly making persons of his books, a
tendency more than forgivable in a librarian.

Some bindings look quite ordinary, but many are splendid and burnished (a lanolin compound is worked into the
leather bindings with a cloth about once in eighteen
months). In the stacks, the individuality of books, each with
its own design and size and presentation to the eye, is a fascinating allurement. There are fine old works to savor, like
decanters of elegant wine.

★ ★ ★

A word written in haste in, say, 1727 or 1814, can be repented at leisure by scholars obliged to decipher an author's inchoate scrawl. Staring the illegible into self-revealing legibility takes time and the full play of imagination upon the possibilities. The magnifying glass set at the end of a long gooseneck arm on one of the reading tables also helps.

On two occasions a word that would, after prolonged and scowling inspection, yield no meaning whatever to my eyes was appealed to Dr. Lola L. Szladits, the Berg Collection's curator since 1969. Each time, the word left her tongue the instant her eye fell upon it. It was as if the collection is the writing of her familiar friends, and in a sense it is.

"She is trained, yet she is educated; she is educated, yet she is cultured," remarked Dr. Vartan Gregorian, the buoyant writer, historian, and linguist who became president of the New York Public Library in 1981. "She is the curator's curator. Her work is like laser surgery—one document, one letter, one volume. The great curators know what is missing and where to get it. Sometimes you have to cultivate someone for fifteen, twenty years to get the piece."

Patrick Lawlor is the cataloguer of the collection. His British accent fits it well. The conservator is Brian McInerney, a published poet.

In the realm of literature, books beget books beget books, though not yet entirely by themselves, and begetting of that sort goes on regularly in this cloister. "Sometimes it seems to me," an editor familiar with the collection said, "that half the world's books come out of that collection."

The great majority of the users are from colleges and universities, with a few nonacademic authors and book editors signing in at the register near the entrance. The ratio runs about eight to one.

Users in a recent period came from the Grolier Club, Worcester Polytechnic, the universities of Michigan, Hawaii, London, and Sydney, Australia, Williams College, Dartmouth College, Wedgestone Press, Rhodes House Library at Oxford, the Department of Psychiatry at Mount Sinai Medical Center, the Macmillan Company, and the United States Naval Academy at Annapolis.

The Berg Collection is not only *in* New York, its origin is wholly *of* New York, and there is a saga to it.

In a sense, it might be said to have been built on the back of one apparently unimportant man. His name was Moritz, and he came out of the Austro-Hungarian monarchy in 1862 and worked as a tailor in New York to support his wife and eight children.

He had wanted to be a doctor, and he apparently instilled that aim in his eldest son, Henry Woolfe Berg, who graduated from City College in 1878. Henry, in turn, influenced the youngest son, Albert Ashton Berg, in the same direction.

Both men had long service at Mount Sinai Hospital here. Both were lifelong bachelors. They collected real estate astutely, and in long evenings in their town house at 10 East 73rd Street, they read to each other from the books that were their mutual absorption.

The younger Dr. Berg—slender, dapper, a skilled hunter of wildcats and bear—was not seen again with the red carnation that had been his daily sartorial flourish, worn even while at surgery, after his brother died.

Dr. A. A. Berg founded the collection in memory of his

brother in 1940. He made certain that it would exceed the glory of even the most exalted private collections, by making it a collection of such collections.

One grand haul included a choice literary antique— Charles Dickens's writing desk, with its slanting top and big globe lamp. A chair Dickens used at work came with it. When Mayor Fiorello H. La Guardia came to honor the collection, he plunked his ample bottom into it and split through the caning.

A ramble through the card catalogue turns up much that is engaging about New York.

If, upon opening a letter addressed to him on March 15, 1928, on the stationery of Sara Teasdale Filsinger at 146 Central Park West, the young critic Edmund Wilson was betrayed by its opening lines into expecting an undiluted encomium, he had only to read on.

Sara Teasdale, as her work was signed, was then near the end of a life that was not to reach fifty years. She was the author of a dozen books of poetry, including *River to the Sea* in 1915 and *Love Song*, for which she won the Pulitzer Prize in 1917.

Wilson, who was then in his early thirties and who would later achieve eminence as a literary critic, was on the staff of *The New Republic* when Mrs. Filsinger dipped her pen in blue ink and expressed herself to:

Dear Mr. Wilson:

I have just finished reading your remarkable article on Proust in The New Republic. I have hoped for years that someone capable of understanding his work would write of him here. You seem to have grasped the whole living mass of

the book, and penetrated its last meaning, and you have expressed it—with possibly one exception. I feel that you scarcely do justice to the sheer beauty of many of the incidents,
the almost tremulous freshness and sheen of the narrator's
glimpse, for instance, of the peasant girl from the window of
his train. . . . But the scope of the work, and the color of it
come to us in your essay in all their astounding and contradic-
tory vividness.

Proust's work had found its great American critic; the
critic had found his voice; and Sara Teasdale, recognizing
genius in both, extended her discerning praise.

Edward John Moreton Drax Plunkett, Lord Dunsany,
the high-spirited British aristocrat whose outpourings for
the stage were eagerly received in New York but often only
coolly so in England and Ireland, where he lived, was in
New York near the end of 1919. He was a soldier, hunts-
man, poet, and a dasher off of many, many plays.

One of his singularities was that he wrote with a quill pen,
and he detested journalists who seized upon that crotchet in
portraying him to the public. He may have used such a pen on
Christmas Eve, 1919, in writing to Clayton Meeker Hamilton
from the Hotel Belmont at Park Avenue and 42nd Street.

The envelope was hand-addressed to Hamilton at "The
Players Club, 16 Grammercy Park, New York." It bears the
postmark: December 24—10:30 P.M.—1919 Grand Central.

Here and there Dunsany's pen stroke left wide trailing
flourishes flowing below the last letters of certain words,
suggesting nothing so much as a raccoon's tail. "My dear
Hamilton," he begins, apologizing for his behavior the
other night in "making so much fuss about so small a bolt in

the armoury of Fate as a slight sick-headache: it is perhaps the very smallest missile that the gods throw.''

Dunsany then got to his real purpose, which had to do, not surprisingly in a writer, with a wish to sack his New York agent, who, he said, had ''only condescended to give my plays a place in his cupboard'' if he also handled world rights.

Dunsany earnestly hoped that Hamilton would sound out William Hull to take on his plays in this country, allowing him to cashier his current agent ''after a tearful farewell.''

In 1892, Duprat & Co. published a limited, numbered edition of *Four Private Libraries of New-York* by Henri Pène du Bois. It came off the press in one thousand copies, two hundred on Japanese paper, eight hundred on Holland paper. Opening Number 625, with its rough-cut edges, one finds oneself in the presence of a most exacting sensibility.

The Berg Collection would not exist for decades, but Pène du Bois wrote words that fit it superbly now:

''The formation of a library is a work of genius, and genius always finds the occasional causes of its creations, since these creations must happen. The same workman shapes genius and chance, and shapes them for each other.''

The idea that a book is well bound only in ''levant morocco with a Grolieresque or Le Gasconesque pattern'' was to Pène du Bois as if ''an edict decreed that a woman shall be well dressed in blue or green velvet.

''She is well dressed in silk, velvet, damask, stuff with pompadour flowers, or lily white lawn, according to the scene wherein she appears, drawing room, opera, park, or library-room. Thus is a book.''

Throughout, Pène du Bois, who seems very like an ebullient professor at his lectern, flails right and left at Philistinism. "The qualities of expression in the art of bookbinding are *musical*," he writes. They are not martial. The widely prized book covers "are not dress, but a uniform or livery," he asserts. To Pène du Bois, matched sets of books are an awful barbarity, esteemed only by "addicts of homogeneity."

A passion of similar force erupts in a denunciation of American food, circa 1870, as variety and abundance massacred in the pot and brought as ruin to the table, by the sisters Catherine E. Beecher and Harriet Beecher Stowe. It was published in New York that year by J. B. Ford and Company as *Principles of Domestic Science . . . a Textbook for the Use of Young Ladies*, an opus on domestic felicity in thirty chapters spread across 390 pages.

There are a couple of calmly reasoned pages on the moral instruction of children in which the Beechers chide the double-standard "notion that it is important to secure these virtues to one sex, more than to the other; and, by a strange inconsistency, the sex most exposed to danger is the one selected as least needing care," they note, meaning males.

But it is on *butter* that the Beechers reach their pitch of fervor, especially on "that unpardonable enormity, strong butter!" One quakes to think what they would have said of margarine.

Strong butter, whether applied to "savage or civilized bread" was seen as a pervasively ruinous influence. Such butter "stands sentinel at the door to bar your way to every other kind of food," they complain, with rising vehemence.

"You turn from your dreadful half-slice of bread, which fills your mouth with bitterness, to your beefsteak, which proves virulent with the same poison; you think to take refuge in vegetable diet, and find the butter . . . polluting the innocence of early peas; it is in the corn, in the squash, the beets swim in it, the onions have it poured over them. Hungry and miserable, you think to solace yourself at dessert; but the pastry is cursed, the cake is acrid with the same plague. You are ready to howl with despair. . . .''

The sisters blanch at the ''thousands and millions of pounds of butter yearly manufactured which are merely hobgoblin bewitchments of cream into foul and loathsome poisons.''

They also get in a good lick or two at what they call ''the mere physical and culinary idea of womanhood as connected only with puddings and shirt-buttons.''

Carl Van Vechten came out of Cedar Rapids, Iowa, early in this century as a young man to win a reputation as a man of the arts in New York City—as a novelist, composer, anthologist, photographer, and critic. With it, he got the friendship of many in the arts, including figures of great celebrity, some of whom owed their early recognition to Van Vechten's prescient writings.

A fleeting, shorthand reference to *The Iceman Cometh*, which was to be recognized years later as a crown of the great playwright Eugene O'Neill, is found in a letter to Van Vechten postmarked Berkeley, California, January 19, 1941. It came from the dramatist's wife, the actress Carlotta Monterey O'Neill.

The letter encloses a most curious document headed ''Last Will and Testament of Silverdene Emblem O'Neill,'' the O'Neills' dog. Its seventy-seven typed lines on two pages seem not unduly long for a dog in a family in which creativity was not often strangled by brevity. The letter with it ran:

> Carlo dearest,
>
> Thank you so much for returning the "Iceman" so promptly. You are a lamb!
>
> Enclosed is a copy of Blemie's Last Will and Testament—for you and Fania [Van Vechten's Russian-born wife, an actress]. It *is* a charming thing, isn't it? And, for those of us who knew and loved Blemie, it is *him!*
>
> Dearest love to you both, from us—

The cursive signature "Carlotta" swings up into half the text of the letter. The enclosure begins: "I, Silverdene Emblem O'Neill . . ." and goes on to reflect on survival:

> I would like to believe with those of my fellow Dalmatians who are devout Mohammedans, that there is a Paradise where one is always young and full-bladdered . . . [with unrestricted access to] an amorous multitude of houris, beautifully spotted . . . where in long evenings there are a million fireplaces with logs forever burning, and one curls oneself up and blinks into the flames and nods and dreams, remembering the brave old days on earth, and the love of one's Master and Mistress.

The will dissents from Mrs. O'Neill's overheard resolve never to have another dog: Blemie suggests a Dalmatian as his successor, grants that it cannot be one of equivalent distinction ("My Master and Mistress must not ask the impossible"), imagines him as a boulevardier on Park Avenue and is "sure he will do his utmost not to appear a mere gauche provincial dog."

This document is found among hundreds of letters addressed to Van Vechten (including twenty by Somerset Maugham, for instance, from 1925 to 1944) at a series of New York City addresses that constitute a profile of a young man's rise from obscurity and near poverty to recognition and reward: from East 19th Street to West 55th Street to 101 Central Park West, with other stops along the way.

Early in his career here, in 1911, he went to a suite in the St. Regis on a newspaper assignment to interview Robert Smythe Hichens, then in his middle forties, a man to whom royalties had accrued by heaps.

Hichens had entered the London cultural scene in 1895 as music critic for *The London World*, succeeding no less a figure than George Bernard Shaw. By the time Van Vechten came upon him, Hichens, who wrote and produced plays, had written a reasonable share of the nearly fifty books that he was to turn out with machinelike rapidity over not quite as many years. His *The Garden of Allah*, published in 1904, was a virtual lifetime annuity. After five printings in three months, it eventually sold a staggering seven hundred thousand copies, was made into a hit play, and was filmed twice—once as a silent, later in sound.

The Garden of Allah cleared a lifetime track for Hichens: When a man's book sells seven hundred thousand copies and a ton of rights, publishers are actually afraid not to publish his next thirty-five books.

The British prodigy was seized by the intelligence and sensitivity of the young American. The impression Van Vechten made was so profound that Hichens was to remark on it again and again for decades, and he wrote him into his next book as a character named Van Buren.

Hichens was an Englishman with whose psyche and constitution England did not agree. "It freezes me up. I feel dry, bloodless, sapless,'' he confessed. He became therefore a man whose last-known address was likely to have been succeeded by another by the time anyone wrote to him. He was a man who lived, as it were, somewhere in a gazeteer.

Indeed, the Berg Collection has fifty letters that he wrote in a bold hand to Van Vechten, starting on December 3, 1911, from the Bath Club. The letters continued from London, Rome, Rapallo, Taormina, Milan, Paris, Algiers, Meadowside in Kent, Marseille, Zurich, Upper Egypt, the Hotel Mamounia at Marrakech, Morocco, and half a dozen other places over the next thirty years, until Hichens was seventy-six years old.

"I suppose it is almost impossible to be really free," he wrote early on to Van Vechten. "And those who, like myself, have a sort of crazy passion for freedom often rivet their chains upon their wrists. If one has a conscience . . . one often cannot choose to be free. . . . I passed through years of nervous misery, probably such as you now endure, poor friend. . . . Your letters breathe dissatisfaction. Mist hangs around them. What a spiders web of human relations we are entangled in. . . . The bells of Rome toll me to bed.''

The portrait of Hichens that resolves from his letters is vivid, amusing, often precisely particularized, sometimes deeply self-revealing, if only on a narrow band. It is, finally, the testimony of a man who needed, and found, solace only in work, who wished to perform on a terrain higher than he could reach, and who continued all his years on the comfortable plateau to which early success had given him title.

"I have done mad things now and then," he confessed, adding not a syllable of the specific. A series of remarks of this tone in the early letters appear to be the cause of a succeeding series, in which Hichens urged Van Vechten to put them to the flame: "Do tell me what you have done with those letters," he wrote from the Italian Riviera in 1912. "They had better be destroyed, as they were only meant for your eyes. BURN THEM LIKE A GOOD FRIEND."

He seems not to have received assurance of this noble arson, for he persisted in the exhortation. A wide gap that opened in their literary perceptions seems never to have strained their friendship.

Van Vechten became a herald of Gertrude Stein's work at an early stage, while Hichens had a low threshold of contempt for new-wave writing, conceding only that "the decorative fool is of value. He sometimes adds agreeably to the variety of life."

In 1914 he wrote, "Don't tell me you admire such painful elaboration of rubbish—such pangs of the inane—for I shall not believe you."

"Oddities are numerous but real originals are very rare," he had warned Van Vechten in 1914. He was still going at Miss Stein in 1935. But Van Vechten remained steadfastly heroic in his service to the Stein legend. Nearly forty years after reading Hichens's first tart reproofs, he edited eight volumes of the writings of Gertrude Stein, ending in 1958, six years before his death.

A small photograph of Hichens tumbled out of a 1936 letter. It showed a proper gentleman, well tailored, rod-straight, with a direct gaze from deep-set eyes—a man sure of himself, sure of his place. He was a writer full-caught in the web of his time, beyond possibility of escape, fed on unceasing success, void of greatness.

Standing in the stacks amid the elephant folios, so named for their size, and the clamshell boxes, named for the way they open and close, Mr. McInerney, the conservator, spoke of a process that may eventually add about a hundred years to the life of the precious papers in his care.

He paused a moment, "But what is a hundred years?" he asked. The silence of the chamber was the only answer, and it was eloquent enough.

CHAPTER 6

....

New Glimpses into the Past

BY MICHAEL NORMAN

We are flying north in the early morning haze, going upriver to Albany in search of the past. Manhattan's past. We need to know the past to know the present; but, in the way of all voyeurs, we are also simply curious. We crave details—the daily scandals and disappointments, the quarrels over land and love, the petty, the ordinary, the source, unalloyed and accessible. You see, we are looking for patterns, links, the long, reassuring nexus.

"A people without history," said T. S. Eliot in the *Four Quartets*, "is not redeemed from time, for history is a pattern of timeless moments." We need redemption. We live in a new space and hear old voices.

Eager to make connections, we have been swept up in the new wave of urban archeology and antiquity. Again and again it seems that someone new is digging up the island of Manhattan and sifting the detritus of its beginnings. An eighteenth-century merchant ship is discovered fifteen feet below Water Street; remnants of New York's first City Hall, Stadt Huys, turn up during construction of a skyscraper on Broad Street; in the heart of Sheridan Square volunteers search for evidence of an Indian settlement called Sappokanican.

We had thought at first to seek the past in an archeological excavation and had consulted with Ralph S. Solecki, an urban archeologist as well as professor of anthropology at Columbia University.

We asked Professor Solecki if he had been able to connect with the past during any of his city digs. He had tried, he said, "really tried to capture it," but acknowledged that it was difficult, even late at night or in the early morning quiet in the streets. "You might be able to capture it in parts of Staten Island," he continued, "but when you stand in the shadow of a skyscraper, it's hard to imagine the farm that once was there."

Seeking something more explicit—memoranda rather than phantasms, perhaps—we are on our way to Albany to find an archivist with tallowy pages pressed between sheets of gauze. The archivist has prepared for our arrival. He works in the New York State Library, on the New York Historical Manuscripts: Dutch. He sits at a cluttered desk in a windowless room on the eleventh floor, translating the New Netherland archives of the Dutch West India Company. He is forty-five. He has been there for ten years and may be there for twenty years more. There are twelve thousand handwritten pages to translate—court records, company council minutes, patents, laws, wills—and the work goes slowly. The ventilation system gives him headaches.

His name is Charles T. Gehring, and he is the scholarly heir to a great body of records that document the earliest days of New Amsterdam, the island, Manhattan. He is a doctor of Germanic linguistics, a translator and editor of colonial documents.

The dry titles worry us. We go to lunch. His midday victuals include beer and raw onions. He lets it drop that he once baled hay for his keep. We feel better about him now, but want to know more and look for an opening. We ask about the translator's lot. It seems a dull one, we say with deliberate provocation.

"Oh, no," he begins, taking the bait. "Translation is a creative process. Most people think it's purely mechanical, but it's nothing like that at all. You're not just dealing with word-to-word transference, you're dealing with finding the correct equivalent, the correct situation or social level of speech. The trick is to do it as fairly as possible without interjecting your own personality in the process. You know the Italians have a saying: The translator is a traitor. They mean he is a traitor to the person who wrote the original. I try to be a traitor as little as possible."

The sluice gate is open now and autobiography comes roiling out. He grew up in Fort Plain in New York's Mohawk Valley, the son of an Italian-American mother and a German-American father. His maternal grandparents spoke Italian, and he developed an interest in learning languages. In high school, Latin and French were offered, but "it was mostly girls who took the courses." The Dark Ages.

Our linguist, it seems, was seized by a "childhood dream to fly" and enrolled in the Virginia Military Institute as a precursor to West Point and flight training. After "one year of terror" at V.M.I., he switched to the University of West Virginia. A year later he became a flight cadet, only to discover that he had vertical double vision, which meant that at night he would probably have ended up landing his aircraft six feet under the runway instead of on it.

Out of money and out of the service, he worked for a while as a signalman for the New York Central Railroad. Then back to West Virginia to finish his bachelor's degree and to pick up a master's degree, then off to Germany on a Fulbright Fellowship to develop a dissertation on the mystics of the thirteenth century and their influence on the High German language.

We are at the University of Freiburg now, swimming in syntax and idiom. A class in Dutch suddenly strikes a chord, and the German mystics give way to New World colonists and a new Ph.D. topic: "The Dutch Language in Colonial New York: An Investigation of a Language in Decline and Its Relationship to Social Change."

Another fellowship is offered, and it is back to the States and Indiana University for a program in languages. We stop him here to ask the obvious.

"How many languages have I studied?" He pauses for a moment. "Let's see, there's Old Icelandic, Gothic, Old High German, Middle High German, Danish, Dutch, Swedish, Afrikaans, Sanskrit, Greek, Latin, French, Italian, Old English, Middle English, Hittite, Hebrew, and Sorbian."

Sorbian?

"Low Sorbian, actually. An old West Slavic language. I got quite a few extremely cheap books on Sorbian from East Germany."

A job is offered at the State University of New York at Albany, but tenure is impossible and after six years it is the old story—out. So in the spring of 1974, this speaker of Low Sorbian takes a job as the curator-guide-janitor of a small eighteenth-century farmhouse museum in St. Johnsville, N.Y. While he is there, he decides to work up a little pamphlet on the role of local farmers during the American Revolution and travels to the New York State Museum in Albany to gather information.

The State Library was, at the time, the repository of the New Netherland archives. Over the years four translators had worked on the Dutch manuscripts, the last in this line being A. J. F. van Laer, who gave up the work in 1911 after a fire destroyed some of the archives and damaged others. For sixty years no one seemed to be able to raise the money or to generate any interest in the translation project. Then, in 1974, Ralph De Groff, a trustee of the Holland Society of New York, managed to persuade the state government to allocate funds to renew the project for one year. And officials at the library learned of an expert in seventeenth- and eighteenth-century Dutch language who might be willing to leave his job in a farmhouse museum and take on the task of continuing the translations and the fund-raising.

Only 20 percent of the manuscripts had been translated since the work began in the nineteenth century, and the previous translators had been interested only in politics and extracted from the archives only those passages that were germane. What is more, their translations were never published. Our archivist has set out to publish the complete record, having translated another 20 percent so far, including in it all the social history of the island, the small anonymous voices that found their way into official records.

Ah, yes, these are the voices we want to hear, the ones that will satisfy our impulse to make connections, our desire to be reassured. We are anxious to begin.

The archivist is sitting quietly this morning. History has

revealed itself so slowly to him, he will not allow us to leap into it. We are given background. We must be patient.

He warns that we will have to work hard at this. Court records and council minutes are not the kind of intimate personal papers and letters that easily yield a life. We must infer. We must get a sense of time.

It is the middle of the seventeenth century and the island, a port town, is under the influence of the Dutch West India Company. North of Wall Street is a wilderness. South of it, in homes with gabled roofs and gardens and orchards behind, live some fifteen hundred people. There is trouble with the English and with the Indians. Director General Peter Stuyvesant, able but ambitious, has problems with the budget and proposes one tax after another. Still, there is a sense in these documents that this is the center of the New World, the terminus of trade lines north and south, a busy place filled with opportunity. It may not be called New York yet, but it is, in every other sense, the city.

Are we ready, now? No, says the archivist. Not quite yet. We must understand the process, the "detective work," the long hours spent combing other sources. History does not wash up on the shore and settle at your feet. It is litter along the dunes. It must be gathered and pieced together. And even then, assembled in one place, it does not yield its meaning easily. Here is the obscure line, the baffling allusion, the situation askew. "I've had some bad moments," he confesses, and hands us a bound reproduction of the manuscript.

Volume V, council minutes, 1652–1654, entry No. 15: "Whereas for a long time now we have received many complaints concerning the inconvenience to which the inhabitants are subjected because they cannot get their grain ground or if ground, then improperly done; and for which reason the inhabitants are subjected to using curses and threats; and in order to prevent subsequent disorders . . . a suitable person will be appointed at a yearly salary to oversee the company's windmill. . . ."

Even then, social history recorded long queues and epithets. Today there are the Bureau of Motor Vehicles, the bank at lunch hour, the opening of a new Woody Allen movie. History gives comfort. New Yorkers have been made to wait for more than three hundred years.

Entry No. 18: "The surgeons request by petition that they alone be allowed to shave. The director and council respond that shaving is actually not in the domain of surgery, but is only an appendix to it; and that no one can be denied this service to himself or doing it out of friendship for another. . . . Whereas last summer two or three serious mistakes were made by the inexperience of some ships' barbers; therefore . . . such ships' barbers shall not dress any wound, bleed, or prescribe any drinks for anyone on land without the knowledge or special consent of the petitioners. . . ."

Now here is as clever a political conceit as was ever practiced at City Hall. The doctors, we can guess, became exorcised when the ships' barbers began to siphon their trade, no doubt for a lower fee, and in retaliation they petitioned to put the ships' barbers out of business, at least on land. Special interests, city politics.

At entry No. 30 and again at No. 54, we meet Jacob Claessen, an apparently unsettled man who has lost control. First he claims that Jacob van Curler owes him thirty-two packs of beavers and will not pay his debt. Then he has trouble at home. "The plaintiff demands to know why his wife

Aeltien Dirricksz, the reason why she will not live with him and remains away from him.'' What has happened here? Was Jacob Claessen insufferable? Perhaps Aeltien grew weary of the place, of pigs roaming the streets, of malodorous tanneries and slaughterhouses and riotous taverns, of the Hondeslager, or dog beater, who with his heavy rod disposed of strays and left the carcasses where they fell. Or did she, like so many stirred by this city, find in herself or in someone else a reason to change beds?

If Jacob Claessen was the victim, then his troubles were not over. ''The director and the council having heard the parties and read the depositions, order that the plaintiff be held in confinement until the ships depart for the fatherland, in order to prevent any trouble.'' So there sits Jacob in jail, a cuckold, perhaps, or a brute with a heavy hand, punished either for his love or for his temper. Should we cry for this schlemiel, this latter-day Gimpel? O Aeltien, what have you done?

Or was Aeltien the victim, finally free? O Jacob, are you a fool of another kind, the unhappy Hondeslager of your household? Now we understand the translator's dilemma; the situation is clearly asked, and the manuscript offers no help. The entry does not specify who it was that finally sailed for home.

Further on in Volume V, there are two passing references to Jacob Steendam. We had hoped for more. Jacob Steendam was a poet, by these accounts, Manhattan's first. Dr. Gehring offers help, a slim volume entitled *New Amsterdam and Its People*, by John H. Innes, a turn-of-the-century translator and an enthusiastic purveyor of local history.

Jacob Steendam lived at 26 Stone Street. ''The love of adventure was strong within him,'' wrote Mr. Innes. He signed some of his verse with the pseudonym Noch Vaster, or ''still firmer,'' which the biographer believes was ''adopted from some fancied appositeness to his own name, Steendam signifying 'stone dam.' ''

In the main, he wielded a rhapsodic pen:

> *North and east two streams supplying, 'Twixt the two my garden lying; Here they pour into the sea, Rich with fish, beyond degree. Or, in summation:*
> *Milk and honey flow; Where the wholesome herbs freely as thistles grow; The land where Aaron's Rod its buds doth show; A very Eden!*

In this Eden, on the eve of Lent at the Feast of Bacchus, the Dutch played a game called ''pulling the goose.'' The live animal, its head and neck greased and its limbs bound with rope, was suspended from a pole. The players, on horseback, would ride at it at full gallop and make a grab for the greased parts. The winner of this contest was the one who managed to hold on and separate the body from its limbs or the head and neck from the rest of the animal.

Entry No. 221: ''. . . It has never been the custom in this country and it is considered completely frivolous, needless and disreputable by subjects and neighbors to celebrate such pagan and popish festivals and to introduce such bad customs into this country, even though, as the mayors and schepen claim, it may be tolerated in some places of our fatherland or winked at. . . .''

There does not appear in modern times to be a single recorded case of pulling the goose, though often at night and on certain holidays, there is behavior in the city—considered frivolous, needless, and disreputable—that is tolerated or winked at by the schepen, or aldermen, and everyone else.

At entry No. 370, we encounter Arent Jansz, the provost marshal and, at first glance, a conscientious public official, who during the course of performing his duties was made to suffer abuse from one Sergeant Juriaen Laecken, who was put in irons for gambling during church service. The council, apparently impatient with the sergeant's chronic misbehavior and angered by his disrespect for the provost marshal, ordered the sergeant "to depart on the same ship which brought him here."

Ah, but like so many public officials after him, Arent Jansz apparently did not always keep to the narrow gate and straight way. Although there is no direct testimony in the records to document misbehavior, circumstances indicate that this particular public official might have succumbed to private desire. At entry No. 455, Mary de Truy, a tavern keeper, complained to the council that when she asked the provost marshal to pay his bar bill, "he responded, 'I'll give you the devil for your sick heart. Get out of here or I'll throw you out!'. . . Grabbing her by the arm, he kicked her outside and pinched her one arm between the doors, threatening to throw her in the hole if she refused to go away."

At this point, however, the matter seems to have been dropped. There is no resolution of the case in Volume V. Perhaps the council was preoccupied with English infiltrators, with drafting labor to rebuild the city's crumbling bulwarks, or with making provisions to help widows and orphans. Or maybe it did not call the provost marshal to testify because it remembered that it had once charged Mary de Truy with prostitution, evidently in the tavern he liked to frequent. "If an American of to-day could be transported back 250 years," wrote Mariana Van Rensselaer, a turn-of-the-century historian, in *The City and Its People* (Chapter 14 of *The History of the City of New York in the Seventeenth Century*, Volume I), "he would find himself more comfortably at home on Manhattan than anywhere else. In some of the English settlements, he would have the chance to exercise more direct political power, but in none excepting Rhode Island would he find as much personal freedom, and in none at all a general mental attitude, a prevailing temper, as similar to the temper of the America of today."

We are headed south now, back through the haze toward the city. We have left the archivist to his pages. He has shown us how to find our timeless moments and in them a redemption from time. In the streets of the city we shall hear the old voices, but now they will sound familiar to us. We are convinced that the character of old New York cannot be captured completely in the crumbling masonry of some Dutchman's chamber. We need more than archeology; we need to hear the noise in the silent page, to smell the streets in the reading room. The past reads well.

CHAPTER 7

·····································

A Tour in a Gilded Age

BY JENNIFER DUNNING

―――――――――――――――――――――――――――

". . . how much every commonplace abode in this city has to tell of the tragedy and comedy of life that has passed within it—how little there is in a world of men that is not far from commonplace or insignificant in itself or its associations. How serious a thing is in any row of monotonous twenty-five-foot brick fronts, if one considers what each of them has witnessed or will witness . . ."

So wrote George Templeton Strong on April 2, 1850. The Museum of the City of New York's Sunday Walking Tours, begun in 1959, are dedicated to the same contemplation of the city's buried history, both personal and public. The museum offers a tour that follows Strong's footsteps, a historical visit entitled "Madison Square: The World of Edith Wharton and George Templeton Strong."

Edith Wharton, novelist and short-story writer, lived from 1862 to 1937, spending most of her later life abroad. But much of her work chronicled the conformist upper strata of old New York society from which she came, the

New York of the late nineteenth and early twentieth centuries. She is best known for *Ethan Frome, The House of Mirth, Old New York*, and *The Age of Innocence*, for which she won a Pulitzer Prize in 1921.

George Templeton Strong never achieved Wharton's fame, but his diaries of New York life between 1835 and 1875 are valuable social records of the time. He lived from 1820 to 1875 and was active not only as a lawyer, but also in the political, religious, and artistic issues of the day. He served as a member of the Sanitary Commission, a civic group that assisted wounded Civil War soldiers in the field, and he helped to shape Columbia University as one of its most progressive trustees. He moved in the same world as Wharton's parents and, like her, recorded its manners and mores.

Beginning in the 1840s and coming to an end with the commercialization of the neighborhood in the late 1880s, Madison Square was the site of the residences, stores, and churches of the most fashionable members of New York society. The area's socially accepted boundaries were from 29th Street several blocks to the east and west of Fifth Avenue to Stuyvesant Square and several blocks to its west.

The museum's tour usually begins at the Church of the Transfiguration (the Little Church Around the Corner) at 1 East 29th Street, and zigzags through side streets along Fifth Avenue, across Madison Square Park to Gramercy Park and ends at Stuyvesant Square on 16th Street at Second Avenue. It may include stops at the Little Church and the Marble Collegiate Church, both of which were familiar to Wharton and Strong, and at the Appellate Division of the Supreme Court of the State of New York and the Metropolitan Life Insurance Company, a part of the world which replaced the one they knew. Precise tour stops and routes are left to individual guides. The guides are all well versed in architectural history, and some even carry such props as books or artifacts of the period to lend the tour a sense of immediacy. For very little is left intact of the worlds that Strong and Wharton depicted so acutely: the elegance of a William B. Astor or Hamilton Fish, or the effete existence of General Scole, in Wharton's *The Spark*, an old gentleman with manners "so perfect that they stood him in lieu of language."

Everywhere in the area, however, are telltale signs of what was known as the Gilded Age, for those who know how and where to look. "There are churches and a few buildings that evoke this interesting period," the guide says. "But it's much harder here to read the urban fabric."

Madison Square is rich in nineteenth-century literary legend. Horace Greeley kept a goat in his backyard on East 19th Street. On sunny days, Herman Melville took his granddaughter for walks across the square. Henry James, William Dean Howells, Oscar Wilde, and Stephen Crane all spent part of their lives here. The area figured little in their works, but Strong and Wharton were its recorders—Strong writing with the compassion and humor of the insider, and Wharton with the irony of one who has accepted exclusion.

Neither the Little Church on 29th Street, where the tour starts, nor the Marble Collegiate nearby, were the most fashionable churches of the time. Strong worshiped downtown at Trinity Church and Wharton at Calvary Church, on Park Avenue South and East 21st Street. But both buildings have interesting architectural features and stories to them.

Walking west on 29th Street and several blocks along Broadway, the tour passes examples of the hotels that began to be constructed on Broadway in the 1870s and which came into their own as the section of Broadway from 23rd to 42nd streets became New York's theater district in the 1880s. On the south side of 28th Street between Broadway and Fifth Avenue is a stretch of five brownstones that are good examples of the kind of house the wealthy then owned, such as the one the Archers of Wharton's *The Age of Innocence* lived in on that very street.

It was not an architectural atmosphere Wharton herself could appreciate, having developed other tastes during her travels abroad as a child. In *A Backward Glance* she would write of "the narrow houses so lacking in external dignity, so crammed with smug and suffocating upholstery . . . the little low-studded rectangular New York cursed with its universal chocolate-colored coating of the most hideous stone ever quarried. . . ."

In 1882, after the death of her father, Wharton moved with her mother into a house at 28 West 25th Street. The "Z" Sewing Machine Corporation has superseded the house on that site, but across the street is the church where Wharton made an unhappy marriage in 1885. Now the Serbian Orthodox Cathedral of St. Sava, it was designed in 1855 by Richard Upjohn in the Gothic Revival style and was then a more accessible branch of Trinity Church for uptown parishioners.

After a glance at the little 1860 Parish House next door, designed by J. W. Mould in the richly ornamented style of the Jefferson Court Market, a guide will accompany his fellow walkers down to West 23rd Street where at Number 14, Edith Wharton was born. The facade has changed, and the building converted for business, but a good idea of its original looks and scale may be had by glancing up at the top three floors of 20 West 23rd Street.

It was a solidly well-to-do neighborhood at that time. Living north of Union Square had once been thought pioneering. Then, as the Narrator of Wharton's *New Year's Day* remembers, from his family home on 23rd Street "the new houses advanced steadily Park-ward, outstripping the Thirtieth Streets, taking the Reservoir at a bound, and leaving us in what, in my schooldays, was already a dullish backwater between Aristocracy to the south and Money to the north."

Directly across from Wharton's birthplace on 23rd Street, where the Toy Center South Building now stands, was the famous Fifth Avenue Hotel, the most elegant in the city when it was completed in 1859. It was frequented by the political, literary, and theatrical figures of the day, and it was there, on New Year's Day, that the dashing Mrs. Lizzie Hazeldean carried on an illicit romance.

In his thirtieth year, Strong determinedly wrote: "I've turned over an entirely new leaf—cut Delmonico's, and put myself on a yet shorter allowance of food, the prelude to an entire abstinence therefrom." The resolution did not last, and he was soon back at the most fashionable restaurant in town. Delmonico's has vanished from the northeast corner of Fifth Avenue and 26th Street, but one can almost see Strong, a man addicted to "long hard walks" all over the city, his sharp eyes missing very little of what went on in every stratum of that urban society, setting off at a brisk pace through Madison Square Park after one of his Delmonico lunches.

Madison Square Park cannot have changed so much since. It is flanked on the north by an impressive Saint-Gaudens statue of Admiral David Farragut, resting on a most unlikely Art Nouveau base by Stanford White, his first

New York project. At the south end of the park stands a much maligned statue of William H. Seward by Randolph Rogers, whose small terra-cotta sculptures were to be found in many of the households frequented by the Archers.

On the east side of the park are three buildings of some architectural interest: Cass Gilbert's New York Life Insurance building (1928), the Appellate Division building (1900) by James Brown Lord, and Napoleon LeBrun's Metropolitan Life Insurance Company tower (1909), with its delicate gilded spire rising high above the neighborhood. But for the devoted Strong–Wharton contingent, the area south from Broadway and 23rd Street to Union Square may hold the most interest, for there, on what was then called the Ladies' Mile, in the most fashionable department store of the period, Deia Ralston of Wharton's *The Old Maid* might well have bought her bonnet with the blond ruffles and Mrs. Strong a furbelow to complete her "elaborate attire" in the Sanitary Commission theatricals.

There, at Broadway and 20th Street, may be seen the impressive facade of the original Lord & Taylor and a block further down, that of Arnold Constable's, where it was de rigeur for old money to shop.

Sometimes the guide will escort his charges through the reconstructed East 20th Street birthplace of Theodore Roosevelt, a friend and hero to Wharton. Five rooms there are furnished in the style of the 1860s, with perhaps a hint of the cultivated ferns, macramé lace embroidery, and glazed ware that crowned the Archer home.

And then, on to Gramercy Park where, although Strong's home at its northwest corner has been demolished, the tranquil air of the community remains unchanged. After a surreptitious look inside an ornate lobby or two and a longer glance at some architectural curiosities on the Square, the tour usually proceeds to its end at the elegant Stuyvesant Square.

For information about this and other tours sponsored by the Museum of the City of New York, call (212) 534-1672.

CHAPTER 8

································

Herman Melville's New York

BY HERBERT MITGANG

Herman Melville did not spring full-blown from the forecastle of the *Acushnet,* bound for the South Seas out of New Bedford Harbor with a harpoon in his hand. He was more of a New Yorker than a New Englander, and (sometimes) proud of it. Telling a friend about the freedom to find one's own voice here, he once wrote:

"I would to God Shakespeare had lived late and promenaded in Broadway. Not that I might have had the pleasure of leaving my card for him at the Astor [Hotel], or made merry with him over a bowl of fine punch, but that the muzzle which all men wore on their souls in the Elizabethan day might not have intercepted Shakespeare from articulation."

Manhattan is full of Melville: Melville the uncelebrated novelist, Melville the saddened family man, Melville the customs inspector prowling among the tall ships during the day, writing his unpublished *Billy Budd* late into the night.

He was born here in 1819, and there is a plaque on the site

of a building at 6 Pearl Street, in downtown Manhattan, that Melville scholars pay homage to once a year. He took his only formal learning here—at the New-York Male High School and at Columbia Grammar School. At age twenty, he boarded his first ship, the trader *St. Lawrence*, as a crew member out of New York, sailing to Liverpool and back. And his first book, *Typee*, was rejected by Harper & Bros., then accepted in 1846 by Wiley & Putnam, publishers whose successors still thrive in New York.

During the last twenty-eight years of his life, Melville lived in a one-family brick house at 104 East 26th Street. Here, while earning a living as a customs inspector, he wrote his first volume of poetry, *Battle-Pieces*, and other poems and stories, but nothing that won as much fame in his own time as *Typee*. He wrote the first draft of *Moby-Dick* while living in Pittsfield, Massachusetts, before returning to New York a sardonic, embittered man, struggling for recognition. When *Moby-Dick* was published in 1851, it received disappointing notices. His lifetime earnings from all his books published in the United States came to $5,900.

Not long ago, a troop of intrepid scholars braved the cold to put up a bronze plaque on the side of a nondescript Manhattan office building just east of Park Avenue South. It reads:

HERMAN MELVILLE
The American Author
Resided from 1863–1891
at This Site
104 East 26th Street
Where He Wrote
BILLY BUDD
Among Other Works

They were members of the Melville Society, keepers of the flame for the great American novelist. Spouting white whales, imprinted in the design of the blue ties worn by several of the thirty-five men and women present, added a touch of color to the street scene. In a marvelous piece of detective work, the society, which has five hundred members and reaches devotees as far away as Japan, had finally pinned down the exact place where Melville lived during one of his most productive periods.

"What about the best thing he ever wrote—his eighteen-thousand word poem, *Clarel*?" asked Hershel Parker of the University of Delaware, one of the professors who had gathered on the sidewalk for the dedication. "He wrote it in 1876 in his house here—why isn't *Clarel* on the plaque?"

"Because we couldn't include everything," said Donald Yannella, chairman of the English department at the University of Southern Mississippi, who is secretary-treasurer of the society. "For the general public, we thought that *Billy Budd* would be his most familiar work."

"Fellow Melvillians," said Edward H. Rosenberry, an emeritus professor of the University of Delaware, a former president of the thirty-six-year-old society. "As you know, *Billy Budd, Sailor*, was not published while he was alive."

"It didn't come out until 1924," explained the incoming president, Thomas Tanselle of the Guggenheim Foundation, to a non-Melvillian.

Someone asked about Melville's working routine here, and Louis Zara, who is writing a biography, pointed to Professor Stanton Garner of the University of Texas at

Arlington. In the branches of Melvilliana, Professor Garner is considered "the Custom House expert."

"Melville was a district inspector in the Custom House Service," said Professor Garner. "He walked from his house west to the Hudson River. In later years, his post was moved uptown along the East River. He probably took the Third Avenue El to work—it was already in existence in the 1880s. It's strange to think of this man, who once sailed in square-rigged ships, riding the El.

"He got into the Custom House right after the Civil War, one of the few men who obtained such a post without a political sponsor. The job he held was one of the lowest in the service—one thousand dollars a year. And he never got a raise—he still made the same thousand when he resigned in 1885. But he used his idle hours near the piers to write on little scraps of paper."

How did Professor Garner unearth these vital details? "I've been spending a lot of time in Bayonne, New Jersey, where the federal records are kept," he said. "There's not too much—Melville was an expert on keeping his name out, which probably helped him to escape the perils of the civil service. Later in his career, he had to wear a uniform while inspecting cargo. It's mind-boggling—Melville wearing a uniform that was just like a city policeman's."

Melville lived here with his wife, two daughters, and two sons (both died while the author occupied the residence). Paul Metcalf, whose mother was a Melville granddaughter, sent a postcard from Becket, Massachusetts, to Charles Neumeier, who teaches at Stuyvesant High School, approving where the Melville plaque was being placed: "Much better he should be a delivery entrance than an armory!"

The 104 East 26th Street address today is the delivery entrance to the office building at 357 Park Avenue South. Right next to the plaque is the rear of the 69th Regiment Armory building on Lexington Avenue. For many years, until research by Mr. Neumeier and Professor Yannella proved otherwise, many people thought that the armory rather than a business building had replaced the Melville house.

In tracking down the exact site, Messrs. Neumeier and Yannella examined tax records in the Municipal Archives and old atlases. There was a certain amount of confusion in the records caused by renumbering; the 104 address had earlier been designated as 60 East 26th Street. Then the tax records unfolded the clues: The Melville home was in the city's Eighteenth Ward on Block No. 881. It occupied Lot No. 82. The listing for 1832 reads: "Owner, Elizabeth S. Melville; Size of Lot, 20 × 98; Size of House, 20 × 45; Stories, 3; Value of Real Estate, $6,500." At the time of Melville's death, the value of the property had gone up to $7,000. It was replaced in 1902 by a seven-story structure.

In 1890, Melville could look up from the stoop of his home and see a nude golden Diana, the mythical huntress, poised on one foot, aiming her arrow in his direction from her tower crown on Stanford White's gleaming new Madison Square Garden.

The Garden site on the northwest corner of Park Avenue South and East 26th Street is now the location of the New York Life Insurance building. The old Garden was razed in 1928, but Augustus Saint-Gaudens's Diana survives atop a grand staircase in the Philadelphia Museum of Art. A copy of Diana exists in the Metropolitan Museum of Art. And a movie Diana appears in the film *Ragtime*, in which Norman Mailer plays the role of Stanford White.

Melville, who had once lectured on the marbles of ancient

Rome, may have approved of Saint-Gaudens's thirteen-foot Diana, mounted on a revolving base like a weather vane, hovering over his neighborhood. The scholars are not sure. However, one incensed newspaper, *The Philadelphia Times*, denounced the sculpture as representing "the depraved artistic taste of New York."

Among the scholars at a later meeting of the Melville Society at Baruch College was Jay Leyda, professor of film studies at New York University and author of the two-volume work that Melvillians consider their bible, *The Melville Log*.

Professor Leyda said: "I've included every document I could find about Melville, and I've had to add material recently—there's always some new detail turning up. He was probably the best-read of any American writer. Of course, questions have been raised about Melville's sanity."

Was the great nineteenth-century novelist, whom fame eluded in his own lifetime, not sane?

"Well, insanity was a very broad diagnosis in those days," Professor Leyda replied. "He had family problems and he couldn't make a living and his work wasn't fully recognized. Let me put it this way: It was a miracle that he held on to his sanity."

On September 29, 1891, a day after the man who today stands in the front rank of American novelists died, *The World* wrote a short notice. The first sentence began: "Herman Melville, formerly a well-known author. . . ."

PART 2

....

9 P.M. to
5 A.M.

CHAPTER 9

....

9 P.M. to 5 A.M.

BY MAUREEN DOWD

You are limited only by your imagination. Or your stamina.

"Every week there's a new club," says the pale guru of the night scene, Andy Warhol. "Every day there's a new restaurant."

The night is crisp with promise. In the boom years, from the repeal of Prohibition into the 1960s, night life was concentrated in a few bright pools. Café society frolicked in the midtown supper clubs whose names evoke the glamorous high life: El Morocco, the Blue Angel, the Colony Club, "21," the Latin Quarter, the Stork Club. In Greenwich Village, Harlem, the East 50s, and along the length of 52nd Street, there were legendary evenings of jazz and comedy. Lenny Bruce worked the clubs here in the beginning of his career, as did Mike Nichols and Elaine May, Shelley Berman, Mort Sahl, Dick Gregory, and Woody Allen.

"You could walk down a single block of saloons on Fifty-second Street and hear Art Tatum, Billie Holiday, and Charlie Parker on a single night," recalls writer Pete Hamill, who did just that as a teen-ager. "And you could go to the Latin Quarter and see girls running around with bananas on their heads.

"On the other hand," he adds, "Babe Ruth doesn't play for the Yankees anymore, either."

The style may be different, but the night is once again charged with energy and romance and, sometimes, raunchiness. Elegance is back in vogue, with soigné clothes and late dinners. The playground has become more diffuse, geographically and, with the expanding presence of European and Latin American arrivistes, culturally. Colorful new clubs and restaurants, in varying shades of sophistication, stripe Manhattan from the Upper East and West Sides through midtown, the Village, down into the formerly deserted business district of lower Manhattan, and even under the Brooklyn Bridge.

The divisions have blurred between young and old, and old and new. Consider Bobby Short and Maura Moynihan.

Short, sixty-one years old, who plays the piano and sings Cole Porter at the Café Carlyle on Madison Avenue and 76th Street, personifies New York sophistication. After he finishes work at one A.M., he likes to change out of his tuxedo and go downtown to dancing clubs like Area and Limelight. "That's where the real night life is," he says. "I love the freedom and casualness of it all. What I do is almost quaint compared to that."

Maura Moynihan is going in the opposite direction. This twenty-seven-year-old daughter of New York's Democratic senator, former member of a punk band and current contributing editor for Warhol's *Interview* magazine, is at the center of the city's young smart set. Yet she is bored with discos. "You can't talk," she says, yelling over the new-wave music at Area. "It's too much of an assault. I'm rediscovering the old New York: The lobby of the Waldorf. The Pierre. The Ritz. The Plaza. The Sherry Netherland. The Rainbow Room."

It is this diverse jumble of places and people and shops and services that makes Manhattan after dark seductive. "You're twenty-four inches away from everything," says David Witt, an Australian television writer, as he eats cheesecake at the Algonquin Hotel. "There are bars for every fad, fascination, social inclination, and sexual preference."

At three A.M., any yen can be satisfied, from eating crayfish stew to buying Connie Francis albums or hand-dyed silk party dresses or used hubcaps, fish scalers or birds of paradise. There are midnight punk hair salons, dentists at dawn, and twenty-four hour therapists, marriage brokers, air-charter services, florists, bowling lanes, and bagel shops. There are some two hundred restaurants and coffee shops open round-the-clock in Manhattan and twice that many delicatessens.

Strange and wonderful confluences lace the night with fantasy. Cynthia Shoss, a lawyer who moved to Manhattan from Cape Girardeau, Missouri, wore her purple Norma Kamali jump suit to dinner at Café Seiyoken on West 18th Street. There, at the nouvelle Japanese restaurant, was Norma Kamali wearing her Norma Kamali jump suit.

"You can see things here," says David Witt, "that you only read about anywhere else."

And you can read about things here that you see on any evening in Manhattan. A journey, of many nights, from 9 to 5.

9 P.M.

Gowned by Blass and jeweled by Bulgari, the lady rushed into the Midnight Sun Tanning Salon on Madison Avenue as it was closing. She unclasped her diamond-and-ruby necklace and earrings and dropped them into the hands of the manager. "Hold these while I tan," she said, darting into a ray room. "I've got to be at a gala at the Met in half an hour." She left on time, glowing golden brown.

10 P.M.

The blond hair was teased high and wide. The stockings were black lace. The pumps, red. The jean jacket was by Levi, not by Calvin, her designing father. And on her arm, Marci Klein wore thirty-five bangle bracelets. "Did you think we were hookers?" she asked, laughing with amusement. "It's important to wear as much jewelry as possible. It adds zing and makes the night more electric."

Marci is a De Tocqueville of the New York night scene. On any evening, she can be found having drinks at a Columbus Avenue café, eating at the latest sushi place, hanging out at the clubs.

"I feel jaded," she said. "I've been going out every night for five years. I was warned by my parents that I'd get really bored if I kept going out. And I am."

Sitting with two girl friends, she surveyed the glittering crowd at the Café Luxembourg near Lincoln Center.

"We wanted a new place," she said. "It's not easy to find good early-night action.

"As I look around," she said, frowning, "I see a few not-so-attractive people."

Her friend Stephanie Watzdorf, a tawny vision in leopard-skin pants and rhinestone earrings, echoed her ennui. "It's sort of an American Art Deco imitation of a Paris café," she sniffed.

Marci suggested that they head down to Studio 54. "Studio's not good at all anymore," she said. "Guys from the Bronx, Brooklyn, and Queens dancing the hustle in Saturday Night Fever white suits. But it's like our living room. We don't go there to dance or get hassled. We go in sweat pants to see our friends.

"It's difficult to keep the night interesting," she said, sipping her Tab reflectively. "I guess the thing is, when you're in New York, you want to be in Europe."

The man going into Elaine's suddenly stops, looking panicked. "Wait a minute," he says, grabbing his date's arm. "What if no one famous is here?"

Not to worry.

Center court, as some call the coveted cluster of back tables in this literati hangout, is shimmering with stars. Installed at his regular table near the cappuccino machine is Elaine's headline attraction, Woody Allen. He's holding hands with an angelic-looking Mia Farrow, who is talking to her mother, the actress Maureen O'Sullivan, who is eating pasta. At the next table are Alan King and his wife, Jeannette. Then Jules Feiffer. Then Alice and Michael Arlen.

Etiquette at Elaine's means not staring at Allen's table.

"New Yorkers are the worst tourists in the world," says David Watson, a theatrical producer who often eats at Elaine's. "We pretend we don't see Woody Allen sitting there when we're really staring at him the whole time. We should all just whip out our Instamatic cameras and get it over with.''

11 P.M.

At long last, New York. They were honeymooners from Waco, Texas, who had been saving their money for this enchanted evening. First, they dined at the Four Seasons. Then they saw *A Chorus Line*. Now, they were sitting in the cozy darkness of the Café Carlyle, listening to Bobby Short.

"He's just like he is on the Charlie commercial," said Maureen Yett in a gentle drawl.

The singer was spinning a silken Gotham fantasy:

> *We are seen around New*
> *York,*
> *El Morocco and the Stork.*
> *And the other stay-up-late*
> *cafés . . .*
> *Like to drink and dance*
> *around,*
> *And maybe kick romance*
> *around . . .*
> *All in fun . . .*
> *Some cocktails, some orchids, a show or two. . . .*

His voice was hoarse from hay fever, and he has been stoking up on tea with lemon. But the Yetts were caught in the magic.

"He's just like I pictured him," Maureen said, "like Tony Bennett, Frank Sinatra, and Dean Martin all in one." David reached over to hold his bride's hand.

"We'll be eating hot dogs for weeks," he said, smiling.

"I almost got trampled on the street today," she said, smiling.

The Rockies may crumble, Gibraltar may tumble. Their love went home to Waco the next day.

Beneath the opalescent globes of the Odeon, ten blocks north of the World Trade Center, New York's downtown café society of artists, actors, and musicians were dining. All were capriciously garbed and many were wearing sunglasses. The theme music from *77 Sunset Strip* was playing. It was New York at its most fiercely chic. It was too much for a young lady sitting alone at the long Art Deco bar, gulping brandy and looking terrified.

"I don't belong here," she confessed to a man next to her.

He was sympathetic. "A girl with your looks? Forget it." He said that he was from Queens, but that he did not like to party in Queens. Anyway, he told her, all of his friends were home watching the Islanders hockey game on television. He tried to give her confidence.

"I have a theory," he explained. "Everybody is a jerk, but there are two kinds of jerks. Some people act cool and glib, like they know what they're doing. Others just party and have a good time and don't care what anybody else thinks."

She nodded. He smiled. They had another drink.

12 A.M.

It was midnight at Roseland and the fox-trot had given way to the Boy George.

Johnny Mulay and His Orchestra had stopped playing ballroom music. With them went the spotlights' mauve glow and the men in gray suits and the women in chiffon skirts and gold shoes. Hal Gordon, an art dealer and regular at Roseland for twenty years, watched with disdain as young people surged onto the floor and began the syncopated movements of electric boogeying under strobe lights. "It's shaking, not dancing," he yelled over the blare of a Herbie Hancock tape. "You don't hold your partner. You don't even need a partner."

Elaine Hardy, a twenty-year-old from Brooklyn, was indeed engaged in a solo, robotlike rendition of dances she and her friends had named for rock stars—the Michael Jackson and the Boy George. She wore a white lace glove on her left hand and a "Where's the Beef?" button on her blouse. "When I get to their age," she said, pointing to the sidelined ballroom crowd, "I'll do the tango. But right now, it's t-o-o-o slow."

1 A.M.

The creamy white Mercedes limousine stretched along Third Avenue, waiting in the moonlight.

A beautiful young woman walked out of Jim McMullen's restaurant, wearing a red drop-waist dress and a drop-dead expression. She tried the back door of a Cadillac parked in front of the white limo but found it locked. Pouting, she flicked her red, zebra-striped hat at the driver lounging against the Mercedes. "Here you are," she said, "and I can't find my driver anywhere. It's totally outrageous."

She sashayed off, but the driver was not looking. Jesse Gislason was running his hand along the flank of the Illustria, the white car he drives for what he proudly describes as "a very elite clientele." Beneath the sunroof sat a television and a rack full of rock video tapes. Three crystal decanters gleamed with vodka, gin, and scotch. A cellular phone sat atop 750-watt stereo speakers.

"This car only comes out at night," he said. "I don't like to drive it during the day because it's too ostentatious. It's an outrageous party car. I take clients to the clubs, and as soon as she pulls up, it's like the parting of the Red Sea. They never have to wait in line."

This night, for fifty dollars an hour, the white car belonged to Don Blackburn, who was in from the Coast to help direct a commercial for Belmont Park Race Track. "Everyone's got to have a gimmick in New York," the driver said.

Don Blackburn was eating dinner at McMullen's, one of the many East Side restaurants cloned from the fabled bar, P. J. Clarke's. The crowd was high-gloss: models and sports stars, politicians and business moguls. Men in blue blazers and striped ties. Women in backless dresses and eight-millimeter pearls, or maybe seven and a half. Peter Ueberroth, the baseball commissioner, was at one table; Andrew Stein, Manhattan Borough President, at another. As a pianist played "As Time Goes By" again, Jim McMullen pointed out other regulars.

"That guy's from Switzerland. He's worth three billion dollars.

"That's Norman Alexander. He invented polyester and the seamless bra.

"That's Lauren Helm. She's a top model."

Lauren Helm rolled her large blue eyes and confessed she and her girl friend had been at the restaurant for eight hours. Lauren said they had been talking about "life, the universe, everyone we ever knew, everyone we can possibly imagine, all at once, going backward fifty years and ahead twenty years."

Next to her, with a felt-tip pen, Norman Alexander was drawing a polyester molecule on the tablecloth and talking about "interpersonal interfacing." His friend, Silvia Simonelli, an alluring Italian journalist, was drawing body parts in a parlor game meant to reveal personality traits.

The restaurateur happily watched the ruin of his linen. "New York night life in the eighties," he said, "is bright, witty, Oscar Wilde conversations."

That could be a matter of interpersonal debate. It was, after all, Oscar Wilde who said: "In matters of grave importance, style, not sincerity, is the vital thing."

As conversations drifted, so did the diners. Outside, the white limo was gone. In its place stretched an ordinary black Rolls, waiting in the moonlight.

You shall know them by their lines, the hot cafés and dance clubs. They begin to fill up just when most places are closing.

The line in front of the Hard Rock Café snaked down West 57th Street. Bobby Zarem, publicist extraordinaire, who attends more openings and events after dark than anyone could—or would care to—imagine, moved past the throng. These were ordinary mortals who held no gold Hard Rock Express cards and so had no assurance of quick entry.

"You've got to give Mickey Rourke and Sean Penn and Liza Minnelli and Michael Douglas and Rod Stewart and Nick Nolte a way to get in without standing in line for forty-five minutes," he explained.

Inside, rock music was pounding. Maureen Starkey, the ex-wife of Ringo Starr, sat sipping Taittinger's at a table overlooking a display of Ringo's old drums.

The café is patronized by the children of celebrity: Julian

Lennon, Jade Jagger, Jenny and Amy Lumet, Anderson and Carter Vanderbilt. Polly Segal, daughter of George (the actor, not the painter), is a waitress. Rock Brynner, son of Yul (one of the co-owners), is a manager.

Elaine Kaufman, whose own restaurant, Elaine's, had already closed, had stopped by for champagne and a cheeseburger. She met Rock and, shouting over the din, told him that when he was born, she was working in his mother's obstetrician's office.

She soon left, saying good-bye to the children of some of her customers on her way out. "At least in my place," she said, reaching the relative serenity of the street, "you can talk."

2 A.M.

Downtown, on an otherwise deserted street, the line outside of Area is so long that it almost intersects the line of people waiting to get into Heartbreak, several blocks to the north. These two clubs, the Brazilian dinner club across the way (S.O.B.'s for Sounds of Brazil, naturally) plus a number of others have all opened within the past few years, brightening the barren, industrial landscape of SoHo and Tribeca (acronym for the blocks between Broadway and the Hudson River, north of Barclay Street, and south of Canal Street—the Triangle Below Canal).

"You've got to have a selective door policy or you get the Bridge and Tunnel crowd," says Area's publicist, Joe Dolce. "We've got a particular problem here because we're so close to the Holland Tunnel."

Clubs are no longer merely places to drink and dance. You gotta have a gimmick, an idea behind the night. At Heartbreak, cigarette girls jive their way through couples jitterbugging to '50s rock 'n' roll. At Visage, near the river on West 56th, mermaids and King Neptune descend on a swing from the ceiling into a pool; close to the dance floor, Hell's Angels ice-skate on a miniature portable rink.

Area, the hottest of them all, is totally redecorated every five weeks, when the theme changes. The club was outfitted with pink flamingos and giant Tide boxes for the suburban period; with wrestlers and trampolines for sports; with Mao posters and a huge sculpture of a hand with scarlet fingernails for the color red.

"The old business of just going to drink seems a bit mindless," says Sylvia Miles, an actress who has been on the club-and-disco circuit long enough to know.

Theme parties—celebrating everything from William Burroughs's seventieth birthday to Grace Jones's thirty-second—lure the famous, poseurs, and pretties. The parties often smack of the surreal. At a designer's party, introducing a beachwear collection, tables were arrayed with Barbie dolls sitting in sand buckets. That night, one writer familiar with the club scene watched in dismay as Anthony Haden-Guest, another writer, bit off his Barbie's head and limbs. Asked why Haden-Guest did it, she sighed, "Because it was there."

Like Chinese boxes, there are themes within themes within themes. On Monday nights, Area offers "obsession" nights—with fixations such as sex, pets, and body oddities. At a recent "sex evening," nude jugglers and whip dancers moved in and out of the crowd while an ex-nun heard sexual confessions in the ladies' room and an old man played with inflatable dolls in a pool.

This evening, the theme is "confinement," and the club is decorated with dolls in pajamas chained underwater, a caged rabbit, and go-go dancers armed with guns and dressed in army fatigues.

"Where's Andy Warhol?" asks a young punk, dragging on a joint and scanning the crowd. "I want to get a good look at him."

"I think he went to Limelight," says his friend. At Limelight, a church-turned-club on the Avenue of the Americas at 20th Street, halolike arcs of light stream from stained-glass windows.

"We should go there," says someone else.

"We should go there immediately," says another.

They scurry off to Limelight, unaware that their quarry, wearing corduroys and a backpack, is standing unobtrusively at the bar.

"This is the best bar in town," Andy Warhol says. "You could take everything out and put it in a gallery."

Matt Dillon, Vincent Spano, and Mickey Rourke, each confident in his role as a teen idol, make their separate ways through the crowd, as young girls reach out to touch their arms, backs, anything. Director Francis Ford Coppola is talking to the actress Diane Lane.

Nearby, Don Marino, an up-and-coming actor, is talking to Brian Jones, an up-and-coming director. "L.A. is a whole different world," the actor says. "You go to the A party, the B party, and you are home in bed by eleven for your five-o'clock call the next morning. In New York, you've got to be seen at night, you've got to get around." The young director scans the room. "I know people Coppola knows," he says. "I wonder if I could go say hi."

Others are working the room in other ways.

A tall blonde in a short dress is talking to a short man in a straw boater.

"Where do you get your antiques?" she asks. "What do you do, go shopping or something?"

"Yes," he says. "What do you do?"

"I'm an actress, of course. Tell me your name one more time so I'll remember it."

"Alan."

"I'm glad I met you, Alan. I definitely need an antique."

"Do you want to get together later?"

"Definitely," she says, moving off into the crowd. "Later."

Rival club owners drop by to check out the competition. Bouncing around the dance floor is Toby Beavers, a garrulous, fraternity-cute thirty-year-old who is one of the owners of the Surf Club, a popular Upper East Side hangout for preppies. It has been suggested that if the Surf Club were hit by a bomb, a whole generation of investment bankers and debutantes would be wiped out.

"This place clobbers the hell out of any club in town," he says good-naturedly. "Have you checked out the ladies' room? All hell is breaking loose in there."

In the ladies' room, men and women are standing around talking, drinking, trading phone numbers, congregating in the stalls. Peter Melhado wanders in and does a double take. "Is this a bona fide bathroom?" the twenty-six-year-old business-school student asks, looking around with disgust. "It reminds me of the fall of the Weimar Republic."

The ladies' room at Heartbreak is all pink and all girls.

Through a fog of hair spray, Christine Rucci teases her hair. "From nine to five, I'm Susie Executive," says the twenty-one-year-old designer, who is wearing a black dress puffy with crinolines, a white cashmere cardigan, and dangling rhinestone earrings. "You go to work, do your job, and at night you go out and do something different. Here, you can be really different."

Heartbreak is a time machine, set for the 1950s, prom night. Records spin behind a cafeteria counter. Mounted swordfish hang above the bar, flanked by posters of James Dean and Marilyn Monroe. There is a stag line of men sporting pompadours and black leather jackets. Everyone chews gum and drinks beer. Smoke gets in your eyes. Mick Jagger dropped by one night to strut around the room, lips jutted, as Elvis wailed. Jeremy Irons was there at the same time, dancing a slinky lindy to Marvin Gaye.

Others may opt for saddle shoes and high-top Keds. Not Katy K. She wears black mules. Always. Miss K., a dress designer, affects the Jayne Mansfield look. She sports a fluffy wig and a low-cut black cocktail dress. "Drag queens dress like this," she says, smoothing the tight dress tighter over her hips. "Why should they have all the fun?"

When asked about the enduring charm of the '50s, she says: "Roles are easy. Boys are boys. Girls are girls. Everybody knows who they are supposed to be. Boys pay for everything.

"America was king in the fifties," she continues. "I mean you wouldn't want all of it back. You wouldn't want Little Rock and communism again. But dating and corsages are fun."

For Christine Rucci, the '50s are only hearsay, but she thinks they're neat. "It's nostalgic, yet it's fashionable," she says. "It could be now, but it's a thing from the past."

"New York knows how to theatricalize romance," says

Eustacia Cutler, sitting in the Art Deco splendor of the Rainbow Room. "This room is the epitome of that."

Moving to the windows of the adjacent Rainbow Grill, with a view of the Verrazano-Narrows Bridge, she murmurs, "Look at the bridge, like strings of pearls."

The city has more lights than ever, and more people are gazing at them, from the Rainbow Room, the River Café, Windows on the World, the Water Club, Beekman Towers, the Top of the Park at the Gulf & Western Building, the Coho at South Street Seaport, even from boats cruising around the harbor.

Eustacia Cutler, a New York writer, and her friend Robert Strange, a retired financier from Boston, are sipping champagne with another couple they had met on the dance floor. Mr. Strange reminisces about the early 1930s, when John D. Rockefeller, Jr., first rented space in his new skyscraper. "The area was all brownstones and whorehouses then," he says. "No one thought this place was a good idea."

The maître d'hotel tells them that it is two A.M., closing time.

Mr. Strange gently asks if they might finish their champagne. It is a special place for him, he tells his companions, because he was once on the board of directors for Rockefeller Center.

Champagne is had by all.

You can buy the best of Lesley Gore and Connie Francis at Big Hit Oldies in the Village. You might pick up a 45 of "When Santa Comes Over the Brooklyn Bridge." You can also pick up rolling papers and used hubcaps for five dollars and lapel buttons with legends like "Preppies from Hell."

"We have," says the owner, Broadway Al, tugging on his fedora, "something for everyone."

By 2:30 A.M., the place has the look of a clubhouse. Broadway Al is harmonizing with Little Joey Juliano to Lee Andrews and the Hearts' 1957 Chess Records version of "Long Lonely Nights." Meat Bones, the resident German shepherd, howls tenor.

3 A.M.

They had dined at Jams, danced at Club A, and capped the evening with burgers and beer at P. J. Clarke's.

But Donna O'Bryan was feeling blue. She had a craving, it seemed, for tulips.

Eager to oblige, the O'Bryans' chauffeur jumped out of the limo and picked up two yellow tulips on Park Avenue. But yellow wasn't quite right.

At home in Newport Beach, California, Frank O'Bryan, vice-chairman of Shearson Lehman/American Express, sends his wife two dozen mauve tulips every Tuesday. And their hotel room at the Ritz Carlton seemed empty without them.

So the limo pulled up to the Rialto Florist on Lexington Avenue. The O'Bryans, glowing with diamonds and happiness and fine wine, sailed in to fetch their flowers.

"My wife," said Frank O'Bryan, "is the only woman in America with no limit on her credit card. And she's exceeded it."

He paid in cash.

The set at the Village Vanguard ended. Slide Hampton packed up his trombone, Ron Carter zipped up his bass. A few people stood around in an alcove near the dressing room lined with empty cartons of beer. It was 3:30 A.M., midevening for jazz musicians and their fans. Marietta Drummond sat at a table rolling a cigarette. Manager of the gift shop at the Cathedral of St. John the Divine, she goes to jazz clubs four or five nights a week.

"It's the improvisation," she said. "The music is happening at that moment, in that way. Some nights the tunes, the sets are magical. And it will never happen again in that particular way. If I don't go, I feel that I've missed something special." She headed off to a jam session. Just in case.

4 A.M.

The couple got into a cab and asked to go to Area.

"Area's bar closes at four," the cabbie said. "Do you want to check out an after-hours joint?" They looked at each other, startled, and said sure, why not. The cabbie turned onto West Houston Street and pulled up outside a building with the sign King Bear Auto Service Center. The street was deserted except for a small cluster of people standing outside a metal door that periodically opened and closed.

A man came out and announced: "If you want to get in, let me see your card from Phil." Several people held up business cards and slipped past. Nick Nolte, wearing a seedy blue raincoat and a Jack Daniel's cap, ducked in without showing a card. So did fellow actor Jan-Michael Vincent.

"I know Phil, but I forgot my card," said a burly, bearded man.

"If you know Phil," sneers the doorman. "If you know Phil, then you call him up. You wake him up. You get a card from him. And then you come back. If you know Phil."

"I don't want to bother him."

"I think," the doorman said, "you're undercover."

With that, the burly one lumbered away, yelling obscenities. The young couple, whose aura was more Ralph Lauren
than undercover, showed their work ID's, submitted to two
frisks for firearms, slipped thirty dollars to a disembodied
hand that appeared from beneath an opaque window, and finally achieved the inner sanctum of Page Six.

John Maksim, a sales representative for F. A. MacCluer,
a sportswear manufacturer, and Leah Wasserberger, a
buyer for Mark Cross, sat wide-eyed amid the palms in the
bar. "I've had many job offers outside of New York, but I
would not take them because I love the night life here," he
said. "Here we were, ready to call it a night, and we stop to
look at a crowd on the street and end up in this place at four
A.M., drinking gin and tonics next to Nick Nolte."

In that city's after-hours clubs, all manner of erotic, auto-
erotic, and neurotic divertissements are offered: gambling,
drugs, heterosexual and homosexual encounters, bondage
and bowling. Page Six is popular and relatively tame, three
stories of bars and a dance floor. Drug use is not blatant. But
the lines to the rest rooms, which are cordoned off and
guarded by a uniformed attendant, move very, very slowly.

By 4:30 A.M., the bartenders began to run out of glasses
and booze. A bottle of Dom Perignon was served with
frosted plastic glasses. The rest room attendant was asked
what time they would close.

"We close at eleven," he said. "But don't worry. There's
a place on Twenty-sixth Street that opens at noon."

At Tiffany's, there is breakfast. It is one of a number
of places—the glossy Empire Diner, the funky Market
diners—that cater to the early-morning hunger of late-night

....

Eating Around the Clock
BY BRYAN MILLER

Of all the all-night spots in Manhattan, the most unfailingly democratic are the three Market diners, all just a short spin from the Hudson River and its tunnels. They are stainless steel anachronisms you would expect to see on Route 66, with wraparound parking lots, gum-snapping waitresses, and single-digit meals right out of the prewar years. All night long, everyone from bone-weary cabbies to exuberant young punkers and fashionably preened partygoers stop by for a jolt of 40-weight java and a wedge of glutinous pie. The good-natured if jaded staff probably would not look up from their check pads if Queen Elizabeth II slid into a booth and ordered a B.L.T. "Whole wheat, rye, or white, ma'am?"

The Market Diner on West 43rd Street at Eleventh Avenue, more fancified than the diner at 33rd Street and Ninth Avenue or the one at West and Laight streets, is, like all diners, just a bit too brightly lighted for comfort. It has a long, L-shaped counter—the box seats of dinerland—from which you can glance through an open window into the kitchen and see the white-frocked cooks rustle up the day's

revelers who don't want to stop. Tiffany II, a twenty-four-hour café on West 4th Street that is filled mostly with male couples, has a menu with 307 items. Sliced tomatoes are forty cents extra. Between ringing up checks, Josephine Kenny does puzzles at her cash register. "Every time I hear Frankie Sinatra sing 'New York, New York,' " she says, "I specials; meatballs and spaghetti ($4.30), pot roast and potato pancakes "with veg. and salad" ($6.50). You can be assured that endive and raddichio never got near this kitchen. And so what if the meatballs have enough bread filling to double as dinner rolls in a pinch? This is an authentic diner, the archetype of American highway cuisine, a gastronomic emergency room for night owls. One should be grateful it has survived the exposed brick and ersatz Roman column assault witnessed in so many Manhattan restaurants.

At the 43rd Street diner, the décor is strictly simulated woodgrain paneling and lots of slippery vinyl. The only concession to interior design is a row of bizarre stalactitelike chandeliers the color of lemon lollipops. The West Street diner is far more modest, though it does have a view of the Hudson. It is patronized largely by cops and taxi drivers who stare into their omelets while listening dreamily to piped-in Johnny Mathis. The chef's specialty is something called a Delancey Street Melt.

As homespun as these diners are, they are not immune to the greedy practice of imposing minimum charges on customers who want to rest the feet with just a drink or something light to eat. On the menu is printed in bold type: MINIMUM CHECK 50 CENTS PER CUSTOMER. Outrageous.

think that he should visit the Village. He should see this madhouse."

5 A.M.

Reeling from the heady task of chronicling New York at night, the writer decided to get some fresh air. She took her date for a dawn cruise on the Staten Island Ferry. The couple snuggled against the wind, drinking champagne and eating potato chips bought at the snack bar. They saw the Statue of Liberty, modest behind a mesh construction screen, and watched the lights of the Manhattan skyline twinkle off. It all seemed terribly romantic until, just past dawn, the ferry docked at Staten Island and three hundred cyclists rolled aboard, bound for a race around Manhattan. The invasion was jarring. The ferry sailed with the sunrise. Reluctantly, the couple turned the city over to the day people. In another sixteen hours, the night-trippers would begin their shift all over again.

CHAPTER 10

....

Guardian of the Gate

BY WILLIAM E. GEIST

"To not get in is to die," Laura Barclay explained.

Miss Barclay lives, thanks to her ostrich-feathered turban. The doorman at the Area Nightclub spotted her top feathers in the roiling sea of human desperation outside the club one night and commanded one of his lieutenants to pull her through the pressing crowd, up the steps from social oblivion, and into the club.

"Oh, thank you, thank you, thank you," Miss Barclay said, as if Joe Brese were the doorman on the last helicopter out of Danang. Mr. Brese has the power to save social lives. With a point of his finger and a word to a security man, he determines who shall pass into this rock club, now enjoying the fleeting status of New York's hottest.

The chosen thank him, kiss him, hug him, and push gratuities into his hand. After a year at the door, his status is such that he can no longer pay for meals in restaurants or for clothing at boutiques, so eager are those in the know to in-gratiate themselves.

Those he has not selected have pulled guns on him nine times, knives six times, and a baseball bat once. A few days ago, a full bottle of wine was hurled at him, crashing against a wall eight inches from his head. He stays a safe distance from the crowd to avoid kicks and jabs. It really is all that important.

"This could only happen in New York," said the mild-mannered Mr. Brese, thirty-two years old, who has worked throughout the country and was lured to this job by the club's owners from his home in San Francisco. "New York is a city of money, power, and big egos that bruise easily."

At an hour when most of New York was going to bed—the club does not even open until eleven P.M.—the crowd out-side Area swelled to several hundred, spilling out onto Hudson Street in front of Number 157 near the Holland Tunnel and mingling with squadrons of arriving taxis and limousines.

Mr. Brese stood at the top of the stairs, wearing a black beret and a long, black coat that lent him a vaguely monklike appearance. As if mounting the steps to a temple, a burly se-curity man slowly walked to him and said quietly: "E. Randolph. Says he's on the list." That would be the list—a computer printout made anew each day and containing the names of those who are positively allowed in. Mr. Brese looked down at the list on his clipboard. He shook his head and said, "Not here," just as he had also shaken his head when a man claimed to be Mick Jagger's son. Someone in the crowd jumped up and down yelling, "Joe, Joe, it's me!" And with that, those who had not had a clue as to his name began yelling, "Joe! Joe! Joe!"

Mr. Brese pointed to a woman and commanded one of the security people standing in the small, cordoned area at the bottom of the steps: "Dmitri! The woman in the red hat." As she squeezed toward the front accompanied by three friends, Dmitri grabbed her hand and opened the velvet ropes for her and three of her friends—while simultaneously holding off a dozen others who said they were with her.

It is not unusual for single men, who have more difficulty getting in because of their great numbers, to pay a fee to such a woman to say they are with her.

Mr. Brese selected people quickly, as if assembling a bouquet. Sure, the women with the clear plastic dresses and white tape over their breasts were selected, as were those with fluorescent, feathered earrings that looked as if they would be useful for deep-sea fishing. But also, he chose Wall Street types in pin-striped suits. Celebrities, regular customers, and Mr. Brese's friends had an edge, as did the distractingly attractive and the obviously rich.

He turned down dowdy women who looked like they were out hunting up a draught beer and young men in T-shirts and jeans who looked as if they had come over to mow the lawn. Rowdy men rarely make it, even though that has meant excluding offspring of the rich and famous who try to have him dismissed the next day. He said he preferred people who showed a little imagination in their dress—the man in a fake-fur tuxedo being a possible example.

"It's hard to describe," Mr. Brese said. "Sometimes it comes down to the way a person walks or the look on their faces."

Loved ones must often be left behind.

"My husband is right back there!" screamed a woman

who was being ushered in. "He has all my money. I won't be able to buy a drink." The security people told her to move along, and an hour later, she was still tugging on Mr. Brese's sleeve asking, "Any hope for my husband? Any hope at all?"

At 12:15 A.M., twelve hundred people were packed in, and Mr. Brese had cut the intake to a trickle. Outside, the mob mounted, undulating and pushing, with those in the front row barely able to stand.

"More rope!" shouted one of the security people, who wanted to widen the cordoned area around the door.

"More stanchions!" shouted another, sounding like a crew member on some strange ship in a storm.

The crowd kept pressing in until the security people stood back to back leaning out against the crowd. "Not one more, Michael!" Mr. Brese yelled to the assistant doorman, Michael Clancy. "No one gets in until you move back!" Mr. Brese yelled at the crowd.

Finally, however, it appeared to Mr. Brese as if the crowd might just overrun his position, and he pulled down the heavy rolling steel door to this converted warehouse with a crash.

Standing inside and catching his breath, one club employee asked: "What do they want? It's as if we were giving something away."

Clearly, they were, something intangible. When some semblance of order was restored, Mr. Brese reopened.

At two A.M., a man in the crowd shouted that his civil rights were being violated and that he would see the doorman in court. At three A.M., one of the few remaining rejects yelled obscenities at him.

At four A.M., two men from England who said they had

been in the country for two hours pulled up in a taxicab and asked, "Is this the place?" Several hundred people still dancing at five A.M. were sure that it was.

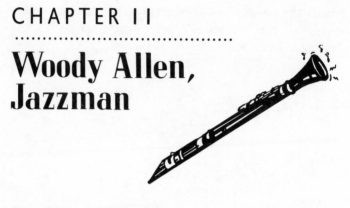

CHAPTER 11

Woody Allen, Jazzman

BY JOHN S. WILSON

The New Orleans Funeral and Ragtime Orchestra, a jazz septet led by the clarinetist Woody Allen, is now in its sixteenth year at Michael's Pub in what may be the longest-running jazz gig in town. For most of those years, Mr. Allen has torn himself away from writing, acting, and directing to be at the band's Monday-night-only sessions for nine months each year. From now on, however, he intends to be there year-round.

"I'm not using ideas for films that require getting away from New York anymore," Mr. Allen said the other night after finishing a set that included "Lead Me, Savior," "Wild Man Blues," and "In the Shade of the Old Apple Tree." "I'm working totally in New York so I can sleep in my own bed every night. I don't even go away in the summer. Sometimes I can play at the Pub right through shooting a picture, particularly if it's a script comedy. But crowd scenes with extras are more grueling.

"It's refreshing to go to Michael's Pub and play," Mr. Allen continued. "But by midnight I begin to get anxious if I know I have to get up at five o'clock. I'm thinking of doing things only in Manhattan, not even Brooklyn or New Jersey, because it tires me to have to get up early, get in a car, drive somewhere, and unload."

Mr. Allen's style as a jazz clarinetist is based primarily on the willowy, quavering lines of the New Orleans clarinetist George Lewis, although the rougher, more aggressive attack of Johnny Dodds, an earlier clarinetist from New Orleans, also creeps in. Mr. Allen, who is fifty years old, was first attracted to New Orleans jazz when, at the age of fifteen he heard the bravura playing of Sidney Bechet on soprano saxophone, an instrument that resembles a chubby golden clarinet.

Like many others, Mr. Allen found he was unable to emulate Mr. Bechet's passionate outpourings, so he switched to the simpler clarinet style of Mr. Lewis. He still admires Mr. Bechet and considers him the greatest of all jazz instrumentalists, including Louis Armstrong.

"Bechet had a more animal style than Armstrong," Mr. Allen explained with relish. "I like crudeness in jazz a lot. Johnny Dodds and Sidney Bechet had a ferocious animal style. George Lewis had a bluesy style with a lot of bad harmonies, and I like that disjointed sound, too."

"Crudeness" has been one of his goals for the New Orleans Funeral and Ragtime Orchestra.

"I try to push this band to greater crudeness," he said. "They're all better musicians than me, and they have to play down to be crude. I have to play up to be crude."

This has given the band a split personality. Mr. Allen likes to play the relatively simple traditional New Orleans repertory of spirituals and blues. Whenever he is not at Michael's Pub, however, the other members of the band indulge their penchant for Chicago jazz of the '20s, the music of Louis Armstrong's Hot Five, King Oliver, and Jelly Roll Morton's Red Hot Peppers.

"When I come back, I kill the fun for them," Mr. Allen conceded. "It's back to the spirituals and blues."

Despite this difference of approach, five of the six musicians who started the band with Mr. Allen in 1970 are still at Michael's Pub every Monday evening. Four are part-time musicians: John Bucher, a stockbroker, plays cornet; Dick Dreiwitz, the trombonist, is a teacher; Jay Duke, the drummer, has a burglar alarm business, and the pianist, Dick Miller, is an English professor at Brooklyn College. The tuba player, Barbara Dreiwitz, the trombonist's wife, is a full-time musician, and so is the incumbent banjo player, Marty Grosz.

The original banjo player was Marshall Brickman, the television and movie writer-director who wrote the scripts of *Sleeper, Annie Hall,* and *Manhattan* with Mr. Allen. He left the band, according to Mr. Allen, "when he became a film director and had two babies." He was replaced by Carmen Mastren, a guitarist and banjo player who had played for Tommy Dorsey and Glenn Miller. When Mr. Mastren died in 1981, Mr. Grosz took his place.

Mr. Allen's clarinet playing was a very private affair until 1966, when he was coming into his own as a nightclub comedian. He took his clarinet, some records, and a record player with him whenever he went on tour. When he got back to his hotel room after a performance, he practiced with his records. While he was playing at the hungry i in San Francisco, he was attracted to Earthquake McCoon's, the club owned by the jazz trombonist Turk Murphy, whose band played there.

"I used to stand outside the club just to listen to the music," Mr. Allen said. "I didn't have the nerve to go in. Not even as a customer. It was my normal entering fear."

When Mr. Murphy learned that the comedian at the hungry i played New Orleans-style clarinet, he invited him to sit in with the band. For two years Mr. Allen resisted.

"I promised him twenty times to bring my clarinet before I finally did," Mr. Allen said. "Turk was so friendly. He wouldn't take any of my excuses of incompetence—that my rhythm was bad, that my harmony was terrible."

But Mr. Allen finally sat in with Mr. Murphy's band, and this encouraged him to form a group in New York.

"We started playing in our apartments for fun," Mr. Allen recalled. "The others wanted to play in public, but I had no desire to communicate with an audience. I was already communicating as a comedian. But I agreed and I found they were right. It's more fun with an audience."

The band made its debut in 1970 at a one-time German beer garden on East 86th Street that, at the moment, was called Barney Google's. A brief stay there was followed by brief engagements at Les Champs, an East Side restaurant, at the Playboy Club, and a slightly longer one at Jimmy Weston's. Mr. Allen attributes these frequent changes to the fact that, while his name got the band bookings, club owners lost interest when people failed to return after they found out that he was playing jazz and not being funny.

"Gil Wiest, who owns Michael's Pub, was the first to realize that, if he kept us for a while, people who enjoy the music would start coming back," Mr. Allen said. "And they did."

Mr. Allen's interest in music began to connect with his film making when, on the soundtrack of *Sleeper*, he used his own band and the one at Preservation Hall in New Orleans, with whom he had played occasionally.

"In selecting music for my films, I use myself as a barometer," he said. "I use what appeals to me, which is jazz, standard melodies by composers like Gershwin and Porter, and classical music—Mahler, Bach, Brahms, Stravinsky. We think what music would be good behind a scene and I put on a record."

Mr. Allen feels that the music he picks for each scene is so important that, once he has found the right record, he cuts the picture to fit the music. On four of his films—*Manhattan, Stardust Memories, Zelig*, and *Broadway Danny Rose*—he has worked with the composer and pianist Dick Hyman, for whom he has great admiration.

"He's a film director's dream," Mr. Allen said. "He looks at the scenes and knows what works. He can do whatever you want. He can be Erroll Garner or Bud Powell or Fats Waller. He has a mastery of the tunes of Jelly Roll Morton and Bix Beiderbecke and the New Orleans style that I love. On *Zelig* we used a mixture of records that I chose, along with scoring behind the newsreels written by Dick. I'm amazed at the scenes with music he has given us." Mr. Allen's interest in jazz and films has led him to toy with an inevitable thought—to do a jazz movie.

"Eventually I will," he declared. "I'm the most qualified person to do a jazz film. I'm a film director and a jazz enthusiast—for New Orleans jazz. I'd like to do a big, colorful jazz film, and I'd do it better than anyone else because I know more about it and I feel more connected with it."

CHAPTER 12

································

Nightclubs with a Latin Beat

BY JOHN DUKA

At ten P.M. Monday, Ottavio was hawking La Carmencita *cigarros* to the people waiting in line outside the Village Gate. White convertibles settled like mosquitoes into double park. Young people carried cassette players as big as suitcases. The line grew quickly, curving from Bleecker onto Thompson Street. Why? The appearance of Ruben Blades, a handsome young Latin singer who is blond, wears tight white trousers, and is currently *numero uno* in the hearts of New York's Latin music fans.

Everyone waited patiently in line to see him, and no one wanted a pack of Ottavio's twenty-four little cigarettes. "You must be kidding," a girl with silk flowers in her hair said to him.

Even without the presence of Mr. Blades, Monday night always jumps at the Gate. While the club is given over to jazz during the week, on Monday it is strictly Latin music, with live bands, margaritas, and a dance floor that explodes with the swivel-hipped energy of mambo, samba, merengue, and cha-cha.

Indeed, the entire Latin music scene that came to life again in New York in the mid-1970s is still salsaing with more bump, grind, and babaloo than Ricky Ricardo probably ever dreamed possible.

At the Gate, the crowd consists of everyone from fashion models to Wall Street brokers to people who have come from New Jersey by train. The club, which has survived from the halcyon days of the '60s when Chad Mitchell and Miriam Makeba used to belt it out in harmony, is subterranean, two flights down from street level. Dress is casual, the cigarette smoke is dense, and competition for space on the dance floor is intense.

"All it takes," said Luisa Delgado, who rested against a pillar and patted her forehead with a handkerchief while her boyfriend went to get her a drink, "is to dance your dance, don't get carried away with how cool you are, and to wear a small bag that won't hit someone in the face when you turn."

The Gate is only one of the clubs for the growing number of people who have foresaken the solitary pleasures of disco for a little touch dancing in the night. "It's a revolving kind of thing with the clubs," said Zenaida Plaza at Ochentas while she waited for the dance contest to begin. "On Monday, everyone goes to the Gate. Thursday night, it's Ochentas. On Friday and Saturday, people go to Justine."

Like many of the clubs, Ochentas has taped music some nights and live on others. There is a dance contest every Wednesday, after which the floor stays crowded till one A.M.

"Listen, this place has the best Latin music anywhere," said Caryl Daniels, who sat sipping drinks with Iris

Garcilazo at a ringside table. She wore tight black pants, heels, and a black net top studded with sequins. "It's not too dressy and it's like a family, the same people come almost every week. And the people dance incredible, you know. Last week, I won the Harvest Moon Dance contest. I won the ballroom, tango, and cha-cha contest at the World's Fair in 1964. So I know what I'm talking about."

Among the other nightclubs that fanciers of Latin music and dance frequent are Justine, Club Broadway, the Copacabana, which has begun holding Latin Tuesdays, and Tony Raimone's Corso, the oldest and perhaps the most famous Latin club in town.

The only thing missing from the Corso are women wearing fruit on their heads. There is a stage with lamé swags and drapes. There is live music every night. There are mirrored columns, walls covered with tiny mirrored tiles, men wearing dark shirts and white ties, women in tiered samba skirts, and Tony Raimone himself, resplendent in a white suit, white shoes, a red shirt with his initials embroidered in red on the cuff, and a gold pinky ring.

"We get all kinds of people," said Mr. Raimone, who sat in his office in the back of the club one night while Johnny Pacheco played out front to the crowd. There were pictures of him on the wall with his son and with celebrities. "Schoolteachers," he said, "business people, dishwashers, stars. We've had Tony Martin, Sophia Loren, Dick Cavett. The little kid who used to be in *The Real McCoys*. Geoffrey Holder used to dance here. They come from all over. Every South American who comes to New York has heard of us. It's a salsa crowd.

"But the scene is changing," he said. "There used to be champagne nights, where the winning couple on the dance floor got a bottle of champagne. There used to be troupes of professional dancers who went from club to club. But the people got bored seeing the same dancers all the time. This club, and a lot of the others, used to have dining and dancing. But that's all passé. Now it's live music if you're lucky and a lot of taped music. And some clubs mix Latin music with Latin disco and just plain disco. Here, we give 'em what they want, and if you get here early enough on Sunday, you get a chance to eat something from the buffet.''

But on that night, no one at the Corso was thinking about food. The floor was crowded, and in one corner Little Jimmy was doing the merengue. Four feet four inches tall, wearing a baseball cap and a T-shirt emblazoned with the words ''I Love Corso,'' he danced with a tall blonde in white Capri pants to the music of Johnny Pacheco.

''I been coming here for seventeen years,'' said Little Jimmy, who produced his card, which said, ''Little Jimmy, the World's Smallest Maître D','' and a book of photographs that he calls his Brag Book.

''That's my name, just Little Jimmy,'' he said. ''I'm an actor, I've been on television, on the *Time Bandits*, on *Bonanza*. I'm the National Leprechaun for Anheuser-Busch. I'm like the mascot of this place. When I go to all the other clubs they say, 'Look, it's Little Jimmy from the Corso,' the Italian dwarf from Brooklyn. I'm proud of it. This place is like home.''

At that, he spotted a young woman that he knew, darted through the crush of dancers, took her hand, and spun her across the floor. No one missed a beat.

The Clubs

Corso: 205 East 86th Street (212-534-4964); Wednesday, Friday, Saturday, 9:30 P.M. to 4:30 A.M.; Sunday, 6 P.M. to 4 A.M. Admission: Wednesday, $7; Friday, women free until 11 P.M., men, $7; after 11 P.M. , $7 for everyone; Saturday, $5 until 11 P.M. , $10 thereafter.

Club Broadway: 2551 Broadway, at 96th Street (212-864-7600); Thursday, Friday, Saturday, 6 P.M. to 4:30 A.M. Admission $7.

Copacabana: 10 East 60th Street (212-755-6010); Tuesday, 6 P.M. to 2 A.M. Admission $3 for women, $6 for men.

Justine: 500 Eighth Avenue, at 35th Street (212-695-9229); Wednesday and Thursday, 5 P.M. to midnight or 1 A.M.; Friday, 5 P.M. to 5 A.M.; Saturday, 10 P.M. to 5 A.M. Admission: Wednesday and Thursday, free before 6:30 P.M.; Friday, $3 before 7 P.M. , $5 thereafter; Saturday $8.

The Village Gate: Bleecker and Thompson streets (212-475-5120); Monday, 9:30 P.M. to 2:30 A.M. (Box office opens at 8:30 P.M.); Admission $8 to $15, depending on who is performing.

CHAPTER 13

·····································

Roseland

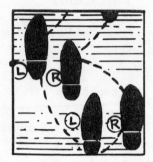

BY WILLIAM E. GEIST

Out of the fog of maroon darkness swept two dancers in tuxedo and taffeta, gliding high on their toes through smooth spins and smart turns that soon carried them back out across the vast dance floor, where they disappeared into the shadowy dancers like some fast ghost ship that had not been seen in many years.

Johnny Mulay and His Orchestra completed the number, and some of the dancers took a break. Robin Strick sat down hard at a table with a sign in the center reading: Hosts and Hostesses—$1 a dance. Tickets Available at Soda Fountain. Miss Strick is a hostess, a taxi dancer, at the Roseland Ballroom on West 52nd Street.

"For a dollar," she says, "anyone can take me out for a spin."

She poured a glass of ice water from one of several large pitchers on the table. After she took two sips, an elderly man came up and reserved her for two tangos and a rumba at eight P.M.

A debonair man—maybe the last in America—approached, wearing a brilliant red ascot, his jet-black hair slicked straight back. He handed her a ticket, she tucked it down the front of her dress, and the two waltzed off to "My Funny Valentine."

Another hostess asked what time it was. The time was five P.M., but the answer came back, "Oh, I'd say about 1935."

With the changing times, six men have joined the ten women taxi dancers, and it now costs a dollar to rent one of the partners celebrated in the 1930 Rodgers and Hart song: "Ten cents a dance—That's what they pay me; Gosh, how they weigh me down! Pansies and rough guys. Tough guys who tear my gown!"

Occupational hazards persist.

"I got kicked good during that Viennese waltz," said Christopher Daniels, a taxi dancer, as he returned to the table. Clods crush their toes.

"We're supposed to smile through the pain," said Shirley Ann Steffee, another dancer. Penny Prucha said that sometimes she goes home limping. Most of the taxi dancers own electric foot massagers.

Waxy buildup on the soles of their shoes causes the dancers to slip and fall. Suzanne Huyot, another dancer, said that old codgers try to lift her and dip her, sometimes with excruciating results.

Another occupational hazard is the occasional masher. "A guy holds me too close," Miss Prucha said, "and I say, 'Hey, no rub-a-dub-dub, buddy.' "

"We need to take a caring, personal approach," said Miss Strick, thirty years old, who gave up her job as a registered nurse to become a taxi dancer and dance instructor, "but this can be misunderstood."

Miss Huyot said that she was recently grabbed by the shoulders and kissed. "Only a fool would wonder why," commented a man who had danced with her.

"In the old days at other dance halls," recalled Ramon Argueso, whose orchestra alternates on the bandstand with Johnny Mulay's, "the taxi dancers used to do more than dance."

Not here, where Florence Forder is chaperone of hostesses and insists on dresses cut no lower in front than the top of the sternum and the uppermost lumbar vertebra in back. Still, taxi dancers are forbidden such things as drinking, gum chewing, and falling in love with customers.

"People think I have a crazy job," said Miss Strick, echoing the comments of the others, "but I just love to dance."

The taxi dancers are at Roseland every Thursday, and when they are not there, they hold a variety of occupations, including housewife, model, dance instructor, and actress. Dwight Carter is a real estate salesman who aspires to the stage. The group had a cake and balloons at the dancers' table in January when Miss Steffee, an associate professor at New York University, received her Ph.D. in psychology.

They reported their earnings variously, from about $20 to $65 for the four P.M.-to-ten P.M. period that they dance. They keep the dollars they receive. The male taxi dancers wear tuxedos; the women wear dresses or slacks.

Mr. Daniels rarely has a chance to sit down. Reaching for the water pitcher, he said: "We've got to talk to the band about playing shorter numbers. Those mambos are killers and some of these women buy ten tickets at a time." One woman after another comes to the table to ask him to dance.

"They tell me," he said, "that I am their Prince Charming."

The quarter-acre dance floor, which will accommodate two thousand dancers, is nearly half full this afternoon, a popular time for many retired people. The rose motif carries throughout, from the rose-colored light bathing the dancers to the cabbage roses, three feet in diameter, in the carpeting pattern. In the lobby, a Wall of Fame contains the shoes of famous dancers, including those of Betty Grable, June Taylor, Ruby Keeler, and Ray Bolger. And there is a scroll of several hundred married couples who first met at Roseland.

Mr. Argueso has been playing at Roseland since 1948, when the taxi dancers cost thirty-five cents. The two band leaders recalled the old days, when a dance marathon was held, and before the police came to break it up, the dancing couples were trucked to a pier and sent out on a boat to complete the contest. Female prizefights were also held to bring in extra money, much as Roseland today hosts rock concerts and has regular disco nights.

"This place is really still the same," Mr. Argueso said. "People still love to dance for all the same reasons."

George Fizer of Perth Amboy, New Jersey, who recalled coming to Roseland in 1938, said, "I come to dance with the hostesses and remember." Irene Fletcher of Queens was recently divorced and said she comes to dance with the hosts and forget.

CHAPTER 14

Night Court

BY ANNA QUINDLEN

The Manhattan Night Arraignment Court, known to law enforcement personnel and felons alike simply as Night Court, is one of the great shifting immutables in this town. Like Grand Central Terminal or cocktail party conversation, the ingredients are always changing, yet the whole always remains the same.

From one night to the next, it seems that the same bored prostitutes are sitting on the same long benches putting on the same coffee-colored lip gloss while the same out-of-uniform police officers wait with the same forms in their hands for the same individual accused of possession of a controlled dangerous substance to be called by the same court officer before the same judge in the same big, brown courtroom.

In fact, this cast of characters is ever changing. Only the signs stay the same. In God We Trust over the judge's head, Police Officers Must Display Shields on one post of the wooden bar cordoning off the bench, and No Firearms Beyond This Point on the door to the holding pens. The signs are the same every night, and the noise and confusion. Night Court is to the usual courtroom administration of justice what madras is to white oxford cloth.

New School Course 506, Criminal Justice, met just after six o'clock the other night in the marble hallways of the Criminal Courts Building at 100 Centre Street, and its members were prepared for this. The instructor is Frederic S. Berman, an acting State Supreme Court justice, and he had briefed the class, and briefed them again outside the courtroom.

"The people you are going to see tonight are people who have been arrested in the borough of Manhattan, probably in the last twelve to eighteen hours," said the judge, whose fourteen students include a retired lawyer, a fashion writer, and the director of the police department lab. "This is their first contact with the system."

Judge Berman handed out a diagram of the courtroom, indicating who was who. Inside the courtroom, everything was just like the diagram, except in garish color instead of black and white.

A young woman in spandex pants and a little disco purse was called up to the table on charges of loitering for the purpose of prostitution. She was sentenced by Judge Martin Erdmann to time served, stepped daintily over the chain dividing the spectators from the participants, shot one of the court officers a smile, and sashayed out into the evening.

A man in a black ski jacket was led in from the holding pens. "Drug possession," whispered one of the police officers, looking strangely denuded of authority in jeans and a plaid shirt. "He gave me the whole rap about how he'd never been in trouble before, and then when we ran his name through the computer, turned out he'd escaped from Rikers Island.''

Some more men were brought in on charges of criminal possession of controlled dangerous substances. One wore a natty suit and carried a briefcase, and, initially, many of Judge Berman's students, as well as Judge Berman, thought he was an attorney, not the defendant.

Another approached the bench with a police officer. Both wore blue jeans and hooded sweatshirts, and it was difficult to tell who was who until the officer's badge, hung on his belt, caught the courtroom lights.

Many of the defendants held their hands behind their backs as though they were handcuffed, though they were not. "That's how you can tell they've been here before," said one of the judge's students.

"Kidnapping in the second degree," said a court officer as three young men were led into the courtroom, blinking a little as though they had been sleeping in the back, and a number of the police officers sat up, and one whistled.

But then the garbled colloquy at the bench revealed that the identification by the complainant might not be entirely solid, and that the complainant was no longer living in New York, and finally that the complainant was a prostitute. The police officer who had whistled exhaled contemptuously. Two of the defendants were released on their own recognizance, and bail was set at $1,000 on the third.

"That was terrible," whispered one of the students. And finally, when the class was almost over—although Night Court still had some hours to run—someone was sentenced to jail. A man with wild hair and a sullen face, who, it was charged, "intentionally broke open the window of a 1981

Oldsmobile with a wire hanger," pleaded guilty to a Class A misdemeanor and was immediately sent to Rikers Island for five months.

An hour had passed, and the judge led his class outside to describe the difference between prostitution and loitering for the purpose of prostitution, and to explain that time served for the prostitutes meant the night they had probably just spent in jail.

"Shouldn't they serve at least three weeks?" said one woman indignantly. "Yes," said another, not waiting for the judge to answer. A third, moving on to the kidnapping case, asked the judge whether someone could indeed be accused of raping a prostitute. The judge said yes. "Judge Berman, that was pretty bad," said one woman as they prepared to leave the marble hallways. "You couldn't tell the good guys from the bad guys."

Back inside the courtroom, some of the good guys and the bad guys left, and new ones arrived, but the scene remained the same. Another prostitute, this one with a long scar along her jawline, was sentenced to time served, and as she stepped over the chain she stuck out her tongue at one of the police officers. The family of a young man accused of car theft had moved up into the seats vacated by the class.

"Nice crowd tonight," said a police officer in the narcotics division, as he waited for the man he arrested to be called to justice.

PART 3

The City Romantic

CHAPTER 15

....

Phil and Molly: The New Romantics

BY WENDY WASSERSTEIN

On a spring morning in 1972, a senior from the Spence School was in Central Park, completing her science project on the reproductive cycle of flowering plants, when she saw an unmarked bus drop off twenty women in silk suits, bow ties, and sneakers on the corner of 89th Street and Fifth. She took note; when she was in sixth grade, sneakers and suits had been cause for suspension.

Meanwhile, on the West Side, a middle-aged but very nice lady was on her way to Barney Greengrass, the Sturgeon King, on 89th Street, when three cars—a Volvo, a BMW, and a Saab with M.D. plates and Save the Whales bumper stickers—pulled up to 87th Street and Amsterdam Avenue. Fifteen young men, whom the lady thought she recognized from her son's protest days at the University of Wisconsin, emerged from the cars. Before the gracious lady could offer them an Entenmann's cake, they jogged into a dilapidated brownstone and immediately began exposing brick and hanging spider plants.

And the city embraced these pioneers, who were dressed in 100-percent-natural fabric. They prospered and they multiplied. From the now infamous drop-offs grew a new breed of New Yorkers, the Professionalites. Only their ratio of men to women, three to four, has remained constant.

What follows is a Love Story in One Act and Six Scenes between two of these sabra Professionalites: Phil and Molly.

CHARACTERS

Molly. Thirty-three years old, single, successful, and quietly desperate. Every Saturday night, Molly sheds her doctorate in molecular microchips and slips into a Zandra Rhodes macromini. On the weekends, Molly is just another girl at Ruelles, a popular café on the Columbus Avenue strip. Just another S.S.D. (Single/Successful/Desperate) face waiting for a discriminating Root Canal Man to invite her for an unfulfilling weekend at his summer share in the Hamptons. Molly, though a native New Yorker, by this point is considering relocating to the Sun Belt.

Phil. A successful creative director at B.B.D. & O. advertising agency. He is thirty-two, single, and having a great time. Every night, after winning another Clio Award for his clients, Phil goes to the Odeon, where he shares poached salmon on kiwi fruit with visual artists, conceptual artists, and performing artists. And every night, after picking up the tab, Phil swears he, too, will become an artist.

Dr. Susan. Molly's psychiatrist.

Dave Tannenbaum. Ph. D. Phil's psychologist.

Her Majesty, The Queen. Ruler of the Helmsley Palace.

SCENE ONE

One night in late August, Phil has a yearning to talk to someone who knows Perry Ellis but has moved on to Issey Miyake. Phil slips into Ruelles, where the number of single women is a plague to the West Side zoning committee. It is here that he first sees Molly, seated at the bar. She is young, she is urban, she is professional. He knows immediately that Molly is the kind of new-fashioned girl he could bring home to his analyst's couch. Phil sits next to her.

Phil. Hi.

Molly. Hi.

Phil. Do you come here often?

Molly. Never.

Phil. I don't either.

Molly. I'm waiting here for a woman friend. She selected this place. I think what's happening to the West Side is outrageous.

Phil. This is really an East Side singles kind of restaurant.

Molly. Yes, but it's here on the West Side, so we have to deal with it.

Phil. You sound like a concerned citizen.

Molly. Did you ever read any Kenneth Burke in college? Lit. Crit.?

Phil. *(Immediately.)* Oh, sure.

Molly. He divides people into observers, spectators, and participants. I'm here strictly as a sociological observer. I love to watch people in New York. But I would never really, really come to a place like this.

Phil. I wouldn't either. In my spare time I write film criticism.

Molly. *(More interested.)* Oh, you're a critic! Who do you write for?

Phil. I write for myself. I keep a film criticism journal.

Molly. I love women in film. My favorites are Diane Kurys, Joan Micklin Silver, and Claudia Weill.

Phil. I love women in film too.

Molly. *(Impressed.)* You're so open and vulnerable. What do you do?

Phil. I'm a psychiatrist.

Molly. Individual, group, house calls?

Phil. Actually, I'm a creative director at the B.B.D. & O. advertising agency. But I think of it as psychology. Dealing with the individual's everyday dreams and desires. I'm in charge of the Scott Paper account.

Molly. Fascinating. I use tissues a lot. I've always wondered why.

Phil. What do you do?

Molly. I'm a systems analyst for American Express.

Phil. Do you know me?

Molly. *(Very straightforward.)* Not very well. But I'd like to.

Phil. *(Looks at her intently.)* Why don't we go somewhere a little less trendy to talk. I can tell these aren't your kind of people.

Molly. No, I don't belong here. This isn't my New York.

Phil. *(Helps her on with her coat.)* That's a nice jacket.

Molly. Perry Ellis. But I've moved on to Issey Miyake.

Phil. *(Putting on a multilayered karate jacket.)* We have so much in common.

Molly. "It's a phenomenon." That's a quote from a song in *Gypsy*. "Small World," isn't it? I love Stephen Sondheim. Have you been to *Sunday in the Park with George?*

Phil. No. I work on Sundays. I'm afraid I'm a workaholic. You know, mid-thirties New York man, longing for Real Relationship with Remarkable Woman, meanwhile finds fulfillment through his work.

Molly. I think I like you. But be careful, I have Fear of Intimacy.

Phil. The New York Woman's Disease. I hear it's an epidemic.

Molly. I'm working with my shrink to get past it.

(Pause as Phil looks at her.)

Phil. I think I like you, too.

(They begin to exit restaurant.)

Phil. What about your girl friend?

Molly. Uh, ah, she told me if she wasn't here by now she wasn't coming.

Phil. Not a very reliable friend.

Molly. No, but she's working with her shrink to get past it.

(They exit.)

SCENE TWO

Pasta and Cheese, a pasta and cheese emporium. Phil and Molly stroll over to the counter arm in arm. It is mid-September.

Phil. *(Ordering at the counter.)* We'll have goat cheese, goat cheese with ash, sun-dried tomatoes with smoked moz-zarella, pesto tart, stuffed brioche with brie, spinach ricotta tortellini salad, carrot ravioli, and a half pound of American.

Molly. *(Surprised, almost disturbed.)* American?

Phil. Have you ever had real American cheese? Not the stuff they sell at the supermarket, but real American. *(He gives her a piece.)* Taste this.

Molly. *(Tasting.)* Oh, that's marvelous!

Phil. I've been rediscovering American food: peanut but-ter, grape jelly, Marshmallow Fluff, Scooter Pies, Chef Boy-Ar-Dee, bologna. It is unbelievable! If it's done correctly.

Molly. *(Softly.)* I love you.

Phil. Excuse me?

Molly. I love blue. I adore Kraft blue cheese dressing.

Phil. Well, if it's done correctly.

SCENE THREE
Molly at her psychiatrist, Dr. Susan. It is October.

Molly. *(Sneezes.)* Excuse me. I'm getting a cold.

Dr. Susan. How do you feel about that?

Molly. Terrible. Tissues remind me of him. He says peo-ple should live together before they get married.

Dr. Susan. How do you feel about that?

Molly. Sigourney Weaver and Glenn Close got married this summer.

Dr. Susan. How do you feel about that?

Molly. Living together was for kids in the late '60s and '70s. I'm a thirty-three-year-old woman.

Dr. Susan. How do you feel about that?

Molly. I need a commitment. I want a family. I don't

want to take a course at the New School on how to place a personal ad. Meryl Streep has two children already.

Dr. Susan. Why do you always compare yourself to movie stars? You're not an actress.

Molly. That's true. That's really true!! That's an incredible insight. Maybe my mother wanted me to be an actress. I hate her.

SCENE FOUR

Phil at his psychologist, Dave Tannenbaum, Ph.D. It is November.

Phil. I don't think I want to make a commitment to Molly, but I'm afraid of what she'll say.

Dave Tannenbaum, Ph.D. We'll put Molly in this chair and then you can answer for her. *(Phil talks to an empty chair.)*

Phil. Molly, I don't think I want to make a commitment.

(Phil gets up and sits in chair to answer as Molly would.)

Phil. *(Acting out Molly.)* That's okay. I'm an observer. This is all a sociological investigation. Kenneth Burke divides people into spectators, partici—

(Phil runs back to his seat to answer Molly.)

Phil. *(Angry.)* Who the hell is Kenneth Burke? That is so pretentious, Molly!!!

Phil. *(As Molly.)* Not as pretentious as keeping a journal of film criticism.

Phil. *(Furious.)* You resent my writing! You want to swallow me up. If I live with you, I won't be here anymore. I'll lose myself.

Dave Tannenbaum, Ph.D. Did you hear what you just said?

Phil. I have it. Goddamn it! I have it. Fear of Intimacy. The New York Woman's Disease. I wish I had burn-out.

SCENE FIVE

Central Park West. The Thanksgiving Day Parade. Phil and Molly are watching as floats of Bullwinkle and Superman pass by.

Molly. *(Overcome by the sight of the floats.)* I love this parade. Gosh, I really love this parade. Reminds me of growing up here and of New York before there was a Trump Organization and chocolate-chip cookie wars.

Phil. I never imagined people actually grew up in New York.

Molly. It was different then. There were real neighborhoods. The ladies on Madison Avenue wore white gloves and ate mashed potatoes at the Kirby Allen Restaurant, Marjorie Morningstar and her family gathered for Sabbath dinners on Central Park West. All artists wore turtlenecks and played bongos in the Village. And every night at seven o'clock, men in top hats and tails tap-danced from Shubert Alley to the Winter Garden Theater. And when a Broadway baby said good night, it was early in the morning.

Phil. Really!

Molly. Well, I like to think so. Now everywhere I go all the women look like me.

Phil. What's so bad about that?

Molly. Nothing, it's just all the same. I like the idea of a theater district, a flower district, a diamond district. The whole city is being renovated into Molly district. Phil, I gotta confess. I hate goat cheese.

Phil. *(Softly.)* Me too. But I love you.

Molly. Hmmmmmm?

Phil. I hate goat cheese, but I love blue. Molly, with Bullwinkle as my witness, I want to marry you. And every Thanksgiving we can bring our children here. And someday they'll tell a fella they met at Ruelles, "I love this parade, I grew up here."

Molly. *(No longer wistful.)* But will our children go to Dalton or the Ethical Culture School? They could probably learn Chinese at Dalton, but there are a lot of show-business parents. Ethical Culture is nice, but maybe it's too liberal, not enough attention to the classics. How 'bout Brearley? There's something to be said for an all-women's education. *(She kisses Phil. Excited.)* Phil, just think! We can have a family of women film makers, women lyricists, women stage managers, even women vice-presidential candidates!!!!!

SCENE SIX

The Helmsley Palace. The Grand Ballroom. An enormous wedding party. Phil and Molly are standing under the altar before Her Royal Highness, Queen of the Helmsley.

Queen. Phil, do you take this woman to be your wife? To love, be emotionally supportive of, have good dialogue with, and a country home in the Hamptons, Connecticut, or consider upper New York State?

Phil. I do.

Queen. Molly, do you take this man to love, and at the same time maintain your career, spend quality time with the children, and keep yourself appealing by joining the New York Health and Racquet Club and, in the summer, Lotte Berk?

Molly. I do.

Queen. *(Addressing the wedding guests.)* I've known this couple for two hours. But I've stood guard at their honeymoon suite. Molly will be able to see her makeup in soft light in the bathroom mirror. Phil will be put at ease by the suit hangers that detach from the closet. And if Phil and Molly decide to get remarried someday, and return to the honeymoon suite, I will keep a note of their room number.

Phil. *(Kisses her hand.)* Thank you, Your Majesty.

Molly. *(Curtsies.)* Thank you, Your Majesty.

Queen. And now by virtue of being Queen of all the Helmsleys, I pronounce you husband and wife. *(She presents Phil with a big gold hook.)* Congratulations! New York is the only place a real New Yorker can hang his or her hat and call home, even if he or she moves away. You may kiss the bride. *(Phil kisses Molly. There are cheers and the band begins to play "Lullaby of Broadway." Five hundred men in top hats and tails begin to tap down the aisle.)*

EPILOGUE

Phil and Molly are now bi-island (Manhattan and Long), bi-point three children (a girl, a boy, and an au pair from Barnard), and bi-career (a shift into management for him, a cottage industry for her). Phil was featured on the cover of *New York Professionalite Cheese* magazine for his distinguished cellar of American pasteurized-cheese foods. Molly, in the twenty minutes of quality time she devotes each day to her own enrichment, began taking tap class from Honi Coles.

Two weeks ago, Phil was offered the position of creative director of Paper Towels International, with headquarters in Zambia. When Molly suggested that this move would perhaps disorient the children, Phil reminded her of the wisdom of Her Majesty, the Queen. Phil and Molly would always be New Yorkers.

CHAPTER 16

....

A Father Rediscovers the City

BY BERNARD KALB

Hand in hand, my daughter and I crisscross the city: I lead her to Times Square, Greenwich Village, and Chinatown, my stomping grounds during the late 1940s and early '50s. She leads me to neighborhoods and landmarks that were not around in my day: SoHo, the South Street Seaport, the Trump Tower.

A glittering new spike of glass, Trump Tower. Ah, I quickly point out, the tower only comes to the waist of my middle-aged Empire State Building, some twenty blocks south on Fifth Avenue. It strikes me that these two structures symbolize the New York my daughter knows, the New York I knew.

Inside the tower, yet another dimension of contrast: I inquire about the price of a suit on display in one of the boutiques. "Seven hundred and fifty dollars." $750! Once we have escaped to Fifth Avenue, I tell my daughter that, when I was a kid living with my parents in the Bronx during the

Depression, $750 would have easily paid a year's rent. She, who came of age during the era of double-digit inflation, says I am joking.

I am a New York aborigine, but it is my daughter, born in Indonesia, who has rekindled the New Yorker in me. Almost three decades have gone by since we, the city and I, have gotten together in any serious way. Outgrowing New York was not the issue; rather, it was my growing away from New York. I mean, far away, all the way to Antarctica. The bottom of the world was my first real reportorial out-of-town assignment, in the mid-1950s. That led to some fifteen years of living abroad, mostly in Southeast Asia, where three of my four daughters were born. Though the archives will show that I was born, bred, and schooled in New York, my footprints on all the boroughs, I know the alleys of Saigon, Jakarta, and Paris as well as I ever knew midtown Manhattan. And, though my work still calls for a bit of globe-trotting, since 1970 my neighborhood has been the Washington area.

Now I find myself living in New York once again—indirectly. My daughter has reunited me with my city. Less than a year out of a New England college and after testing Western Europe, the Middle East, and the Southwest United States, she zeroed in on my hometown and became, *mirabile dictu*, a happy little apple in the Big Apple. She found a place to live on the Upper West Side, and I found a seat on the Washington–New York shuttle. The result has been totally unexpected: the exhilaration of exploring three New Yorks—my daughter's New York, my old New York, and our New York. Her New York centers on the Upper West Side. Her loyalty is touching. She is an absolute chauvinist. We stroll.

"Just look, Pop," she exclaims, waving her arm to take in crowds of Saturday-morning shoppers. We pass Korean vegetable stands heaped with pyramids of bok choy; fish markets featuring sashimi; ice-cream parlors with imported flavors ranging from mango to jungle fruit (her favorite is still chocolate, she confesses). Bakeries offer Viennese Sacher tortes, Middle Eastern pita, cinnamon-raisin bagels, and croissants. And restaurants serve a confusion of cuisines—Japanese, Chinese, Pakistani, Mexican, Indian, Vietnamese, Thai, Jewish, Italian, Hungarian, German.

Some of this variety was here in my day. But the main ambition of foreigners then was to melt into the melting pot. Now, wherever I look, I see New York proudly advertising its diversity. "Foreign" has become "ethnic"—genuine, spirited, without additives.

My daughter cannot wait to display Columbus Avenue, as if it were her own handiwork. "A lot of people my age live in this neighborhood," she says. "More relaxed, more casual. You never know what's going to happen from minute to minute. Makes me chortle every time I walk down this street."

True. I have heard about the renaissance that has overtaken this once-shabby avenue, but I am not prepared for the chic bistros and boutiques, the glass-enclosed cafés commandeering the sidewalks. "And you," my daughter says forgivingly, "wanted me to live on the East Side."

We step into McGlade's, an old-fashioned saloon on the corner of West 67th Street and Columbus. With its brass cash register and faded blowups of old prizefighters, McGlade's, dating back to 1887, is clearly an outpost of a bygone era.

"I remember the days when you couldn't walk down

Columbus Avenue unless you had a blackjack or a baseball bat," says Hy Halpern, the owner of McGlade's. "There was a hotel on Seventy-second Street. They used to throw bodies off the roof there." But the opening of Lincoln Center in the 1960s triggered a dramatic change; people started investing in real estate and rehabilitating old buildings. Now you can leave your baseball bat at home.

Up the street at Banbury Cross, cotton pin-striped shirts sell for $47.50 and wool sweater-vests for $110. "Used to be a Japanese restaurant," a salesman tells me cheerfully. The young man, who says that he defected from Philadelphia, "a town," to come to New York, "a city," points to shelves of neatly stacked clothes. "No combination polyester. Everything is a hundred percent linen or a hundred percent cotton. Guaranteed to wrinkle."

Haberdashery can be a clue to the economic swings of a neighborhood, but the idea is to go beyond the trendy togs, the nouvelle cuisine, the glass towers to the central force behind these changes. I find myself more than paternally curious about just what it is now, compared to my own day, that has intensified New York's magnetic draw on people. As if on cue, we run into a couple of my daughter's friends. We talk about jobs, places to live, social life, money, and the ways the city, for all its liberating appeal, is more than a bit intimidating.

The first, who met my daughter in New Hampshire a couple of summers ago, is trying for a career on the stage. As I begin my quiz, my daughter gives him an I-have-nothing-to-do-with-this look. He talks about the challenge of New York. "It's so big," he says, "that it's an effort to make plans. I never had that experience before, coming from a small town like Hanover. New York has taught me that I have to be more aggressive; it has made me confront myself more. Sometimes it's exciting, sometimes it's despair. A mixed thing."

The second, from the Washington area, works at a bank. "This city is a jolt of lightning," he says.

I ask him for adjectives describing the West Side. He answers without hesitation: "Spirited. Imaginative. The best-looking women live there." And the East Side? "Preppy. Old money. A barren intellectual wasteland."

My daughter chortles.

I cajole my daughter into crossing the East-West divide of Fifth Avenue. On the way, a memory surfaces, dating back to the early '60s, when my wife, my daughter, and I were living temporarily on East 79th Street; I had a fellowship between overseas assignments. A friend had come from the West Side to visit us. No sooner had she entered our apartment than she asked for two aspirin. "Every time I come to the East Side," she said, "I get a headache."

We revisit our old apartment building, between First and York avenues.

"You had your first birthday party here," I tell my daughter.

"Here?" she asks, incredulous.

We stroll past antique shops and cafés along Second and Third Avenues, boutiques with designer clothes on Lexington. I confess that I still find the East Side appealing. Maybe it has to do with age, I say. But before I can decide which side of Manhattan I would prefer, if I were to live in New York, I feel a tug at my sleeve. My daughter feels a headache coming on.

She asks to see some of my old bachelor haunts, so we head down Fifth Avenue toward Greenwich Village. First stop, a three-story town house at 132 MacDougal Street, where a close friend once lived. The exterior has been freshened up; otherwise, the building looks the same, although whatever was standing to the north of Number 132 (a grocery store?) has been demolished. I tell my daughter that I recently discovered that Louisa May Alcott had lived at Number 132. *"Little Women?"* she asks. I nod, and then suggest that Louisa's ghost must have been shocked at some of our carryings-on more than thirty years ago.

Quick as a wink, before she can quiz me, I guide her across the street for a cappuccino. The coffee machine on the bar still plays the same hiss-and-gurgle tune it did in my day. I tell her about the old Village, about writers and artists, the Provincetown Players, all-night talks. About how that close friend of mine, a hick from Lancaster, Pennsylvania, could teach me, a kid from New York, something about prose and women. I talk about a studio I once had on Morton Street, and conjure up a picture of myself as host at what I had decided would be a formal party; guests in fancy dress slicing kosher salamis that were strung from the ceiling.

Our visit to Washington Square Park provides the starkest contrast between Greenwich Village, 1984, and Greenwich Village, circa 1950. As if a nickelodeon were flashing snapshots, with all rough features blurred, I see the park of a generation ago. Young mothers with waist-length hair and sandals. Guitar-strummers. People playing chess. This Saturday afternoon, the chess games are still in progress, but the background music is hard rock blaring out of portable stereos. The population is predominantly male. The park looks like a way station for the rootless. The innocence I remember is gone.

My daughter nervously pulls me along a littered path to the street. I stop at a parked patrol car.

"Crowded, isn't it?" I comment to two police officers sitting in the front seat.

Both men give me a surprised look.

"Empty!" says one. "If it were warmer, the place would be jammed. But don't worry. The people here won't bother you. There is probably less violence for this size crowd than you'd imagine. Sure, lots of drugs—but beat."

" 'Beat'?"

"Yeah, beat. Fake. Some wrapped-up leaves with birdseed and stale tobacco they try to palm off as the real thing."

"How long have you been doing this?"

"Four years." The officer looks up at me wearily. "Do you want to offer me your condolences?"

Chinatown, Saturday night. Mott Street is a confetti of people, and the pungent aroma of ginger and garlic wafts up an image of Wah Kee, once my favorite Chinese restaurant. Instead of ordering by dish, my friends and I used to order by amount, say, $1.50 a person, since we were never exactly flush. (I tell my daughter that, just a few years ago in Peking, I asked my Chinese government escort to help me choose some Sichuan and Hunan delicacies for a banquet. "Let's make it easy," he suggested. "How much do you want to spend per person?" *In Peking.)*

Our group used to descend the steep flight of stairs into Wah Kee and look for a waiter who had once been introduced to me as "Louie." One evening, we couldn't spot Louie. So I asked one of the waiters whether Louie was working that night. He laughed. "Which 'Louie' do you want?" he asked. "I'm Louie, he's Louie, everybody's Louie!"

Anyway, I can't find Wah Kee, so I stop at a souvenir shop on Mott Street to ask directions.

"Wah Kee," says a gentleman sitting in the doorway on a porcelain garden stool. "I know the place. Closed a few years ago."

I tell him we used to ask for a waiter named Louie.

"Which 'Louie' do you mean? There were four Louies, all brothers. One of them died just a couple of weeks ago."

He watches a group of tourists pass by. He recommends a restaurant halfway down Elizabeth Street. "Ask for Mr. Wong. Tell him I sent you." He gives me his name.

I thank him and tell him I am from Washington.

"Washington? I know Washington. I'm a graduate of the Georgetown School of Foreign Service, class of 'forty-nine." He stands up and shakes my hand. "Have a good dinner."

We walk through the crowded, tangled streets in search of Mr. Wong.

"Small world," my daughter chortles.

I must confess that I was concerned by reports of violence and drugs in New York, particularly after I learned that the junction of West 72nd Street and Broadway, a few blocks from my daughter's first apartment, was once a notorious heroin center nicknamed Needle Park. "Don't come home at night alone, but if you must, stick to the middle of the sidewalk," I warned her when she first moved to the city. "Don't walk too close to the buildings, with their open doorways and cellars." She was amused, told me not to worry. But I remember the day she anxiously telephoned Washington to report that the boyfriend of a girl she knew had been mugged on Wall Street at high noon.

Mayor Koch, whom I met at a reception in Washington,

tried to allay my fears: "People unfairly think of New York City as a high-crime city. It is not. We were the tenth down in terms of crime."

He did add that, in the last ten years, New York City's population has dropped from 8 million to 7 million. Had the missing million moved to Philadelphia, I wondered. "Well, we really don't know what happened to them," the mayor said, "but wherever they are, I'm willing to give them amnesty and they can come back."

My own reentry so far has been mostly confined to the lower half of Manhattan; I still have not revisited the places where I lived with my parents and sister and brother in Washington Heights, Brooklyn, and Queens, or my old schools, DeWitt Clinton (coed since last year) and City College of New York. I have not been back to Crotona Park in the Bronx, where, as a very young boy during summer nights of the '30s, I sold sunflower seeds, two jiggers for a penny, to unemployed sweatshop workers who sat on park benches and prayed for the coming of the Messiah. Or even to the Hayden Planetarium on West 81st Street, where I used to watch pinpoint stars manipulated against a stainless steel sky and dream of other worlds.

Now, whenever I shuttle to the city, I find each visit a part of a homecoming mosaic of discovery and rediscovery. With my daughter, born at the other end of the world, as my trusty New York guide.

CHAPTER 17

....

A Mother Introduces the City

BY JOYCE MAYNARD

New York has always been a city I come to from somewhere else. I lived there, very briefly—owned a good black suit and three silk blouses, rode the subway to work, bought my dinner at a deli every night on my way home, and ate it in a Pullman kitchen overlooking Gramercy Park.

But when I think of New York City, the images that come to mind are not these once-familiar close-ups; I summon versions of the skyline as a traveler sees it when entering the territory from one direction or another: New York as seen from the Franklin D. Roosevelt Drive heading south; New York across the Hudson River from the Palisades; viewed off in the distance like a crystal formation from a car idling on the Pulaski Skyway, or rising up from the industrial flatlands of New Jersey or down below a shuttle landing at La Guardia. On a visit a while back, I leaned against a fence on the Promenade in Brooklyn Heights, where I was walking with my two young sons, and recited the names of skyscrapers. "New York City," I said, summing things up. And Charlie, age two, answered softly, "Like on the news."

Like my children, I was born and raised in a small New Hampshire town. Some of my neighbors fear and even hate the very idea of New York City: Haven't been there, haven't wanted to. To them, "the city" means Manchester, where the malls are. But mine is another tradition, starting with my grandfather, who made New York his destination from Odessa, Russia, back in 1916. My own feeling for New York, as a child growing up far away from it, was always one of interest and longing. New York was where they filmed *The Ed Sullivan Show* and *To Tell the Truth*. Where you could buy the clothes featured in *Seventeen,* and maybe spot Jackie Kennedy walking down the street. If I could just get there, I could audition for commercials, buy raspberries in December, see the windows of F. A. O. Schwarz I had always heard about.

I came to New York City first by bus. I was eleven years old, and the trip took seven hours. We wanted, my mother, my sister, and I, to visit the 1964 New York World's Fair. Friends put us up in their little apartment on East 31st Street—two bedrooms above a funeral parlor—and I stayed awake most of that first night, listening to sirens and waiting for the sky to turn black. The next day we took a train out to Flushing Meadows, but, except for a three-minute escalator ride transporting us (after nearly an hour's wait) past Michelangelo's *Pietà,* I can remember nothing of the fair. My fond images from that trip are of the city itself, at its grungiest. I remember sitting on that old Greyhound in a cloud of carbon monoxide, driving in through Harlem. I remember pressing my face against the glass, looking down on the sidewalks, wanting to be there. I remember thinking how someday I would live in New York. I remember feeling my heart beat.

We came back to Manhattan after that, once a year, at Christmas. We had a set of ritual stops that strikes me now, knowing the city better, as a funny, oddball itinerary. We always went to Ohrbach's basement (Macy's being more than we could handle). We always hit a shop uptown that sold nothing but buttons, not so much because we needed buttons, I see now, as because we found there another basic element of the New York shopping experience: specialization. We ate date-nut-and-cream-cheese sandwiches at Chock Full O'Nuts. We rode buses and subways, never cabs. I remember affecting a blank, bored expression as we rattled uptown, staring out the windows of the Fifth Avenue bus, hanging onto my mother's purse strap and hoping I looked like a native instead of a hopelessly excited rube. We went to see Alexander Calder's wire-sculpture *Circus* at the Guggenheim Museum, bought postcards, visited the Dennison's Party Bazaar on Fifth Avenue to buy pipe cleaners or felt in colors we never saw back home. I used my savings for a Chinese kite one Christmas and for Mexican tin ornaments another year, and always we brought back bags full of city tastes and smells: halvah and bagels, a fancy bar of soap from the Caswell-Massey apothecary. Usually I acquired one piece of clothing that would put me right on the cutting edge of fashion back at school after vacation: fishnet stockings before they had traveled north, a vinyl skirt. It was known, in my town, that I had been to New York.

All through high school and beyond, I made my annual pilgrimage, taking in new sights: record stores in Greenwich Village, Bloomingdale's first floor to try on makeup. And another element was added to my feelings about the city.

....

The ambition to acquire Diane von Furstenburg dresses in every available pattern was gradually supplanted by the ambition to develop the sort of life a person lived in a Diane von Furstenburg dress.

Riding that bus into New York (and later driving there), I would find myself wanting to be one of those women wearing perfectly accessorized outfits, shopping in Henri Bendel's, and going out to lunch. Wanting to swing a briefcase, hail a cab, file into a Broadway theater, get messages on an answering machine. Manhattan always drew me in. First just to be there. Then to survive there, find my way around the subway, locate the bathing suits at Macy's and the dinosaurs at the American Museum of Natural History. But finally what I wanted from the city—like most people who come there from someplace else—was to succeed in it.

Inevitable, then, that I'd try living in New York. But if a visit rejuvenated me, a protracted stay wore me out. I know some people who successfully made that transition from short-term visitor to long-term resident, but I never got the hang of it. I came to New York and my temperature rose. I walked faster, as if there were a Walkman planted not on my head but in it, playing reggae tunes nonstop. I never got accustomed to the idea of leading a regular life in the city—going to a job, going home, cooking meals, going to sleep.

When there were no limits imposed on how much I could take in, I found I could not impose my own. Every time a derelict spoke to me, I ended up engaged in full-scale conversation. Every store window I passed, I had to look in. (And every dress I saw looked good to me.) I never perfected that beautiful, trancelike meditation of so many subway riders, who spend their minutes on the train as if on a Tibetan mountaintop: eyes open and staring straight ahead but thoughts turned inward until, miraculously, they get up at just the moment their stop appears.

So I moved back to the country and resumed my status as an out-of-towner. Sitting by my wood-burning stove in a house so quiet I can hear our dog breathing two rooms away, I read the New York papers, study photographs of unwearable clothes, note concert dates and theater openings to take place on nights when I'll be at day-care-center pot-luck suppers. It matters a good deal to me that at any moment I can get in my car and five hours later I'll be crossing the Triborough Bridge. I act on that impulse so seldom I might as well live in Milwaukee, but in my mind the distinction, and the importance of something like proximity to Manhattan, remains clear.

Like every ex-New Yorker, too, I pride myself on having once lived in the city. When I make a friend, that fact comes up. Knowing a person has lived in Kansas City or Cleveland does not, I think, convey as swift and rich a sense of her as knowing she has lived in New York City. New Yorkers are not even close to a type, to be sure, but the simple fact of their residence gives them one important trait in common: an appreciation of how hard it is to survive in their city. Plenty of people never manage it. But if you do, that sense of mastery never leaves you.

It comes from all sorts of small victories: locating, amid the city's ten thousand navy blue blazers, one that fits just right, on sale. Having a token ready when you get to the turnstile. Discovering a cool and private spot in Central Park. Finding—this, most of all—a few good friends. I managed all those things once, and feel, still, when contemplating my accomplishment, like a rabbit who has successfully got through a bramble patch. A person could study the lapels on my good black suit and know how many seasons have passed since I was a New Yorker. But now my oldest child dreams of the city. Born at the end of a dirt road five miles outside a town with no movie theater or traffic lights, surrounded by woods and streams, my daughter says a country walk is boring because there are no buildings or people to look at. When she grows up, she tells me, she's going to live in New York.

Audrey's first real visit to New York came when she was three. I took her to some of the ritual places, naturally: to the Central Park zoo, and the Museum of the City of New York to see the same dollhouses I'd studied when I was a little girl. (The Stettheimer house, whose rooms I had memorized, is still my favorite, with its original Duchamp painting and flapperish maids.)

But what my child loved best, as I had known she would, was simply life on the streets. And she saw it all fresh, the way I had, having come from someplace else. She would stop and study a sidewalk grate with steam rising from the subway and want to lie flat on her stomach to peer through the cracks. She loved the 14th Street subway station and the cut-rate parking lot on Pier 40, where we leave our car, with its view of the Statue of Liberty. Once, a wild-looking shopping bag lady stopped her and asked her name. My daughter said, "Guess. It begins with *A.*" The woman made just one wrong guess before asking if her name might be Audrey. "Yup," said my daughter happily, and "Bye," and then moved on, unamazed by one more magic-seeming event in a city of so much strangeness.

The city is never more magical than at Christmas, so last December, when Audrey was five, my husband and I drove her down for a three-day visit. It was just about sunset when we approached New York, and the skyline glowed. Audrey thought Co-op City looked beautiful, studied the houses alongside the turnpike, saying, "Aren't those people lucky?" and wanted personally to hand over our toll money at the Triborough Bridge as if it were our admission fee not simply to the bridge, but to the city.

The next day, my husband took her to see the Calder *Circus*, now at the Whitney Museum, and I took her to the Metropolitan Museum, where we studied the Christmas tree and the Ming-style Astor Court. We bought her a pretzel on the street and stood in front of the windows at À La Vieille Russie, choosing our favorite jewels. I took her to the ladies' room off the lobby of the Plaza Hotel (she reminisces still about the uniformed woman who handed her a fresh towel after she washed her hands). She wanted me to read her all the advertisements on buses and was outraged when she saw someone sitting in a seat designated for the handicapped. We tried out a zillion mechanical toys but spent hardly any money. She viewed the entire city, I think, as one large museum. Possession wasn't the point, for once.

On our last night in New York, my husband and I took Audrey skating at Rockefeller Center. She had seen the Christmas tree on television and now here she was, skating just below its branches. I was seven months pregnant, her ankles were bowed in; we did not, either of us, bear much resemblance to the spinning figures in skating skirts at the center of the ice. But still, the night felt pretty dreamlike. So when I pointed out the girl who played the little sister in *E.T.*, skating directly ahead of us, Audrey just nodded: Naturally we would see movie stars here.

Near the end of our money, we turned in our skates and planned a dinner at McDonald's, but first I thought we would see one more set of Christmas windows and take Audrey through one more revolving door, at Lord & Taylor. As we got in the door there, a man acting a little strange pushed in next to us. We didn't think about it until fifteen blocks later. Then, having ordered our hamburgers, I reached into my purse for my wallet and realized it was gone.

We had been cleaned out. My husband had only change enough for a packet of french fries before the long, cold walk back to the car. Audrey did not say much, except to ask quietly if the theft meant that we'd be poor forever. Then we got to the block where we had parked and the car was gone— towed away from a poorly marked No Parking zone.

The upsetting things that happened on the last night of that trip were bona fide New York experiences. I never did acquire all the protective devices seasoned New Yorkers use to insulate themselves against the harsher aspects of city life, but Audrey knew, more than I had given her credit for, that not being entirely safe is also part of the adventure of the city. Back in New Hampshire, when she tells the story of her trip, the thief and the tow truck feature prominently. But she also includes the triumph of retrieving our impounded car. (Imagine: It disappears from one spot and turns up fifty blocks away, surrounded by unfamiliar vehicles, with the same inscription drawn in the dust on its door: "Wash me.")

At home, where the danger but also the excitement is diminished, we catch glimpses of New York in the movies and on television. Audrey says with satisfaction, "I was there."

CHAPTER 18

The Mating Game and Other Exercises at the Vertical Club

BY WILLIAM E. GEIST

A young woman in a leotard stands at the juice bar in an East Side health club, enjoying some low-fat Dutch Apple yogurt. A remarkably handsome, sweaty stranger with really good deltoid definition sidles up and orders carob peanuts and freshly squeezed grapefruit juice, large. He turns slowly, looks her in the eyes, and speaks.

"Yogurt is mucous-forming," he says softly.

"My name is Sharon," she replies.

They repaired to their respective locker rooms for grooming and departed healthily into the night from the Vertical Club, a glamorous, celebrity-studded health club that has become so much more—serving not only the physical conditioning needs but, members say, also the social, psychological, occasionally professional, and even spiritual needs of the Upper East Side.

"We have no fat people here," says Tom DiNatale, the manager. That is his pledge. "People join other health clubs to get in shape before they join here," explains Heidi Halliday, a supervisor at the club. "The Vertical Club is today's Studio 54," says High Voltage, a person, and a bizarre hybrid of the show business and physical conditioning industries, with glitter in her hair and sequined leg warmers. "Same people: same scene," she says, "Only positive instead of destructive. People are getting up when they used to go to bed. Five A.M. I was there."

As an aerobics instructor to the stars here, this little ganglion of a woman has become something of a celebrity in her own right. She always gets the best table at Elaine's, regardless. She has the disconcerting habit of constantly doing stretching exercises, even in restaurants, and she sometimes rises from her desk during a conversation and flies into the splits.

Michael Rodriguez, an assistant manager at the club, sits calmly cutting up important little white slips of paper in the center of a vast, open, teeming room aflutter with hundreds of exercise disciples. "Pure Fellini," remarks Ron Haase, a program director. The gleaming room of mirrored walls and wraparound neon is filled with energizing rock music— "You might as well jump!" prods a Van Halen recording.

The club membership grunts, discreetly, on more than 250 of the very latest chrome exercise machines, kept glistening by a squad of cleaning personnel. The members jog on a bouncy track that seems almost to run for them. They furiously pedal exercise bicycles, with digital calorie burn-rate readouts, on their way to where they are going. An already anatomically correct club member, Leslie Arden, pedals wildly toward her goal of looking great in her swimming suit on Memorial Day at Southampton.

Mr. Rodriguez is a gregarious, twenty-year-old conditioning expert who is attending to the important task of replenishing the little white slips of paper at the desk. He said the exercisers keep coming over and grabbing them in their sweaty hands and scribbling down the names and telephone numbers of someone they have just met who can be useful to them—socially or professionally or in providing the name of a good plumber.

"People see someone they like," said Mr. Rodriguez, "and they ask me things like the person's name, telephone number, job, marital status, sexual preference, whether they rent or own in the Hamptons, things like that. Two couples I introduced are married."

Although there are hundreds of members, Mr. Rodriguez happens to know the correct answers. Through his orientation sessions at the club, he gets to know all of the members, who he said range from professional models and athletes serious about exercise to socialites and dirty old men whose attitude during orientation is one of cardio-schmardio, where are the dancing aerobics girls?

Some club members say health clubs are replacing the networking function of the old men-only clubs. Jack Krenek, a professional model, attests to this, saying he met his accountant here as well as his insurance man and an advertising executive who gave him a modeling job.

Theresa Echeverry, an admirer of his, is a twenty-five-year-old restaurant hostess who comes to the club during the day. "That," said Mr. Rodriguez, "is when I advise women looking for rich men to come." He tells of several members who scrimped and saved for the $1,150 to join so that they might find a well-to-do mate here. Several members remarked that the cloakroom at the club looks like a fur vault in the winter.

Miss Echeverry wears gold necklaces and bracelets while exercising. She and other female members say space at makeup mirrors in the women's locker room is often strongly contested by women about to take the exercise floor. "Sport perfumes" and "sport jewelry" are applied. A $1,500 gold Cartier bracelet is a current favorite. Reebok sport shoes and Ellesse sportswear—a sweat suit selling for $325—are the vogue.

Miss Echeverry says she is weighing several offers from fellow exercisers for lunch this day. Putting her arms around the owner of two restaurants, she said, "Everyone around here owns something." Phil Suarez, co-owner of Bob Giraldi Productions, quipped, "Guys can't get on the elevator with her unless you make seven figures."

"People come to see and be seen," Mr. DiNatale said of his club, where even the sauna has glass walls. There is also a communal spa, a bar and restaurant, and a rooftop sunning area for socializing.

"It is better socially than a singles bar because it's not so obvious," said Miss Arden. "You also don't meet as many low-life creeps and insistent drunks. It's safer. The only problem here is that a lot of these people look like they'd rather go home and look at themselves than somebody else."

CHAPTER 19

....

Romance in Bloomingdale's

BY WILLIAM E. GEIST

"We're going in," said Martin Gallatin to the fifteen apprehensive men and women under his command, one of whom confessed that he would just as soon be parachuting into combat.

Mr. Gallatin had seen his people freeze at this door, but this day the brave charged ahead and the timid swallowed hard and followed, popping into the revolving door at Bloomingdale's, one after another.

This was the culmination of their training in Mr. Gallatin's class, Finding a Mate in Bloomingdale's, a $25 seminar for single people seeking to meet members of the opposite sex.

At a briefing before entering the store, Mr. Gallatin had denounced singles bars, computer dating services and the like as largely ineffective ways to meet people for New York's estimated two million singles.

Rather, Mr. Gallatin teaches tactics for meeting "mates"

naturally, in such places as museums, laundromats, food stores, buses, and Bloomingdale's. Said Mr. Gallatin: "You avoid the 'If-you're-so-great-why-are-you-here?' question."

Mr. Gallatin, a bearded, bespectacled sociologist, likes Bloomingdale's "because it is a kind of Disneyland, with interesting displays and gadgets to aid conversation.

"The sixty thousand people in the store on a busy day mean a lot of prospects," he said, "and the demographics are right." A class member, Howard Kaplan, said with a moan, "And I've been going to Syms all these years."

The class entered the fray ever mindful of Mr. Gallatin's philosophy: "This is highly competitive. You must use sales and marketing skills to sell yourself."

They took mental and written notes from the lecture with them: opening lines, such as "What do you think of this tie?"; and store geography, such as the best departments to find mates. They fanned out quickly to the electronics department, the men's department, household goods, and the card shop—all recommended by Mr. Gallatin—but not to the first floor, crowded with tourists, and certainly not to cosmetics, where Mr. Gallatin said "Very serious business is being conducted."

The instructor was available for consultation during this practical exercise. A twenty-seven-year-old class member cornered Mr. Gallatin behind a pile of designer handbags for some quick advice. He had struck up a conversation with a married woman, and Mr. Gallatin reminded him that this had been covered under "Special Problems: Married/Attached."

Richard Smith stooped to read a greeting card, remarking to a young woman that the cards were impractically displayed.

"You need binoculars to see them," he said. "Yeah," she replied without looking up. But he somehow continued the conversation for a few seconds before she stopped responding, and Mr. Gallatin said enthusiastically, "See, they will talk to you."

Other members of the class were self-consciously unbuttoning their coats to give a more casual appearance, body language that Mr. Gallatin had recommended, as well as making obvious attempts to gauge distance between themselves and their prospects, a recommended twenty-five inches.

To warm up, some could be seen talking to demonstrators of perfume or cooking utensils, as had also been suggested. "They have to talk to you," Mr. Gallatin told them.

A few class members quoted Mr. Gallatin's opening lines verbatim: "How do you like this tie?" one woman said to a male customer. "I don't," he replied, turning away.

Bob Howard came to Mr. Gallatin and said he had gone all the way to the sixth floor "and couldn't think of anything to say about pots and pans." Mr. Gallatin suggested he pick out some sort of utensil and ask someone what it was used for.

"I keep seeing prospects," complained one man, "who are with other women. Women are like cops, always in pairs."

Most in the class had carried conversations through the greeting, response, and main body stages, as discussed in class, but were unable to make the transition to the critical closing stage—"that's the hard part," explained one class member, "where you go from 'nice Mixmaster' to 'how about a date.' "

The twenty-seven-year-old class member, who said he

had just returned from a Club Med trip to Martinique, said that next time he would try "the women's lingerie department, because the conversation transition from product to personal would be easier."

Michael Posner seemed to be doing well, having given out three cards with his name and telephone number on them, after animated conversations in the electronics department.

"Everyone is interested in the new gadgets," he said, "and no one understands them."

The group gathered in the back of the store for a scheduled departure. When some members of the class failed to show up, Mr. Gallatin worried: "These sessions are hard. Some never come out." As it turned out, three had gone to the Alexander's store down the street by mistake.

The group went to a nearby delicatessen to discuss the exercise. "Don't worry about rejection," Mr. Gallatin told them. "Success is the ability to talk to people, so that one rejection won't mean so much."

The group lingered, most saying they had no plans on this weekend evening, and the discussion turned to the problem of meeting members of the opposite sex in New York.

"If you are friendly in New York," said Helen Keating Lopez, a forty-two-year-old widow, "you arouse suspicion, but subtlety doesn't seem to be getting anybody anywhere."

Mr. Gallatin had told them to "show interest, not need" in meeting prospects at Bloomingdale's, something class members said was easier said than done. "I've tried everything," said Mr. Kaplan, staring into a coffee cup, "I feel like giving up sometimes."

Said another man: "I've been having this discussion about not having anyone to date for fifteen years, since high school. My relatives always ask if I've met somebody. It's like a disease that won't go away.

"It's tiresome," he said, leaving the table, walking through the door of the delicatessen and pulling his collar up against the blustery chill of an autumn Saturday night.

CHAPTER 20

·····································

Mad for Manhattan

BY DAVID FROST

Even if you are lucky enough to spend a lot of time in London, New York is still quite simply special—from the moment you arrive. The airports are named after politicians, of all people. (Mrs. Thatcher will have made a note of that.) The cars are three feet longer, the limousines three yards longer, than the last ones you saw seven and a half hours ago—a thoughtful touch, since smaller cars have difficulty negotiating the potholes on the Van Wyck Expressway.

If your flight from Heathrow is the last of the day, arriving at J.F.K. at 9:30 P.M., there is the immediate visual bonus of the Manhattan skyline by night—along with Sydney's Opera House and Harbor Bridge, one of the two greatest man-made views in the world. Then there is your arrival at the hotel and, at 10:30 P.M. (3:30 A.M. London time), the reception clerk's disorientating, though oddly sincere, instruction to "Have a nice day." (The greeting to the weary traveler returning to the hotel at half-past midnight will have been somewhat updated to "Have a nice evening.")

New York is special, in so many ways. I always try to have my first New York meal in a steak house. A New York steak is unobtainable in Europe. The size over there is all wrong—it's too thin and too small—and so is the taste.

Then there is Broadway. For me, it has an excitement that the West End lacks. A hit on Broadway is like a hit nowhere else. Somehow, *Noises Off, The Real Thing,* and *Cats* all seem bigger when acclaimed on Broadway. Success on Broadway seems to matter more in the life of the city: The Broadway star who arrives late at a dinner party is saluted, and the hostess immediately makes a place for him on her right. The West End star who arrives late is apologetic, and the hostess consigns him to wait in a room where coffee is going to be served, while the diners continue with their dessert. Major stars seem happy to take over the lead in a Broadway hit even after it has been running for two years or more. In London, such an offer provokes an identity crisis for actor and agent.

Even restaurants in New York are theatrical, intent on putting on a show as well as a meal. The atmosphere of Sardi's is an obvious example, but it is equally true of restaurants away from the theater district. There is a razzmatazz about the Russian Tea Room, Maxwell's Plum, and Windows on the World that is copied elsewhere, but seldom reproduced. All over town, captains "dress the room" with the care and flourish of Broadway set designers.

The nonclub clubs are special, too. The camaraderie of "21" could scarcely be equaled if there were a ten-year waiting list for membership. And you can have a late-night —even early-morning—meal in New York without the nagging fear that chairs are about to be placed on all the tables surrounding you. One New York friend says that, when in London, he always has the feeling that he should have a taxi waiting, with meter running, outside the theater so that he can make a headlong dash for nourishment as the curtain falls. No such problem in New York.

New York means many different things to me. It certainly means cheesecake, more species of cheesecake than I ever knew existed: rum, orange, hazelnut, chocolate marble, Italian, Boston, and, of course, New York. And it means Madison Square Garden, which, by its very name, evokes for the visitor a hundred stirring memories of sporting legends like Joe Louis, Jack Dempsey, Gene Tunney, and Muhammad Ali.

Some people find New Yorkers rude, but that's not been my experience. I well remember, on my first visit to New York, my sense of shock when, having said "Thank you" to a shop assistant, she replied, "You're welcome." "Thank you," I repeated, in astonished gratitude. "You're welcome," she said again. "Thank you," I said again. If I had not been late for the airport, I might still be in her shop now.

Then, there is New York pride, a form of unabashed localized patriotism. It is difficult to imagine an "I Love New York" type of campaign taking off in London. Maybe it all has to do with the shyness and understatement of Londoners versus the openness (and even brashness) of New Yorkers. New Yorkers don't mind being seen in a singles bar—it is a healthy pursuit. Singles bars in London have never caught on: To a Londoner, it would be almost as bad as being caught in a dirty raincoat entering a strip club. Instead of an "I Love London" campaign, Londoners' only response over the years has been a series of tuneful songs about nightingales singing in Berkeley Square. London pride is rarely permissible, and then only because it has been "handed down to us," as Noël Coward was forced to explain.

New York has soul. The gift of gab of those well-advertised New York characters rarely lets you down. Cabdrivers are probably more consistently entertaining than their London counterparts: I think immediately of one cab ride, on a boiling July day, in a New York traffic jam that held us stationary for twenty minutes while we just sat and sweltered. I bore it in silence, because there just seemed to be no words to express our misery. The driver, however, found them: "Better, maybe, we never *invented* the wheel, huh?"

So far so good. I have listed a number of the delights of New York, but I still have not yet satisfactorily explained its specialness to myself. Why is it that I look forward to any trip to New York with such anticipation? Why do I return home from New York so invigorated? What is it that gives New York that special buzz that no other city can quite emulate?

The answer, I think, is ideas. Ideas matter in New York. I am certain that more conversations in New York are about ideas than anywhere else. Not just vague theories, but ideas that New Yorkers have the will, and the clout, to do something about. Indeed, it could be argued that the business of New York is to take in information from other places, reprocess it with New York know-how, and sell it back at a profit. Ideas are regarded—and respected—as the most basic commodity of all.

And the interchange of those ideas is aided and abetted by the geography of the place. The island of Manhattan is remarkably small—22.6 square miles—and people actually walk. The result is that New York is the international capital of face-to-face encounters. I run into more friends and acquaintances on the streets of New York than anywhere else. And, indeed, those friends are just as likely to be from London, Rome, or Sydney as from Westchester. And all about us, as we talk, is the visible evidence of that willingness to take a chance on something new, symbolized by the self-confidence of the modern architecture shooting up on almost all sides.

That's it, isn't it? The buzz that I find in New York is the buzz of ideas, the willingness to have a go, the willingness to take fifty-fifty as good, rather than unacceptable, odds.

Dr. Samuel Johnson said, "When a man is tired of London he is tired of life," and he was probably right. But when a man is tired of New York he is tired of work. And thought. And cheesecake.

CHAPTER 21

....

Best Views of the New City of Lights

BY PAUL GOLDBERGER

New York has never been a dark city, but never has it been so obsessed with light as now. The city has become brightly, intensely lit up—every month, it seems, a new skyscraper top goes ablaze with floodlights, every season a new facade takes on a nighttime presence. It is difficult to believe that it was only half a dozen years ago that the energy crisis was turning off public displays of light all over town, for now there is little thought of limits, little thought of restraint. We are at a moment when the more light we have, the more we seem to want.

It is, by and large, a positive addition to the cityscape. There is nothing that is more naturally appealing, and seems more completely right for New York, than the lighting of the skyscraper crowns that are the city's very symbol. Some of the new wave of lighting that has come over Manhattan is no blessing at all, however—such as the garish floodlighting that illuminates the bases of the four buildings at the corners of Fifth Avenue and 57th Street. There, the romantic fantasy that night lighting should be becomes an all-too harsh reality, shooting off ugly glare for blocks around and making one of the city's most dignified corners feel like Shea Stadium during a night game.

All of the new lighting, from the best to the worst, is of a very different sort from that of only a few years ago. For now the lights of New York are not simply those of Broadway, the blinking bulbs of theater marquees and the garish neon of Times Square advertising signs. Those lights are present as much as ever, but so is an altogether different kind of lighting, a kind of lighting that exists not as a thing in itself, the way an electric sign does, but is there to glorify and transform those parts of the city that we see by day. Right now, at least a dozen of the city's skyscraper tops are lighted after dark, and so are the fronts of many prominent buildings. Unlike a neon sign, which is but a ghost in daylight, these buildings are things we see all the time that take on a different existence under the beam of artificial light.

To light the tops of skyscrapers is so natural an idea that it is a wonder it was not done years ago—the city's towers are its equivalents to the Beaux-Arts public buildings of Paris, which have been lit for years, and their illumination now represents much the same kind of act of civic celebration. Indeed, in New York the lighting of important buildings has been a clear affirmation of the city's improved sense of itself. It is not likely that flooding the city's skyscraper tops with light would have seemed credible in the depths of the city's financial troubles a decade ago, for that time was a crisis of image as much as it was one of substance. Now, though the substance may not be so much improved, the city's image certainly is.

There is another reason that we are wallowing in light these days. The city's great skyscrapers of the 1920s and '30s have always been objects of fantasy as much as of commerce, buildings that express the sense of flamboyance, of theatricality, that is central to the city's spirit. In the 1950s and '60s, as the glass boxes of modernism took over the skyline, that sense of fantasy was lost; practicality alone seemed to dominate the cityscape. It is no accident that the lighted buildings are, with but one exception, skyscrapers that reject the sharp forms of modernism—what point is there, really, to lighting the World Trade Center? Now, the pendulum in architecture swings away from modernism, and we not only struggle to recapture some of the sense of earlier decades in new buildings, but we also appreciate more the theatricality of the skyline we have inherited.

Indeed, the goal of much of the current lighting is to make the city's skyscrapers look still more like objects of fantasy. The goal is to render a building a magical presence by night, to turn it into something that glows with a beckoning and distant fire.

Most of the lighted skyscraper tops, thus, are better seen from a distance. They have been designed to entice us, to cause us to turn thoughts of a city rational into visions of a city seductive. This illumination works its spell at odd moments, and often from surprising and unexpected locations—only rarely can a lighted top be seen from the base of a skyscraper itself, or even from across the street.

EMPIRE STATE BUILDING

The Empire State Building's floodlit top is surely the most celebrated in New York, and the lighting project that began the current wave. The Empire State's lighting was designed by Douglas Leigh, the venerable impresario of Times Square neon signs who has since turned his attention to skyscraper lighting. Celebrating more than fifty years as a visual designer, he has become as dominant in this infant business as he was in his earlier one, and most of his efforts have been splendid.

The Empire State's lighting is simple and elegant—the tower's great profile, the work of the architectural firm of Shreve, Lamb & Harmon, is bathed in an even light from the 72nd floor to the top. It is the perfect way to light this building, since it emphasizes what is most special about the Empire State—the profile that has become a virtual symbol of New York. The lights are placed on setbacks, and there is no sense at all as to where they come from—the building's light seems there by magic. And since at Fifth Avenue and 34th Street the Empire State stands relatively free of other tall buildings, its tower can be seen from all sides. The best views are from downtown both east and west.

If there is any problem to this lighting, it is in the much ballyhooed ability of this sytem to change color. For some years now, New Yorkers have watched the Empire State's lights turn red and green at Christmas, red and orange for the autumn, and blue and white for the Yankees. None of these colors look so good as pure white does, and it would be nicer if the building's management would save itself the trouble.

CHRYSLER BUILDING

As venerable a symbol of New York as the Empire State, and perhaps even more beloved, the Chrysler Building's extraordinary top was unlighted from the building's completion in 1930 until four years ago. It was worth the wait—this lighting has become one of the most pleasing presences on the skyline, intensifying the Jazz Deco lines of the crown.

By day, the stainless steel spire of the Chrysler, with its arching groups of triangular windows, is perhaps New York's greatest icon of the 1930s. The firm of Di Giacomo Associates—which created the lighting scheme based on designs left by William Van Alen, the Chrysler Building's architect—wisely chooses to outline the existing detail instead of bathing it in overall light. Now, neon tubes in white trace row upon row of the triangular windows at night.

The Chrysler is at the corner of Lexington Avenue and 42nd Street and, like the Empire State, can be seen from all sorts of vantage points. This lighting looks best from a few blocks in any direction, so that one is distant enough to see the crown as a totality, and close enough to feel a sense of pulsing energy from the white neon lines. One good vantage point is 43rd Street between Fifth Avenue and the Avenue of the Americas, looking east; another is looking downtown on Lexington.

HELMSLEY BUILDING

Completed in 1929 to the designs of Warren & Wetmore, the Helmsley Building was originally the New York Central Building—headquarters of the great railroad that built Grand Central Terminal. It sits astride the tracks and right in the middle of Park Avenue at 46th Street, but far from disrupting the order of the city, this remarkable structure has always seemed to enhance it. Its pyramidal tower, topped by an elaborate cupola, was Park Avenue's great punctuation mark; it accented, rather than blocked the street.

Even the arrival of the wretched Pan Am Building in 1963 could not destroy this building's strong and benign presence, and now it looks better than it has in generations. The developer Harry Helmsley renamed it, but also made a gift to New York of a cleaned facade, a lot of gold leaf, and a floodlit top that enhances the richness of this ornate crown. Douglas Leigh was the designer, and if the building does seem too gilded by day, it could not look better at night, when the new lighting helps it regain from the Pan Am Building its traditional role as the presiding presence of Park Avenue.

GENERAL ELECTRIC

The lovely, slender General Electric tower at Lexington Avenue and 51st Street—completed in 1931 to the designs of Cross & Cross—was originally RCA's headquarters, and its crown of laced stonework was intended not to represent Gothic architecture but to evoke radio waves. If this symbolism seems a bit strained after half a century, the building remains a pleasing and gracious element on the skyline, and its lighting reflects its character—gentle, friendly, and urbane. The tower is seen best from Park Avenue at 50th Street, where it rises gracefully and harmoniously over St. Bartholomew's Church.

CITICORP CENTER

Hugh Stubbins's Citicorp Center at Lexington Avenue and 53rd Street, completed in 1977, was among the first of the current generation of skyscrapers to reassert the importance of a sculptured profile at the top. With this sleek, aluminum tower, the idea has been interpreted a bit simplistically—the top is sharply raked in one great, dramatic slice—but there can be no question of its success as an identifiable symbol.

The lighting—also designed by Douglas Leigh—is simple floodlighting, and it makes the silvery aluminum facade, which is rather demure by day, seem far more exotic and powerful. It glows with an almost futuristic presence now, all the more in bad weather.

WALDORF-ASTORIA

Schultze & Weaver's Waldorf-Astoria at Park Avenue and 50th Street, completed in 1931, is too often overlooked in catalogues of the city's great skyscrapers. It is a splendidly massed mountain of limestone capped by two Art Moderne towers, and a few years ago the towers received pleasant floodlighting. They are not easily seen from the street, although they can be viewed from a few blocks up Park Avenue and from here and there to the east; one of the best views, oddly enough, is from the Queensboro Bridge, where the towers provide a soft counterpoint to the harsher lighting of Citicorp Center.

CROWN BUILDING

Like the Helmsley Building, the Crown Building is a case of a new name bringing new lighting. This tower at the south-west corner of Fifth Avenue and 57th Street was built in 1925 to the designs of Warren & Wetmore as the Heckscher Building. It later became the Genesco Building, and, under Douglas Leigh, it has been gilded and floodlit, and renamed the Crown Building.

The reference is not to any person, but the elaborate spire the building culminates in, not unlike that of the Helmsley Building, though less symmetrical and graceful. The rehabilitation of the Crown Building has both the faults and the virtues of the work done at the Helmsley Building—it is too gilded, particularly on the lower floors, they look not unlike a person with too much makeup. But near the top, distance reduces the garishness, and the effect is splendid.

The Crown Building looks best from north on Fifth Avenue, in part because the crown itself is oriented toward the north. But it also serves as a beacon for a substantial distance up the avenue, pulling the eye down to midtown.

METROPOLITAN LIFE

The seven-hundred-foot Metropolitan Life Insurance Company tower on the east side of Madison Square, a variation on the campanile in St. Mark's Square in Venice, was built in 1909 and designed by Napoleon LeBrun. Once the world's tallest building (a title it lost in 1913 to the Woolworth Building), it has always been one of the most pleasing eccentricities on the Manhattan skyline, with one of the largest four-face clocks in the world.

The lighting was designed by Al Piotrovsky, the Metropolitan's own electrician, and it is quite sensitive to the architecture—like the best lighting designs, it enhances rather than overshadows the building's basic architectural features. The thirty-fifth to forty-ninth floors of the tower are lighted in white, and the golden roof at the pinnacle is illuminated in sodium vapor lights to enhance the color. The tower can be seen well from midtown and lower Manhattan, and from close by on Madison Square.

CON EDISON

The tower of the Consolidated Edison headquarters at Irving Place and 14th Street was designed in 1926 by Warren & Wetmore, the architectural firm that seems to have provided more business for the floodlighters than any other. This is not one of the most distinguished efforts by the firm that also designed Grand Central Terminal—it is an awkward cross between Beaux-Arts monumentality and modernist sleekness—and it may be one of the only buildings that is not merely different under its night lighting, but clearly better. The lighting was designed by Douglas Leigh, and it gives the tower a zest that it altogether lacks by day. The tower is visible from east and west along 14th Street, and also from most points in lower Manhattan.

AMERICAN INTERNATIONAL

The American International Group's building at 70 Pine Street, originally the Cities Service Company headquarters, is one of Manhattan's Art Deco gems, and one of the buildings that has been a crucial part of the classic lower Manhattan skyline. Completed in 1932 and designed by Clinton &

Russell, the lighting is simple and elegant. A lovely translucent glass crown forms the top of the Art Deco setback spire, and at night it glows softly in the midst of the somber financial district.

MUNICIPAL BUILDING

The Municipal Building, a modern skyscraper with a classical temple on top, was designed by McKim, Mead & White and completed in 1914. A remnant of the day when the City of New York commissioned the noblest and grandest architecture for public use, it remains one of the city's most distinguished eclectic skyscrapers—all the more so since its cleaning and rehabilitation. As part of that program, the building's many-tiered crown of classical columns, topped by Adolph Weinman's statue *Civic Fame*, has been softly lighted.

57TH STREET AND FIFTH AVENUE

The one noticeable failure in the current wave of lighting is the plan created by Douglas Leigh that lights the facades of the four buildings at the intersection of Fifth Avenue and 57th Street—Tiffany & Company on the southeast corner, Bergdorf Goodman on the northwest corner, Manufacturers Hanover Trust Company on the northeast corner, and the base of the Crown Building on the southwest corner. (The top of the Crown Building is lighted like many other skyscrapers around town, and is far more successful.)

What has happened at 57th Street is an effort that, alas, may give the whole business of lighting the city's buildings a bad name, for it is both unattractive to the passing observer and irritating to occupants of many Manhattan buildings both nearby and as far as a mile and a half away.

The idea was to light the facades of these four buildings, all the way down to the street, by means of floodlights aimed from each building to its neighbors. Tiffany, for example, lights Manufacturers Hanover, which, in turn, lights Bergdorf Goodman. The first problem with this system is that it requires lights that are visible from the street, not to mention from office and apartment windows, and there is an astonishing amount of glare, even as far away as Central Park West in the Eighties. This might be a price worth paying if the lighting were esthetically pleasing in itself. But it has none of the graceful aura of most of the other lighting schemes.

The facades of these buildings at Fifth Avenue and 57th Street do not appear to glow, as properly lighted buildings should; they shriek, with a kind of light that one observer has compared to a used-car lot on a commercial strip.

The problem is partly the kind of light—a harsh white—and partly the fact that this type of lighting totally obliterates the very architectural features it is intended to enhance. Harsh, straight-on lighting eliminates shadows and any sense of texture in these facades and makes them all feel flat and cold. Moreover, the nature of the placement of these buildings removes all distance between us and the lighting. One reason that floodlighted skyscraper tops are so enticing is that they are far away, untouchable, and slightly magical. These facades are too close, and looking at them gives the same illusion-destroying effect as sitting in the front row of a theater and seeing the footlights.

RCA BUILDING

There is one new lighting scheme in midtown Manhattan that is a total success, however—perhaps the best thing of its kind since Mr. Leigh's original lighting of the Empire State Building top back in 1977. It is the floodlighting of the RCA Building at 30 Rockefeller Plaza, the seventy-story limestone slab that is the tallest and most important building in Rockefeller Center.

The lighting here was designed by Abe Feder, and it is elegantly simple. The building glows, in cool white light, from the first setback a few floors above the street all the way to the top. From Fifth Avenue, the lit shaft provides a lilting backdrop for the Rockefeller Center Christmas tree, but it looks every bit as good when the tree is gone and the building stands alone.

Thirty Rockefeller Plaza is one of the world's greatest skyscrapers, the heart of the complex that is, in many ways, the heart of Manhattan. It is only in the last decade or so that scholars have been willing to give this building, whose design brilliantly melds modernism with Beaux-Arts classicism, the ranking it deserves. It is the peer of the Woolworth Building, the Guaranty Building, and the Chrysler Building, and to see it illuminated in a way that respects its architectural qualities can only be cause for celebration.

Abe Feder has certainly not gilded the lily. The 30 Rockefeller Plaza lighting is most impressive in its simplicity: It is all invisible (the floodlights are mounted on setbacks or on the roofs of adjacent buildings) and it is all white. So it does not change the architecture of the building except, of course, to the extent that anything as dramatic as this does render some changes in our perceptions. But the effort here has been to excite our sense of the existing architecture more than to change it.

CHAPTER 22

....

Around Town with New Yorkers in the Arts

BY LESLIE BENNETTS

Neil Simon likes to wander through Bloomingdale's on weekends and to lunch nearby at Serendipity. Judy Collins goes on movie binges—three a day, and it would be four if her boyfriend didn't draw the line. Cynthia Gregory plays pool and goes to the racetrack. Beverly Sills likes to duck into the American Museum of Natural History to visit the dinosaurs—or whatever else might catch her eye.

For most New Yorkers, the weekend offers a blessed reprieve from all the things they have to do in their workaday lives and a chance to do some things just because they want to. As a cultural mecca of endless richness and diversity, the city is home to a stellar array of figures in each of the arts, and like their less-famous neighbors, they, too, cherish the time to enjoy the pleasures New York has to offer.

First, and always, there is Central Park, which holds as much fascination for famous New Yorkers as it does for the throngs of ordinary citizens who flock there each weekend, particularly in good weather. One Central Park regular is Dustin Hoffman, who is up with the dawn for a long run; on a recent weekend, he and a male friend accidentally crashed a women's mini-marathon and ran 13.2 miles in the midst of fifteen hundred women, several of whom were irate. The unrepentant Mr. Hoffman reports gleefully, "I'm proud to say I finished with the first three hundred women."

When he's not running, Mr. Hoffman is often walking. "The weekend is not the time to be in a museum; it's the time to be on the street," the actor says. "It's theater, and it's wonderful."

Mr. Hoffman also uses his weekends to seek out old movies. "I love catching up on ones I've missed," he explains. "There's no excuse not to see a good movie in New York, because so many old ones are playing at the revival houses. I love the Thalia, the Regency, the Carnegie. I read about people watching cassettes at home, but I like going out and sitting in a movie house with regular people."

When he gets hungry, Mr. Hoffman tends to head for a pizza place on the Upper West Side (Ray's or American Pie), or Victor's, or—if he's with his children—to Nanny Rose. "If you go to Nanny Rose, you get to write on the tablecloth with crayons," he explains. "We all write on the tablecloth."

Jill Krementz, the photographer, says that come fall, she and her husband, Kurt Vonnegut, like staying in the city far better than heading for their country house on Long Island, as they do in summer. "The air is charged with so much energy now, and I love walking everywhere," Miss Krementz says. "With Central Park right here, I feel I can have both aspects in my life. Going to the park is like going to the country for a few hours. I like to go to the carousel with our daughter, Lily. There are lots of other children and mothers there. I love the atmosphere; the carousel is so romantic, and the music is so pretty. The whole thing seems like a magical outing.''

Another dedicated walker is Joseph Papp, who spends a good part of his Sundays strolling in lower Manhattan. ''I particularly like to go down lower Broadway to Bowling Green,'' the producer reports. ''I go over to Delancey and the East Side area; I go through Chinatown, way across to the West Side; I go to NoHo. There are a lot of street fairs and flea markets around the city, particularly along Canal Street, and I run into them and hover around. I like the hustle and bustle of it. I enjoy any kind of crowd situation where people gather.''

Mr. Papp, a resident of the East Village, is loyal to the southern reaches of Manhattan Island. ''I find uptown very uninteresting,'' he says. ''There's a sterility about those big buildings; individualism is what I look for. I love the buildings downtown, and there's such an interesting energy there. There's a tremendous mix of humanity downtown. I watch, and I listen, and I think; it's one of the few times I don't think about working. I feel I can breathe. It's very, very exhilarating.''

For those whose work often takes them out of town, a weekend in the city can be a special pleasure. ''I'm always excited by New York,'' Judy Collins says. ''It makes me feel like a kid, going out on the weekends with the city at my feet. For me, a New York weekend is a real treat.''

Saturday morning often starts with a visit to the Metropolitan Museum of Art, one of the singer's favorite haunts. ''I love it,'' she says. ''The collection is endless and wonderful; the world of art is brought to me on a platter here. I'm particularly enchanted by the Impressionist group, but there are so many others; there's a collection of musical instruments that's just astonishing." On Saturday afternoons, Miss Collins often takes in two movies, and after dinner she heads for another.

Not surprisingly, many of those prominent in the arts find themselves gravitating toward weekend activities that correlate with their work. When the artist Philip Pearlstein can drag himself away from his studio, he likes to check out exhibitions and cruise through art galleries, usually in the 57th Street area and in SoHo. "I find it extremely useful," he says. "I like to know what other artists are doing and see what new directions there are. I enjoy other people's work; there are always new ideas at work, and there's a lot of feedback I can get from it. Going to a gallery is like going to the theater. It's one of the chief entertainments of New York City."

Browsers along Madison Avenue might well spot Liza Minnelli and her husband, Mark Gero. "Because my husband's a sculptor, we walk along Madison and visit the galleries," she explains. "Then we go to lunch, if we can find a little French or Italian restaurant that's not too crowded. I like Fiorella's, on Third Avenue, and La Petite Ferme, on Lexington. And I love going to the street fairs and festivals, like the Italian festivals or the Irish festival. They're fun; everybody's in a good mood."

One reason Miss Minnelli likes to mingle with such throngs is her work: "I like looking at people, and if you see something that's interesting in somebody, you can recall it and use it in a role," she observes.

On Sunday afternoons, she likes to go to off-Broadway

theater. "There's so much off-Broadway, and it's so good, you've really got to work to keep up."

While some avoid museums and department stores on Saturdays because of the crowds, Neil Simon is drawn to them. "I love to look at the people; they're fascinating," he says. "I like to go in the stores; I'll go in Bloomingdale's for sure, to watch the people and see what's come in that's new."

Bookstores are another magnet. "I'll go from one to the next," the playwright says. "Biographies fascinate me. I don't buy any fiction, though. My second favorite stores are stationeries. They're filled with all those pads and pens; it's like the beginning of something."

Serendipity on East 60th Street is a frequent stop-off point for lunch, including "something chocolate" for dessert, and very often the Whitney Museum is a must on Mr. Simon's afternoon itinerary. "I go to look at the Edward Hoppers," he explains. "The paintings they have of his are so beautiful. You just want to see them again; it's like putting on a favorite record and hearing it again. They're so evocative, they put me in a new mood and make me think of things. Almost all his paintings bring back some kind of memory to me. There's one painting called *Sunday Morning*, of an empty street that reminds me of every summer morning I ever spent in New York. When I was growing up in Washington Heights, I was always the first one out on the street, and it was lonely—but it also meant you kind of owned the street."

In the evening, Mr. Simon is likely to be found dining with friends, "nine times out of ten at an Italian restaurant like Elio's, Tre Scalini, Patsy's, or Gian Marino," he reports.

Alan Pakula is another bookstore devotee, and the film director's customary weekend trek is a stroll along Madison Avenue with his dog, Sam, a Komondor. "My favorite bookstore is Books & Company," Mr. Pakula says, "because it has a personal, eccentric character to me, a feel like an old Dickensian bookshop. Sam sits quietly while I browse and buy books for a rainy day, which means I buy more than I could possibly read."

Mr. Pakula—who also likes to film in New York—says that the city's street life is a major reason he decided to move back here after years in Los Angeles. "The great joy of living in New York is people-watching," he says. "As a director, it keeps me in contact with human behavior. In New York, you see people with varieties of life entirely different from your own; there is not that sense of being in some kind of gilded ghetto, cut off from the major part of the human race. Here I'm just one small cog in this extraordinary mélange of humanity, and I find it very satisfying."

One person who wants to get as far away from work as possible during her free time is Beverly Sills. "I try not to listen to any music on the weekend, because I'm absolutely saturated," says the City Opera's general director with a laugh. Like Judy Collins, she is a self-described "movie nut" who fills her weekends with "lots of movies and lots of Chinese restaurants.

"I'm crazy about movies," she says. "It's sheer escape; I can sit there in the dark and look at Paul Newman and pretend he's all mine."

Miss Sills and her husband, Peter Greenough, love Chinese food—"We can eat that for breakfast, lunch, and dinner"—and tend to frequent Shun Lee West, where the chef prepares "all the fattening things I like," she says rue-fully.

They also like to walk across Central Park at 81st Street and stroll down Madison Avenue, popping into boutiques for clothes and galleries for the French naïf art that Miss Sills collects.

The American Museum of Natural History is another lure. "We frequently drop in; I love the dinosaurs and all the Indian stuff," Miss Sills says, "and I love the gift shop, where I do a lot of my Christmas shopping. The museum re-laxes me, gets me away from the telephone, and brings me into a whole different art form. It's a change of ambience, which is what I need."

Eli Wallach and Anne Jackson also have a passion for Chi-nese food, but the acting couple like to go to Chinatown, to wander through the winding, colorful streets with their son, Peter, a film maker and artist, who has a loft on Eldridge Street. "My son is very into all the little restaurants none of the tourists go to," Miss Jackson says proudly.

When she's on her own, she likes to meander with her camera, particularly in Greenwich Village. "I take pictures of trees," she explains. "I'm mad about trees. They're sculptures. I could tell you all the trees in the city that are worth photographing." The Village is also the scene of Mi-chael Tilson Thomas's weekly pilgrimage through the streets. "I'm studying and practicing all the time, and when I start going crazy I just wend my way through the streets," says the New York-based conductor. "I have a little route I follow that incorporates old bookstores, especially ones that specialize in theater materials, and antiques shops, which we're totally surrounded by down here. There are little espresso places and falafel places I stop into, and I go by the

Sephardic Jewish cemetery at 11th Street and Sixth Avenue and say hello. I especially like to get lost in the tangle around where West Fourth and West Tenth streets meet."

One obligatory stop is Balducci's, "to see what outrageous new fresh mushrooms from Outer Moldavia are available."

Mr. Thomas finds his walks a welcome antidote to an overplanned and structured life. "I always leave the house with some very knotty problem in my mind, and I make my way through these streets which mirror my state of mind," he remarks. "By the time I come back, I'm much happier, and I have a sense of real adventure. What I love down here is that I always discover some little cul-de-sac or mews that I never knew existed. I've been doing this for years, but it's just inexhaustible. I find my walks enormously relaxing— the tempo, the ramble of it."

The endless variety of the city's food markets are a lure for Suzanne Farrell of the New York City Ballet. When she is not dancing, Miss Farrell likes to stay home on weekends and read or cook. But she will venture out to shops on the Upper West Side—to pick up some veal at her favorite meat market at Broadway and 68th Street, or fish at Citarella at Broadway and 75th. "I guess it's Mr. Balanchine's influence," she observes. "He was a wonderful chef. I like to eat, and if I can't eat, I like to feed somebody else. Mr. B. taught me how to cook veal, he always told me you have them wrap the fat around the meat and roast it that way, and he was right."

Another ballerina, Cynthia Gregory of the American Ballet Theater, enjoys less domestic weekend pursuits, such as playing pool and going to the track.

"Dancers do so much physical work all week that when

you have some time off, you don't want to jog or play tennis," she comments. "I love to play pool; it's a nice, quiet game. And I love the racetrack; I go to Belmont or the Meadowlands. I have a gambling streak in me. I know all the jockeys, and I get so excited if my horse is winning that I jump up and down and scream, and everyone looks at me. I get very emotional about it." She sighs. "I'm sort of a poor loser, though."

PART 4

Capital of Art
and Music

CHAPTER 23
....
City Art: Lessons for a Critic

BY JOHN RUSSELL

When I was growing up in London, long, long ago, my friends and I used to get together of an evening and wonder what New York was like. People told us first one thing and then another. We listened, we read, we went to the movies, and we looked at the few specimens of American painting that came our way.

Art did not get us far. It was, in fact, mysterious to us that American painters had such trouble with New York, and not until many years later did I piece together the history of the involvement of art with the city. There was no painter, it seemed, who had summed it up, once and for all, the way first Canaletto and later James McNeill Whistler summed up the waterfront of London, Bernardo Bellotto summed up Warsaw and Vienna, and Carpaccio summed up the rooftops of Venice.

If we wanted to know about the ever burgeoning New York of the nineteenth century, it was the engravers who did most for us. Closer to mapping than to what was once called "an artist's impression," their work evidenced an all-seeing mastery of physical detail. Like birds unknown to Audubon, they swooped this way and that, seemingly high above the city, when the great bridges were going up, one by one, and that majestic novelty, the Dakota apartment house, backed on to open country that ran straight down to the Hudson River.

Pondering the look of the Dakota, we found in time that painting in New York had often done better indoors than outdoors. Eastman Johnson was not a major painter, but in the 1870s he had a way with the overfurnished, tightly buttoned, and firmly bolted houses of the moneyed New York bourgeoisie that gave even the young Henry James a run for his money. (His *Not at Home* could, in fact, be an illustration for the last pages of James's novel *Washington Square*.)

Still on the subject of interiors, painting eventually taught us that, at the end of the nineteenth century, there were painters in New York who lived very well indeed in a high bohemian style that was international in its derivation. One of them was William Merritt Chase, and his New York studio scenes had an ease and an amplitude that suggested that New York could be a very pleasant place in which to live. All sense of struggle and bustle had been edited out of them, as if Chase wished to suggest that even painting itself was no more than a pastime for gentlemen, and nothing in life was more important than the correct choice of a fan, a stuffed duck, or an Oriental silk for the sofa.

Still, New York was a place in which the out-of-doors was terribly important. In that context, painting picked up at the start of our own century. Every newspaper went shopping at that time for men who had trained as artist-reporters.

William Glackens, John Sloan, Maurice Prendergast, and their colleagues looked with the eyes of practiced newsmen at the life of the city; when Glackens introduced us, in his *Hammerstein's Roof Garden*, to a life-style that had long since ceased to exist, we trusted him.

Something of this versatility, this feeling for the immediate, became common form among New York artists. The early American modernist Joseph Stella knocked himself out, over and over again, trying to paint the Brooklyn Bridge in what was then thought to be an experimental idiom. (But Hart Crane did better, in just two or three lines of his great poem "The Bridge.")

Not long afterward, Edward Hopper brought an inimitable tristesse and a sense of beached vacancy to the look of the New Yorker, whether male or female. Working with an empty street and a candy-striped barber pole, or with a deserted station on the elevated railway, he brought his own unmistakable elegiac quality to the metropolitan scene. Mark Tobey, another veteran of the hard school of newspaper draftsmanship, looked with wonder upon the tumultuous Broadway of the 1930s, and Reginald Marsh caught the *moto perpetuo* of life as it was lived during the Depression in burlesque houses and on the beach at Coney Island. Meanwhile, the great illustrators of the 1920s and '30s were doing as much to record the look of New York, year-round, as almost any of the painters whom we saw in museums and galleries. Rarely in high art did one find as accurate an indication of things to come as could be found in Peter Arno's portrait of the prototypical jogger, first published by *The New Yorker* in 1931. Covers such as these led us to think of New York as a combination of trysting-ground, nursery garden, and adult playpen.

With hardly any paintings to consult in the late 1930s, we fell back on first-hand accounts of what it was like to be in New York. Some of our friends were half-American and, for that reason, had visiting rights. And when they told us about watching a prizefight in Madison Square Garden, sitting in the old Metropolitan Opera House, skating on the frozen lake in Central Park, and eating chicken hash, we turned emerald with envy.

Longing to know more, we were balked at every turn. Hollywood in those days had barely heard of location shooting. Television did not exist. Knowing nothing of photography, we had no idea that Berenice Abbott had just completed what was probably the single finest survey of New York ever made, *Changing New York*. We knew that there was a marvelous piece of music by Charles Ives called *Central Park in the Dark*, but you could wait forever to hear it in London. (Not until the 1950s, when the playwright S. N. Behrman took to passing through London, did I learn to recognize the inimitable wryness and the well-concealed sense of wonder with which a true New Yorker cuts the fat off conversation.) When something that was truly fresh from the New York stage turned up in London, it took us quite by surprise. We had our first editions of Damon Runyon, and one of us thought that the metric scheme of "You're the Top" was the very epitome of New York. But when a Bernstein-Robbins ballet called *Fancy Free* came to London just after the end of World War II, it might as well have come from another planet, such was our disorientation after long winters of *Giselle* and *Swan Lake*. We knew that during a visit in 1855, William Makepeace Thackeray, the author of *Vanity Fair*, had written to a friend: "There is some electric influence in the air and sun here that we don't experience on our side of the globe." But to have that electricity blowing the fuses in the Royal Opera House was something else again.

News came to us around that time of a great painting that had just been completed by a great European artist who had arrived in New York toward the end of World War II.

The painter in question was Piet Mondrian, a refugee from Europe, and the painting, finished in 1943, was his *Broadway Boogie-Woogie.*

Mondrian had been working for many years with simplified geometrical forms that hewed to an irregular grid. (Curves were outlawed.) Those plain rectangles in their asymmetrical arrangement looked to be as abstract as paintings could be, but, in point of fact, they were summations of a long lifetime of looking at architectural forms, human forms, botanical forms, and the interlocking forms of pier and sea.

In *Broadway Boogie-Woogie,* Mondrian distilled not only his experience of New York street patterns, but his delight in the jazz records that he played over and over again in his studio. All of New York is in this painting, if we know how to look for it. As to the question "Why are there no great paintings of New York?"—it no longer needed to be asked.

The Mondrian was the first thing that I went to see at the Museum of Modern Art when I finally stepped ashore in New York, and I cannot believe that it will ever be superseded as an all-purpose emblem of the city. Since I came to live in the city ten years ago, I have, like everybody else, acquired a private anthology of things seen—in art, in photography, at the movies, in newspapers and magazines, even in signs trailed from very slow aircraft—that are fundamental to my notion of New York. I cannot walk into the Plaza

Hotel without remembering the opening scene of Alfred Hitchcock's *North by Northwest*. Bowling along the F.D.R. Drive, I remember the jogging scene in *Kramer vs. Kramer*. Padding round in half-converted industrial buildings, I have trouble forgetting what nearly happened to Jane Fonda in *Klute*.

Scenes from *Butterfield 8* by John O'Hara and *Mr. Sammler's Planet* by Saul Bellow—to mention two novels only—are as vividly present for me as if I had seen them at the movies, though I know them only from the printed page.

Among our record collection at home, an all-time favorite is a vintage rendition of Leonard Bernstein's "New York, New York" from *On the Town*, in which the bray of the brass section is as evocative of New York as George Gershwin's *An American in Paris* is evocative of Paris.

If New York remains a problematical subject for painting, the fault does not lie with our city alone. All great modern cities, without exception, are problematical subjects for painting. There are no great paintings of Paris or Rome, Amsterdam or Florence, in the 1980s. It is a fact of life that painting now addresses itself to other issues and other subjects and no longer tackles big cities directly.

There are exceptions. I never go into a downtown bookstore without thinking of the one that Red Grooms recreated for the Hudson River Museum in Yonkers.

And there are the painters who have made an impact on New York, rather than the other way round. It was a happy day when huge portrait heads by Alex Katz began to appear above our heads at the corner of Seventh Avenue and 42nd Street. Wind, weather, and other things in combination put an end to Katz's mural, though not before it went into a second edition.

Richard Haas has won himself a large constituency with the paintings, each one "as big as a house," that he has made on blank walls all over the city. Wind and weather—and, in some cases, the wrecker's ball—have done their worst with them, too. The most conspicuous of his paintings was beyond a doubt the one at the south end of Times Square on a building that has lately been pulled down, but Haas is in business all over the city and his work is not likely to go out of favor.

Haas's murals have brought a sense of fun and fantasy to what would otherwise have been dead corners of the city, just as on the Lower East Side there are outdoor mural paintings that have become the focus of the neighborhood immune to the activities of vandal and graffitist.

Among other artists who come to mind: Yvonne Jacquette has worked with the image of New York after nightfall as it appears from the windows of the aircraft in which we grind round and round in a holding pattern. Alice Neel was best known for portraits in which forthright human sympathy is allied to a disconcerting candor in matters of physical detail. But from time to time she painted the view from her window on the West Side with a richness and a fullness of response that few New Yorkers have equaled.

George Segal in some of his bone-white sculptures has caught the elegiac quality of the moments that life in New York suddenly presses down hard upon the bereft and the lonely. And even painters like the late Fairfield Porter, who in his art was a countryman through and through, have brought a fresh, clear eye to the city.

Sometimes for pleasure and sometimes in the line of my professional activity, I have ingested these paintings and these sculptures the way an ostrich ingests a Cartier watch.

None of them has said the last word on New York, but neither have the poets, the novelists, and the moviemakers. For me, the printed work still has primacy—as when E. B. White, in that great essay, "Here Is New York," speaks of the city as "the concentrate of art and commerce and sport and religion and entertainment and finance, bringing to a single compact arena the gladiator, the evangelist, the promoter, the actor, the trader, and the merchant."

CHAPTER 24

....

Galleries: The Seedbeds of Tomorrow's Art

BY JOHN RUSSELL

People in the 1980s play art the way they play horses. They also play art the way they play the stock market, at no matter what level. Art in recent years has been judged by whether or not it "performs." As a hedge against inflation, the paintings of J. M. W. Turner have "performed" in spectacular style, whereas the pound sterling has not. As a repository for hot money, moreover, art beats real estate, beats the stock market, and beats the gold bar.

This is neither a distinguished nor even a reputable attitude, but it is widespread. It is the basis of almost every dinner conversation that turns to the subject of art. Every newsstand has magazines that cater to it, and they can't all be losing money.

Besides, art is prestigious. Even today, it stands for exalted achievement. Just as you are what you eat, so you are what you have on your wall. To own a late Van Gogh may not put you up there with Van Gogh in the scale of human achievements, but it links your name with his. No longer are you simply Judson Jinks. You are the owner of the Judson Jinks Van Gogh, and the beneficiary thereby of a satisfaction on which no price can be set. You don't have to stick to established values, either. If a twenty-five-year-old painter called Christopher Cannibal is the talk of every table in town, what greater bliss than to hear it said that "Jinks was in there early with Cannibal"?

But how to get in there early with Cannibal? Thirty years ago there were just two or three galleries to go to. Today you have to begin on Madison Avenue above 79th Street. From there you work the terrain, fanning out to left and to right, all the way down to 57th Street. On 57th Street you are in heavy territory, both to the east and the west. Chelsea cannot be ignored. SoHo and Tribeca have to be covered in depth. Nor should the area around Tompkins Square, in the East Village, be left out.

There's just no knowing where Cannibal, the new young man of the hour, may surface. There may be a uniformed security man at the door, and the walls may be covered with best quality brown velvet. You may have to endure the ordeal by elevator that is a speciality of 57th Street. Elsewhere, white marble may surround the work of Cannibal, and the view may extend over sixteen square miles. But Cannibal may also be found in a broken-down den to which no former function may decently be assigned. It is the prerogative of Cannibal to be everywhere and nowhere.

Walking along the streets that are part of the New York art world, you will everywhere feel a tingling sensation, as if energy were infiltrating your toes. The source of that energy is other people's ambition, bubbling up through the soles of your feet. Not even in Paris in the 1920s were there quite so many artists—arrived, arriving, or aspirant—as there are in New York today. And Paris in the '20s was by comparison an easygoing, low-keyed, slow-moving sort of place. Ambition in New York is ferocious, unrelenting, implacable, and it bubbles today as never before.

The ambition in question does not reach us in raw form. It comes processed. In the downtown cooperative galleries, artists do the processing themselves. In invitational shows like the Whitney Biennial, curators do it. But primarily it is the dealers who cope, and every one of them has a different way of going about it.

Art dealing has its conglomerates and its international cartels. But fundamentally it is a bastion of individual effort. No one tells you what to do. You rent the space. You get it painted, furnished, and lit. You hire your staff, and you hang up whatever shingle is permitted in your neighborhood. Thereafter, you're on your own.

People become art dealers in every imaginable way, and they come from every conceivable milieu. Pierre Matisse is the son of one of the greatest of all French painters. Sidney Janis sold shirts. Leo Castelli was in the Olympic class as a mountain climber. Klaus Perls was a trained art historian, with a book on Jean Fouquet to his credit. Joan Washburn was the daughter of a gifted hoofer, and inherited her bounce in full measure.

Nor is there any limit to the guises in which art dealers can confront their public. The dealer as statesman, as dreamer, as autobiographer, as exiled patriot, as predator, as stand-up comedian, as historian, as young man in a hurry, as den mother, as Diaghilev, as Salome, and as Dowager Empress— all come our way. (For an insider's view of this, and one that is as amusing as it is incomplete, I recommend *Tracking the*

Marvelous: A Life in the New York Art World, by John Bernard Myers [Random House, $17.95].)

Motivations are many, likewise, and they are often more complicated than people suppose. There is nothing in the American Constitution that says it's a crime to make money fast, and the art world in recent years has undeniably had elements of the gold rush, the national lottery, and the coiner's den. It has its big spenders, but it also has its consummate hoarders who know just when to unload. Like every other profession, it has its black sheep, some of whom we could spot across a five-acre field, but it also has here and there an unreconstructed idealist.

Furthermore, it has people who believe that to be first with the new is to perform a public service. They believe that someone in New York is going to do for living art what the first publishers of *Ulysses* and *The Waste Land* did for literature. That person does not have to operate out of a tall town house in the East Sixties, either. Ambitious young people remember that when Daniel-Henry Kahnweiler had the exclusivity of Picasso, Braque, Juan Gris, and Fernand Léger in Paris before 1914, he operated from the kind of tiny shop near the Madeleine that would otherwise have specialized in a rather dubious kind of hatpin.

There are precedents of that kind in New York, too. What Alfred Stieglitz did with his gallery at 291 Fifth Avenue has never been forgotten. People remember the apostolic simplicity of the gallery, the high level of much of what was on view, and the uncompromising stance of Stieglitz himself. They also remember how after World War II there were pioneers—Charles Egan, Betty Parsons, Richard Bellamy, and Eleanor Ward among them—who went to work single-handedly at a time when galleries for new art were few and collectors even fewer.

Times have changed, of course. Eleanor Ward gave up because she thought that the art world was getting too commercialized. John Bernard Myers gave up for the same kind of reason. About this, as about everything else, people in New York are delighted to take a high moral line. "Commercialization" is the cant word in this context, and there are people who have been complaining of commercialization ever since the first American artist made a living wage.

To hear them talk, you would think that it has been all downhill since the days when Alfred Dove had virtually no income at all from his work, Marsden Hartley was begging the Museum of Modern Art to buy something from him at no matter how low a price, and David Smith didn't make enough money to have to fill in a tax return. Nor is this a phenomenon confined to New York. Only last month a well-known European collector said to me, "When Giacometti drawings cost in the hundreds, I bought them. When they got to be in the thousands, I gave up."

Beyond a doubt there has been a change since Stieglitz sat in his sanctum at 291 Fifth Avenue. There has also been a change since the audience for Jackson Pollock, Willem de Kooning, and Mark Rothko had trouble climbing into three figures.

So in one way or another an untold amount of money is rolling round our city, the way a roulette ball rolls around before falling into this hole or that. Money is magnetic, and the instinct to get some of it while it's still there is very strong in human nature. That instinct in action is not always a pretty sight. Nor does it necessarily favor the production of high art. High art, like the mushroom, may need a secret darkness in which to ripen. If Bonnard and Braque produced more than a few of the greatest paintings of our century, it was in part because they disdained to hurry. But the art world, like every other world, takes on the colors of its time. For this reason not many galleries now count on the kind of expectation of life that enabled the Midtown Gallery on East 57th Street to celebrate its fiftieth birthday a couple of years ago, let alone the 128 years that the Graham Gallery on Madison Avenue can boast. There was a time when art dealers were believed to get better and better with age, like family lawyers. But since World War II the idea has got around that those who deal in new art may burn out after just a few years, like racing drivers or experimental mathematicians. There, too, there are distinguished precedents. Kahnweiler did not find a new painter of any consequence after 1914, though he lived for another sixty years and more. The more intense the initial experience, the more difficult it is to renew it. What the seventeenth-century French aphorist La Bruyère said is still true—"We only love once. The other times are less involuntary."

To burn out, whether as artist, dealer, collector, curator, or critic, is never agreeable. To be seen to have burned out is even worse. Wherever there is acrimony in the New York art world, burning out may well be somewhere behind it. The dealers who stand out in the history of modern art are as often as not the ones who defended their own generation, as Lawrence Rubin (now of Knoedler & Co.) did when he ran the Galerie Lawrence in Paris.

Anyone who has enough money can come along later and consolidate what has already been won. But for the distinguished beginning there is no substitute. What Pierre Matisse did for Balthus, what Leo Castelli did for Jasper

Johns, what Miani Johnson of Willard Gallery did for Susan Rothenburg, what Anne Freedman of Knoedler's did for the sculpture of Nancy Graves, what Paula Cooper did for Jonathan Borofsky, and what Mary Boone did for Julian Schnabel is there for others to parallel as best they can. As to where it will happen, and who will be behind it, is matter for a soothsayer, not a critic.

But there is no way for it not to come about. The dealers' galleries relate to the central nervous system of the city. Working in a city that redefines itself every year, they necessarily take on something of its character. New York would not be New York without the pandemic paranoia that hangs over the city like an umbrella that everyone has forgotten how to furl. "Different has to be better," people say, and they act upon it.

It helps that you really can start from nowhere. Padding along, north and south of Tompkins Square, we should take time off to admire the north side of the square itself, which with its great tall house fronts may well be the most distinguished thing of its kind in Manhattan. The art galleries, when we find them, are in brownstones, in former shops, and in nameless holes in the wall. By uptown standards, presentation is minimal and the neighborhood rough.

But then we remember that when Ernst Ludwig Kirchner and his friends in the *Brücke* group helped to turn European art around before 1914, they showed their work not in a conventional art gallery but in an ad hoc space in a lamp factory in the suburbs of Dresden. There is no such thing as an impossible space in New York City, any more than there is any such thing as a space that has been hallowed once and for all.

Twenty-four West 57th Street was beloved of many people because Betty Parsons had her gallery there. Not only had she found more good artists in her time than just about anyone else, but she knew exactly how to treat them, and they loved her. After she died, her longtime lieutenant Jack Tilton took over the gallery.

He might have kept it as a shrine to Betty Parsons, but he didn't. He changed the architecture, reverting to a design originally made for Mrs. Parsons by the late Tony Smith, who was an architect as well as a sculptor. He also decided to stand on his own legs and choose a whole new team of artists.

And quite right, too. There should be a place of honor for the gallery that has played a historic role in the development of living art, but the dealer's gallery that we must seek out and succor is the one that is dipped in the dyes of the new. This is not—as is sometimes said—because a dealer's gallery thrives on fashion, like a dress shop. It is because it depends on an almost clandestine society of artists, collectors, curators, and critics. It cannot be programmed or planned for. No amount of money can bring it into being, though sometimes quite small amounts of money can save it. It is a combination of listening post and proving ground, talking shop and alchemist's den. Print can help, but even print is not indispensable to it. It depends on something intangible and impalpable—an energizing minimum of good talk and goodwill.

No one person can find, launch, or sufficiently talk up either a new gallery or an individual new artist. It is the first duty of the critic to point the way, but the reader can get there first if he is smart enough. Good hunting!

CHAPTER 25

···

A Critic's Walk Through the New Modern Museum

BY MICHAEL BRENSON

The Museum of Modern Art is the most important museum of its kind in the world. It has more major works by more major nineteenth- and twentieth-century artists than any other institution. There is so much ripe artistic fruit by Pablo Picasso, Henri Matisse, Giorgio de Chirico, Joan Miró, Jackson Pollock, and others, the museum is an Eden of modern art.

Any ambitious permanent installation, however, is a very special and eccentric garden. If a large installation is going to make sense, it must be held together by a particular point of view. As a result, while the reopening of the Museum of Modern Art in the spring of 1984 after a period of reconstruction gave us back many of our artistic roots, it is also necessary to consider just how those roots have been presented to us, and which ones have been extended, watered, trimmed, and cut.

Make no mistake about it, the painting and sculpture that

is the glory of the museum has been cultivated by a very particular hand. William Rubin, director of the department of painting and sculpture, has approached his task with all the courage of his formidable conviction. Knowing that the present installation of two floors and forty-odd galleries of painting and sculpture may be his legacy to generations of artists, Mr. Rubin has left nothing to chance. He has enmeshed every work in a complex, didactic network of correspondences and cross-references. His installation has a density and control that almost oblige the visitor to consider it as a work of art itself.

All the galleries were designed with their installations in mind. The first three-quarters of the painting and sculpture installation, from Post-Impressionism through Abstract Expressionism, will change very little. The installation of art done after 1960 will rotate three times a year.

What follows is a walk through the painting and sculpture galleries that suggests the thinking that went into it. The focus will be on aspects that this visitor found surprising, with an occasional look at the other more or less permanent installations of architecture, design, and photography.

SECOND FLOOR

In any new installation, surprises are created by changing the placement of familiar works. For example, soon after entering the second-floor galleries, visitors now see *The Sleeping Gypsy* by Henri Rousseau from 1897, with its reclining magilike nomad, suspicious lion, and seemingly bemused moon, alongside such icons of the museum as Paul Gauguin's 1893 *Moon and the Earth* and Vincent van Gogh's 1889 *Starry Night*. In a Post-Impressionist gallery that also includes dreamlike and expressive late-nineteenth-century paintings by Odilon Redon and Edvard Munch, the exotic, imaginary world of Rousseau makes sense. The juxtaposition also emphasizes the visionary quality in the paintings of Seurat, Van Gogh, Gauguin, and even Cézanne, which remains relatively inaccessible when their works are discussed primarily in Impressionist terms.

Perhaps the turning point of modern art comes three galleries on, where the visitor is confronted suddenly with Picasso's 1907 *Demoiselles d'Avignon*, which helped lay down the rules and set the tone for all the radical art that followed it. The immediate preparation for this painting is Picasso's 1906 *Two Nudes*, in which two naked female figures emerge from the introspection of the Blue and Rose periods and begin to swell with the violence and energy of Analytic Cubism. The sense of rupture that is still experienced between these two works, done only one year apart, dramatizes the convulsive character of the *Demoiselles*, of Picasso's art and indeed of early-twentieth-century art in general.

From this corner gallery, which is loaded with insight and information, the visitor can turn left and find refuge in the ease and silence of Monet's *Water Lilies*, among the few works in the same gallery as before. The placement of the *Water Lilies* in a private pocket reflects the artistic position of the paintings in their time. While they were being painted, during the development of Cubism, Monet was working essentially on his own, well outside the mainstream, and these works were not in the artistic eye at all.

If an installation can clarify a historical moment, it can also clarify great works. A striking example is the vista across the Cubism galleries onto Picasso's 1921 *Three Musicians*, a painting in which jagged and jovial Pierrot, Harlequin, and monklike figures play music in a closed space in which the festivity and darkness of age-old ritual seem to have been concentrated. The visitor approaches this work through a number of Cubist Picasso paintings and constructions, primarily of Harlequins and guitars. The *Three Musicians* becomes the point at which the directions leading into the painting converge.

Next to Picasso's 1915 *Harlequin*, a key marker along this vista, is a 1915 Cubist sculpture by Jacques Lipchitz called *Man With a Guitar*, made soon after Lipchitz saw the *Harlequin* in Picasso's studio. The juxtaposition of an exceptional painting with an unexceptional but representative Lipchitz sculpture not only makes a point about the relation of Cubist sculpture to painting, but also suggests how derivative Lipchitz's art tended to be. Beyond Brancusi, Expressionism, and Futurism is another highlight of the new installation, an unassuming gallery devoted primarily to Mondrian, which feels far more like a shrine than the huge and somewhat pretentious Matisse gallery, past the stairwell ahead. Mondrian's richly austere 1939–43 painting *Trafalgar Square*, on view for the first time since 1960, provides a key link in the chain of Mondrians that includes the severe diamond-shaped 1926 *Painting I*, the compositional tour de force of the 1936 *Composition in White, Black, and Red* and the jumpy and radiant 1942–43 *Broadway Boogie-Woogie*. Seeing these first-rate Mondrians together is a reminder that his work has that combination of precariousness and toughness that is characteristic of so much major modernist art beginning with Cézanne.

The gallery after the Mondrians, in which Russian Suprematism and Constructivism compete for the visitor's attention with a staircase, is a shock. It is one thing to argue, by placing Mondrians near Suprematist abstractions by Kasimir Malevich, that Malevich is not the abstract painter he is made out to be. It is another to relegate Malevich to a crossroads of the museum and to install the best-known Constructivist sculpture on display, Naum Gabo's *Head of a Woman* (circa 1917–20), in a corner, under the stairs, without light.

There is a shock, as well, in the splendid corner gallery ahead, largely devoted to Picasso, which includes such influential works as the 1930 *Seated Bather*, the 1932 *Girl Before a Mirror*, the 1939 *Night Fishing at Antibes*, and the 1944–45 *Charnel House*. The gallery also includes key sculptures, including the 1932 plaster *Head of a Woman*, a gift from Jacqueline Picasso, and the one sculpture in the second- and third-floor installation that can be seen entirely in the round.

What is jarring here is the treatment dished out to the distinguished Spanish sculptor Julio González. The only two welded-steel works of his on exhibit have been placed alongside welded-steel sculptures by Picasso, in a corner. As a result, González seems little more than a footnote to Picasso.

The last major vista on the second floor leads onto Joan Miró's large 1925 painting *The Birth of the World*, which has never looked stronger. With its simple forms, elemental subject matter, and innovative spilling and blotting techniques, this painting is a bridge between pre-World War II European modernism and Abstract Expressionism. *The Birth of the World* also shows us that when the playful and inventive Miró felt like it, he had access to a fiery and brooding world that few other twentieth-century artists have been allowed to enter. More than any other department, the photography department, on the right near the second-floor entrance, seems to have decided to present everyone and everything. All the photographers are crammed together, from Eugène Atget to Dorothea Lange and the recently deceased Garry Winogrand. There are familiar portraits of Rodin by Gertrude Käsebier, Vladimir Mayakovsky by Laszlo Moholy-Nagy, and James Joyce by Berenice Abbott. There are welcome century-old glimpses of the cathedral of Notre Dame, the Arch of Titus, General Sherman's trail of destruction through the South, and New York's City's Bandit's Roost. This installation will be permanent, except for slight changes.

THIRD FLOOR

The focus of the second half of the painting and sculpture installation, upstairs on the third floor, is what Mr. Rubin calls the "American Renaissance." There is little European art of consequence on this floor apart from Fernand Léger, the ubiquitous Picasso, and an important series of Matisse cutouts called *The Swimming Pool.* There is also a gallery reminding us that in the wake of World War II, Jean Dubuffet and, above all, Francis Bacon and Alberto Giacometti were producing works with a conviction and intensity equal to anything being produced on the other side of the ocean. Bacon's 1952 *Dog* and 1953 *No. VII from Eight Studies for a Portrait* are pitched so high that they seem inconsolable and chilling.

Leading into the gallery with the Bacons is one that goes a long way toward suggesting the Abstract Expressionist inspiration. The placement together of works by Adolph Gottlieb, Willem de Kooning, Seymour Lipton, Robert Motherwell, and Jackson Pollock makes it seem as if post-World War II American painting originated as a journey into the heart of darkness. Using the vocabulary and methods of Surrealism, carefully defined by Mr. Rubin in previous galleries, paintings and sculptures like these helped pioneer a raw, untamed territory. The settlement of that territory went hand in hand with the development of post-World War II American art.

The development of American art from Abstract Expressionism through Minimal Art is clearly plotted. Except for the particularly American element, which really cannot be suggested because the museum owns so few pre-World War II American works, the essential ingredients of Abstract Expressionism are laid out early: Surrealism, Primitivism, pure, expressive line, and pure, expressive color. Almost all the Abstract Expressionists were affected by Surrealism and by some kind of Primitivist orientation. The interest in line could break off into Franz Kline, the interest in color into Mark Rothko and Ad Reinhardt. Pollock and de Kooning, the artists in whose works the greatest number of these elements collided, were the Abstract Expressionist giants.

At the end of the Abstract Expressionist galleries is Pollock's *One (No. 31, 1950)*. This monumental "drip" painting looks back over the entire expanse of its vast post-World War II gallery, across the charged lines of David Smith, Barnett Newman, and Franz Kline, Clyfford Still's sharp and free-floating attempts to capture the sublime, and the huge waterfall of running color by Sam Francis. By the time we have reached this Pollock, there is no longer any artistic limit of subject matter, technique, viewer involvement, or scale. We are ready for Pop Art, Minimal Art, Color-Field painting, and everything else that follows.

FOURTH FLOOR

The architecture and design galleries on the fourth floor fulfill an important function now, not just because of the professional interest in the subject but also because of a revival of artistic interest in the problem of making public art that can be both visually rich and functional. The architectural models of buildings such as Frank Lloyd Wright's Falling Water (the Edgar Kaufmann House) suggest this century's continuing interest in the relationship between form and function, in work with a distinct identity that nevertheless fits into a particular place. In the context of a union between form and function, look at Arthur Young's Bell-47D1 helicopter. This irresistible fragile-winged, bug-eyed creature looms so conspicuously over the escalator that there may be a tendency to look the other way.

CHAPTER 26

....

The Metropolitan Museum

BY GRACE GLUECK

Exploring the Rockefeller Wing

When the Metropolitan Museum of Art, prodded by the late Nelson Rockefeller, decided in 1969 to commit itself to the "primitive" arts of Africa, the Pacific Islands, and the Americas that it had long eschewed, it went all out to create for them what is probably the world's most spectacular showcase. The result, more than a decade in the making, is the $18.3 million Michael C. Rockefeller wing. Of great architectural drama, the installation in which this fragile art is displayed is also a conservator's dream. "Never," as one Met official bemusedly puts it, "has so much expensive high technology been lavished on a display of 'primitive' art."

Nearly an acre of sophisticated, temperature- and humidity-controlled glass cases has been painstakingly built to display two thousand-odd objects, the vast majority made of such perishable organic materials as wood, bark, bone,

231

straw, hides, feathers, and fabrics. The dramatic floor-to-roof wall of transparent glass that forms the south side of the wing has been screened to minimize damage from natural light, and ceiling filters have been placed to remove all traces of destructive ultraviolet rays. The harmful effects of ordinary vibration on these delicate objects have been reduced by placing them on pedestals within pedestals. And the numerous galleries, discreetly painted and carpeted in anonymous beige, have been conceived and arranged so as to focus maximal attention on the exhibits.

From the very beginning, the wing was primarily Nelson Rockefeller's project. It was he who, by giving the Met the contents of the old primitive museum, provided a raison d'être for the wing's construction. It was he who decreed that it be named for his son, Michael C. Rockefeller, who disappeared in 1961 on a collecting expedition among the Asmat people of Papua New Guinea when his native boat overturned off the coast and he attempted to swim ashore. The former vice-president and New York governor was consulted by Met officials on every concept and detail until his death in 1979. Mr. Rockefeller did not, however, provide any funds personally for the building. That was raised by the Met from other members of the Rockefeller family, foundations, including the Rockefeller Brothers Fund and the Vincent Astor Foundation, the National Endowment for the Humanities, and individuals such as Nathan Cummings and the estate of Alice K. Bache.

Although the Metropolitan had begun to collect "primitive" art in the nineteenth century and acquired a number of Mexican and Peruvian antiquities, it lost interest as its acquisitions in other areas grew, and around 1914 the primitive objects were bundled off to the American Museum of

Natural History. During his term as trustee at the Met, Nelson Rockefeller, who began his primitive-art collection in the 1930s, campaigned for the mounting of primitive exhibitions. He even offered to help sponsor a joint expedition of the Met and the Museum of Natural History for pre-Columbian archeological digs. But the Met was not interested, and he began to collect more actively himself. By 1954, the depth and volume of his private acquisitions were such that he set about founding the Museum of Primitive Art in a converted brownstone on West 54th Street.

The installation unites that small museum's collections with the Metropolitan's objects, which include a group of 80 Dogon sculptures of the Western Sudan from the Lester Wunderman collection, approximately 150 pre-Columbian gold objects from the bequest of Alice K. Bache, and some 600 Peruvian ceramics from the Nathan Cummings Collection. Also included are Mr. Rockefeller's personal holdings. In all, the Met now owns some 7,000 objects, not all of which, to be sure, are of exhibition quality. Douglas Newton, formerly director of the old museum and new chairman of the Metropolitan's department of primitive art, thinks that the installation will change people's view of primitive art. "When they see it placed in context with other cultures here," he says, "they'll realize it isn't a backwater, but a major theme in art history."

The wing, with 42,000 square feet of exhibition space and a 14,000-square-foot mezzanine, containing offices and a library, is almost as large as the entire Whitney Museum of American Art. It is divided into equal areas for each of the three major divisions—African, the Americas, and the Pacific islands. There is also a special area for temporary exhibitions. A range of ceiling heights, occasioned by structural necessities, provides theatrical changes of space, running from 50 feet in the area adjacent to the glass wall, where the Pacific material is placed, to 11 and 26 feet in the areas of Africa and the Americas. The Pacific material, coincidentally, contains the tallest pieces, including a group of nine elaborately carved Asmat *mbis*, or memorial, poles, ranging up to 21 feet high, which were collected by Michael Rockefeller. One selling point to Nelson Rockefeller was that as a tribute to his son the poles and other Asmat material found by him would be given most prominence within this space. Lighted at night, the display would be stunningly visible to the outside world.

The point of entry to the installation is in the African area. There, in an introductory gallery, the viewer immediately confronts a number of Dogon sculptures of Western Sudan, including a seven-foot-high male figure with raised arms that is one of the Met's masterpieces. Flanking this open display are glass cases, some wall-mounted, some freestanding, containing smaller objects. In an adjacent area, a raised platform is backed by a wall handsomely mounted with masks and other works from Cameroon.

Other African objects of note include a strongly carved stool by a Zaire tribesman known only as "The Buli Master," a splendid sixteenth-century ivory mask from Benin, and a Fang reliquary head that once belonged to the sculptor Jacob Epstein.

In the Pacific area, which runs lengthwise along the great window wall, a platform presents the *mbis* poles. Behind them, a gallery recreates the ceiling of a Papua New Guinea ceremonial house, with bark paintings, done for a dollar a sheet by Kwoma villagers at Douglas Newton's behest. Among the other prizes here are a twenty-five-foot-long crocodile effigy from the Karawari River region of Papua New Guinea, a temple drum with an elaborate openwork stand from the Austral Islands, plus a group of standing drums and figures from the New Hebrides.

A "treasury" in the Americas area clusters in glass cases a group of gold objects. On open display are such items as a large, elaborately carved stone panel from an eighth-century stele found in the Piedras Negras area of Guatemala and an Izapan altar, circa first century B.C., carved in the shape of a jaguar from a rounded lump of rock. A highlight of the collection is a figure of a kneeling priest or dignitary from the Early Classic Maya period (A.D. 400–500). From Veracruz there is a wonderful group of elaborately ornamental stone objects associated with the ritual ball game of several Mesoamerican cultures.

The design for the Rockefeller installation was begun in 1976 by a team that cut its teeth on the lavish blockbuster shows—the first, "In the Presence of Kings," featured treasures from the Met's collections—mounted during the reign of Thomas Hoving at the Met. Among the other endeavors of the team—Stuart Silver, principal designer for the installation and now vice-president, design communication, at Knoll International, Clifford La Fontaine, design associate and project coordinator, and LeMar Terry, lighting designer—are the Met's Islamic wing, the André Mertens Musical Instruments Galleries, and a long series of exhibitions, including "Treasures of Tutankhamun." The trio worked under the supervision of Mr. Newton and in coordination with Arthur Rosenblatt, vice-president for architecture and planning at the museum, who oversaw the wing's construction.

As an unalterable given, the team had the wing itself, designed by Kevin Roche John Dinkeloo and Associates, architects for the Met's master plan, as a twin to the Temple of Dendur at the north end of the museum rather than around the objects to be displayed within it. And, as Mr. Silver points out, "the change in ceiling heights gave us three different buildings. We've tried to tie them together by means of design techniques—the orchestration of objects, lighting, cases—in a kind of visual rhythm." Mr. Newton credits Mr. Silver with "making the installation look as if it were designed for the architecture in the first place. If it were done less skillfully, it would look improvised, but, as it is, the appearance is very coherent."

An immediate major difficulty was the vast glass wall, an imposing but intrusive presence because of the heavy shadow pattern projected by its strong window grid. Mr. Rockefeller apparently had mixed feelings about the wall. On the one hand, it would provide a proscenium, so to speak, for a dramatic night view of the Asmat objects. On the other hand, he felt that "the idea of creating a museum to look into the park is the silliest one I've ever heard."

As far back as 1970, Mr. Rockefeller had written to Thomas Hoving, then the Met's director, expressing concern that the window wall—even though a metal screen had been designed to cover part of it—would pose conservatorial problems. "But nothing really registered," says Mr. Newton, "until the building was completed." By that time, the Met's conservators had also begun to worry about the effect of heat and sunlight—greatly intensified by the wall's southern exposure—on the perishable wood and fugitive paint of the pieces. Unlike objects of Western art, a good many of the works, particularly those from the Pacific Islands, were not created for the ages. But, paradoxically, their museum enshrinement demanded that every preservatory precaution be observed. Tests were made, readings were taken, and a good deal of angst ensued. Mary Morgan, Nelson Rockefeller's daughter and Michael's twin, who headed a committee to smooth the transition between the old primitive museum and the Metropolitan installation, was instrumental in bringing in, as a consultant, Garry Thomson, scientific adviser to the National Gallery of London. His suggestion: Shield the entire wall.

According to Arthur Rosenblatt, the architects set to work and came up with the present solution: a motorized screen of vinyl-impregnated nylon that covers the entire surface and can be rolled up or down, depending on the intensity of the sun's rays. A network of ultraviolet filters has also been placed in the ceilings of the installation. "If this were on the north side, where the Temple of Dendur is," says Catherine Sease, conservator in charge of the installation, "we'd have fewer problems." But the temple was placed in relationship to the Met's Egyptian galleries and there has been no thought given to a switch.

A related concern was the reflecting pool—160 feet long—designed to match one in the temple wing. Plans were to deploy water-related objects, such as canoes, around it, but there was worry about the heat and humidity hazards posed by a combination of moisture from the pool and direct rays of the sun through the window wall, and the idea was scrapped. But, says Mr. Silver, "we didn't want to lose the effect of a special, dedicated space that was not the floor, so we raised it by decking over the pool." Among other objects, the long, low platform carries a 50-foot Asmat canoe. Not so easily resolved was the question of what to do about the André Meyer galleries for nineteenth-century European art on the balcony above the primitive-art installation. To guarantee isolation of the Asmat material as a tribute to his son, Nelson Rockefeller insisted on a total visual separation of the area. "To insure that no one could look over the balcony," says Mr. Newton, "we raised its parapet and deepened the ledge." A further distancing was achieved by the creation of a large, blank facade whose center portion runs to the Meyer ceiling and whose lower areas permit Meyer visitors a vista of Central Park. "It was costly," concedes Mr. Newton, "but it added considerable wall space to Meyer."

Mr. Rockefeller was, however, dissuaded by the installation's architects and designers from paving the galleries with Astroturf, and from his suggestion that a giant photomural, blown up from a view of an Asnat village taken by Michael Rockefeller, serve as a backdrop for the *mbis* poles. Imbued with the "old-fashioned" Bauhaus esthetic of less is more, Mr. Newton and the designers had originally thought in terms of an uncrowded installation, each piece set out at a comfortable remove from its fellows. "But Rockefeller wanted as much as possible on view," Mr. Newton reports. "We originally wanted to display thirty percent of the collection, and have changing shows. But he insisted that we bring it up to eighty percent. Part of the design challenge was: How do you display all these things and still look elegant?" The designers managed. They have put on view a wealth of nearly two thousand objects without giving an impression of overkill.

Except for the very large pieces, most of the works are kept under glass, both for preservation and for reasons of security. "Almost everything was out in the open in the old primitive museum," points out Mr. Newton. "But here it's out of the question, because of the different character of the Met, and its heavy traffic. And besides, values for these works have gone way up in the intervening years."

Nelson Rockefeller was also concerned that the installation reflect what he referred to as "a sense of intimacy," by which he meant there should be as little distance as possible between the viewer and the object. Working toward that goal, the designers tried to deemphasize the architecture and installation furnishings. In the African introductory gallery, for instance, displays are kept close to the floor, with ceiling height reduced by a suspended grid. In a smaller adjacent gallery, tall, glass-walled cases are clustered in what Mr. Silver calls "minienvironments," to give a sense of privacy. Throughout the installation, wall cases create a "psychological" intimacy by means of recessed glass fronts, with slanted ledges on which the viewer can lean as he peers in at the objects.

On the technical side, each glass case is what Mr. Newton calls a "microenvironment," with temperature and humidity maintained at 70 and 50 degrees, respectively. Many have walk-in backs for easy maintenance, and all cases and pedestals are equipped with containers of silica gels to aid in drying out the air.

Illumination—except for the main gallery, which has natural daylight thanks to the glass wall and ceiling panels—has also been tuned to "private" viewing with a combination of accent and ambient lighting that focuses on the objects and tends to make the architectural background disappear. The general, or ambient, light in each gallery is enhanced by accent lights focused, where appropriate, on objects or groups of objects. Highlights thrown dramatically on a part of an object—a beak, a belly, the fingers of a carved wooden baboon—add further enrichment. Lighting is even used for the subtle direction of traffic. "For instance," Mr. Silver points out, "we want to establish a traffic pattern in the direction of the case bearing Senufo bird masks, so we built very theatrical lighting into it to draw people there."

Because light acts as a catalyst on organic materials, esthetic considerations sometimes had to give way to conservatorial concerns, as with the very delicate Peruvian textiles in the collection and the famous Benin ivory mask. "In such cases," says Mr. Terry, "we lower the ambient lighting, or play a weak light on the object and lower the wattage on those surrounding it to give the illusion of brighter illumination on the object in question." But the most laborious task facing the designers and curators was the actual, highly complex process of placing each object in its proper case or mount, a five-year endeavor in which trial and error played a role. In consultation with Mr. Newton and Mr. La Fontaine, Stuart Silver produced an architectural layout of cases. The initial choice of what might go into each case was made by the curator for each area—Mr. Newton for the Pacific Islands, Julie Jones, curator for the Americas area, and Susan Vogel, associate curator for the African area—whose concern was with chronological and geographical layouts that were curatorially sound. Since the objects themselves were in storage—the Asmat material in a cow barn on the Rockefeller estate at Pocantico Hills—the project coordinator, Clifford La Fontaine, prepared a dozen volumes of photographs of the items. "Then," he explains, "we went through the books, rating each object as to . . . its rarity or esthetic value, then its relationship to other objects, and third, its general appearance, size, shape, and texture." That done, he made small, detailed drawings of the selected objects, cut them out, and, using them as maquettes, worked with the curators in placing them on scale drawings of the cases. "We then made a further selection of objects," Mr. La Fontaine says, "thinking of their relative position in each case, with regard to their size, scale, color, texture, etc." Once a case arrangement was decided on, Mr. La Fontaine would record it in a finished drawing that contained a description of the mountings needed.

"It shouldn't be inferred," put in Mr. Silver, "that these decisions were all sunshine and roses." In fact, he and Mr. Newton hotly debated the installation of a Bangwa royal-ancestor figure from Cameroon on the imposing "open" wall. Mr. Silver pushed for removing the figure from its pedestal and "floating" it on the wall; Mr. Newton wanted it to remain on the pedestal as a floor piece in front of the wall. And that is the way it appears.

One of the toughest installation problems was that of the nine *mbis* poles. The problem, as Mr. La Fontaine describes it, was their size—twelve to twenty-one feet high—and top-heaviness. "We had to devise a method of support that would put minimal stress on them and at the same time provide minimal visual interference. We finally did it by providing two or three holding points for each; some of the poles are virtually hanging, rather than standing."

An even more complex installation, taxing the ingenuity of the conservation department, the designers, and the lighting people, was the ceiling of some 150 bark panels, or *spathes*, used for the Kwoma ceremonial ceiling. For starters, the *spathes* posed perplexing conservation problems. "We had about two hundred and sixty to begin with," notes Catherine Sease, supervising conservator for the installation. "They were painted on very thin bark that responded immediately to temperature and humidity changes. Also, the paint had become powdery.'' After working on the problem for nearly a year, a member of the conservation staff came up with a solution. Each of the 260 bark pieces was cleaned individually and sprayed three times with an acrylic resin. Because each was also covered with painted dots, creating raised areas of pigment, further applications of consolidant had to be applied to cover each dot. ''Then,'' Miss Sease explained, ''each *spathe* had to be strengthened structurally, the cracks and breaks reinforced with Japanese paper. . . . The whole thing took about six months.''

Installing the *spathes*, a number of which were eliminated for lack of quality or inappropriateness of configuration, was another headache. ''We had to figure out, given the varying dimensions of each, how it would be supported from the ceiling, creating at the same time a uniform pattern and richness of variety,'' says Mr. La Fontaine. The *spathes* were finally pierced with holes and then suspended from the ceiling with twill tape so they can move in response to temperature and humidity changes. ''Considering the time and effort we put into them, by the time we got finished, their purchase price of a dollar each went up to maybe a thousand dollars,'' jokes a staff member.

Now, more than a decade after its planning, the wing is finally completed, and no one speaks more feelingly about the results than Mary Morgan. ''I'm happy that it's finished and thrilled about how wonderful it looks,'' she says. ''All the problems were well worth it. Father wanted these objects to have the art-world recognition they deserved, and I think this achieves that goal.'' And she adds, ''There was a lot of sadness involved in the whole business about Michael being lost. But to see these objects in their setting, bearing evidence of his sensitivity, turns the sadness into pride."

Quiet Pleasures

What, you've never laid eyes on the *spinettino* made in 1540 for Eleanora d'Este, Duchess of Urbino? Or the fifteenth-century Annunciation tapestry with the "sliding Christ child" image? Or the bronze Mosan *aquamanile* depicting Phyllis, beloved of Alexander the Great, perched on the back of Aristotle, who crawls on all fours?

These are magnificent objects at the Metropolitan Museum of Art that can be seen without battling the crowds that frequent its more publicized attractions. With minimal effort, you can avoid the well-beaten paths to more touristed galleries, and through serendipitous strolls in some of the Metropolitan's other departments, find marvelous objects to ponder without hustle or hassle.

The *spinettino* (little spinet), for example, in the shape of a writing desk and still in perfect playing condition, may be encountered in the André Mertens Gallery of Musical Instruments on the second floor. Tastefully decorated with mother-of-pearl inlay, carving, gold, and ivory adornments, its delicate craftsmanship makes it as pleasing to the eye as to the ear. And it bears an admonitory inscription in Italian: "I'm rich in gold and rich in sound; Oh, touch me not if no good tone is found."

Next to it, and not to be overlooked, is a double virginal dating from 1581, the oldest extant work by Hans Ruckers the Elder, head of a renowned family of Flemish harpsichord makers. The virginal actually consists of two instruments, the smaller inserted like a drawer under the sound-board of the larger and removable for traveling, housed in a single case with a characteristically charming scene of out-door musical festivities painted on its inner lid. These are only two of the many treasures in this astonishing collection, numbering more than four thousand music makers, from Stradivarius violins to rattles made by the Kwakiutl Indians. More than two-thirds of the collection is non-Western, and it includes such exotica as a Syrian *tombak,* or drum, a *saw sam sai,* or fiddle, from Thailand, and a bowed sitar from India in the form of a peacock.

ISLAMIC TREASURE

You needn't be a carpet fancier to savor the sensuous Persian silk rug from the Safavid period (first half of the seventeenth century) on view in the Met's Islamic galleries. Known as a Polanaise, or Polish-type, rug because in the Islam-ignorant nineteenth century these rugs were thought to come from Poland, it has the appeal of an abstract painting, with its subtle mixture of yellow, salmon red, green, brown, silver, and gold—a gorgeous object, worthy of the nobleman's palace for which it was probably made.

While you're among the Islamic installations, pull up a chair to one of the glassed-over tables housing pages from Persian manuscripts and examine some lively illustrations from the *Khamseh* (translated as "Quintet"), five poems written by Amir Khosrow of Delhi from 1298 to 1301. In one of them, the enraptured hero steals a look at a maiden as she bathes in a pool, and in another, a Moslem pilgrim on the way to Mecca encounters a Hindu Brahmin, from whom he learns a lesson in piety. At another table, you can see pages from the *Shah-Nameh* ("King's Book of Kings"), commissioned in the early sixteenth century by the Persian ruler Shah Tahmasp for his royal library to tell the story of the ancient Iranian empire. In this group, don't miss *The Battle of Pashan Begins*, one of the busiest war scenes ever painted, exploding with color and movement.

NIMRUD IVORIES

In the galleries devoted to ancient Near Eastern art, there's a group of beautifully stylized objects known as the Nimrud Ivories, dating from the thirteenth to the seventh centuries B.C. These small, eloquently carved pieces are from the royal city of ancient Assyria (now Iraq) known as Kalakh (or Nimrud) and include a snarling lion's head and a winged sphinx, whose spirited presence rivals that of works ten times their size. Not far from them, the vigor of Sassanian art is revealed in a cluster of works that includes the powerful head of an unidentified king, sculptured in silver in the late fourth or early fifth century, whose highly symmetrical face and bulbous crown give a good account of the skills of Sassanian metalworkers.

"BLACK FIGURE" GREECE

There are, of course, great riches in the Greek and Roman galleries, among them the famous Euphronios krater, whose purchase by the Met in 1972 is still controversial. But turn your attention as well to a case full of vases adorned by a delicately witty potter and limner known only as the Amasis Painter, circa 560 to 525 B.C. In the eight "black figure" vases (so called because the figures on them are painted in black) on view here, in a wide range of shapes, there are charming scenes of a wedding procession; women at work folding clothes, spinning, and weaving; the return of a hunter; and a warrior leaving home, all done with a fine eye for details of armor, jewelry, and dress.

THE MEDIEVAL CARVER'S ART

There are always finds in the Met's medieval galleries, even for those who know the collections well. One exquisite acquisition is a small, polychrome wood figure of St. George, South German or Austrian in origin and dating from 1475. Blond and pink-cheeked, with an appealing clumsiness engendered by a head and hands out of scale with his body, the saint stands in a relaxed pose holding a lance upside down, indicating the defeat of the dragon that lies at his feet.

Among objects of longer tenure in the department, there is a small, polychrome oak sculpture of the enthroned Virgin and Child, dating from the twelfth-century School of Auvergne (France). A formal, iconlike work notable for its rich surface pattern chiseled from the wood like the strokes of a drawing, it's said to be one of the finest pieces of Romanesque sculpture in this country. You might also pause at a small, silver-gilt reliquary box of St. Thomas à Becket, made in England circa 1175–80. Its magnificent craftsmanship is revealed in the beaded bands, hinges, and floral decoration of the front- and back-lid plaques, and its brilliance of design in the composition and modeling of figures by means of sharply drawn drapery folds.

And then regard the famous Annunciation tapestry, one of the Met's most important, a fifteenth-century Franco-Flemish creation in which the Virgin Mary, seated in a room, is approached by the Angel Gabriel. Above this tableau appears God the Father, who dispatches the infant Jesus, bearing a cross, down from the Heavens toward the Virgin, an example of a recurrent motif known to scholars as the "sliding Christ child."

AMUSEMENTS IN PORCELAIN

Those in search of lighter fare will find amusement in the less-frequented galleries of European sculpture and decorative arts. Among their serendipities is a piece of sixteenth-century Italian majolica ware that served as a salt and pepper dispenser. But the salt and pepper dishes are minor items in a sculptured tableau that shows a richly clad gentleman leaning forward with his head stuck into a funnel over a hot caldron, taking a facial steam bath. Among other goodies is a salt-glaze stoneware piece of English Staffordshire, dating from 1745, known as a "pew group" and very Pennsylvania Dutch in feeling, which depicts a comically courting couple sitting side by side. A number of glass and jewelry items in the gallery labeled jewelry, goldsmith's work, and horology are eminently viewable, including an opulent lorgnette made by René Lalique in Paris around 1900 and boasting gold, colored glass, jade, and diamonds, and a nineteenth-century Swiss watch of gold and enamel, in the form of a beetle with huge red wings. And don't fail to check out the many porcelain figures—of people, dogs, birds, and other beings—made by German and Italian craftsmen, in the Lesley and Emma Sheafer Collection, bequeathed to the Met in 1975 and including more than four hundred examples of German and Austrian porcelain.

MARBLE NYMPH'S COIFFURE

A superb cluster of seventeenth- and eighteenth-century French sculptures is deployed in the Josephine Bay Paul galleries on the main floor (just preceding the entrance to the Lehman Collection). Among the naiads, cherubs, and maidens in which this work abounds is an impressive wall fountain, adorned with a coy nymph drying her hair. Of marble and gilt bronze, with the nymph wringing her tresses (oh, for a Conair blower!) and a pair of bronze serpents spitting water into a large basin, the fountain was made in 1763 for the château of the Duc de Chevreuse at Dampierre where, apparently, scale was no problem.

SMALL LEHMAN MARVELS

Now that the novelty has worn off and multitudes no longer mill about at the Lehman Collection, that controversial gazebo added to the Met in 1975, its magnificent paintings can be looked at in relative comfort. Concentrate on the small period rooms, where you will find such High Renaissance masterpieces as Botticelli's tiny *Annunciation* (1490), Giovanni di Paolo's *Expulsion from Paradise* (1445), with its terrifying figure of God; Petrus Christus's *St. Eligius as Goldsmith* (1449), with its detailed depictions of jewels and other precious objects, and a late-fifteenth-century painting by the Master of Moulins, *Portrait of a Young Princess*, thought to be Margaret of Austria. For comic relief, take a look at the bronze *aquamanile* (a decorative vessel used for the washing of hands and placed on the dining table for the entertainment of guests), made around 1400 and depicting the seduction of Aristotle by Phyllis, supposed wife or mistress of Alexander the Great.

EUROPEAN PAINTINGS

With your appetite for paintings whetted by the Lehman Collection, you might venture next to the European paintings galleries on the second floor, which give new dimension to the phrase "embarrassment of riches." Browsing along, you might look into the area devoted to English painting of the eighteenth century, where among the splashy finery of grand lords and ladies, John Hoppner's feisty 1787 portrait of a boxer named Richard Humphreys stands out. Bare to the waist, clad only in knickerbockers and posed in a landscape with his meanly dukes up, Humphreys, aged twenty-five, has already beaten Will'm Smith, James Bentley, Sam'l Martin, and Dan'l Mendoza, we are told in a caption by the artist.

Drifting along, you'll come to *The Fortune Teller*, by Georges de La Tour, an early, full-daylight work by an artist who specialized in dramatically lighted nighttime paintings. Thought to have been done between 1616 and 1620, or 1630 and 1635, it portrays a skeptical young nobleman having his fortune told amid scheming women, one of whom stealthily picks his pocket as he holds his hand out to a wizened gypsy.

VERMEER

In the Dutch and Flemish galleries, search out a painting by the never prolific Johannes Vermeer, a portrait of a sweet but sickly-looking young woman dressed in blue, who regards us over her shoulder with a wistful smile. An installation of Venetian painting boasts, among other treasures, a portrait of the sculptor Alessandro Vittoria, painted about 1566 by Paolo Veronese. Vittoria, who represented the Venetian classical style of the late sixteenth century, holds a marble statuette of St. Sebastian, almost identical with a small Vittoria bronze from 1566 of the same subject, which is also in the Met's collection.

RENAISSANCE WINDOWS

A Botticelli, *The Three Miracles of St. Zenobius*, offers three scenes in one panel in which the saint, Bishop of Florence in the fifth century, revives the dead. Its brilliant colors and flat, posterish painting style with many architectural details, give it a curiously modern aspect. Other works, chosen at random for their high pleasure quotient, include a Raphael altarpiece, *The Madonna and Child Enthroned with the Young Baptist and SS. Peter, Catherine, Lucy, and Paul;* a *Hunting Scene* by Piero di Cosimo, a wild, not-for-the-squeamish bacchanale in which humans, satyrs, and centaurs disport in a wood, dispatching animals; *Meditation on the Passion,* by Vittore Carpaccio, depicting the sages Job and St. Jerome in a symbolic landscape with the dead Christ, and the charming *Man and Woman at a Casement,* by Filippo Lippi, an engagement or marriage portrait in which an adoring swain regards a very self-satisfied young woman through a casement window.

OLD CHINA AND EGYPT

Stop, before leaving the Met, for a look in the Arthur Sackler Gallery of Oriental art at the giant *Standing Bodhisattva* of polychrome sandstone, from the Northern Chi dynasty in China and dating between 550 and 557, and note, among the Chinese objects on display in glass vitrines along the balcony over the Great Hall, a lively little *Reclining Dog,* in red earthenware, from the Han Dynasty (A.D. 25–220). Don't miss, in the Egyptian galleries on the ground floor, the wonderful, lifelike series of Faiyum tomb portraits, masks of the deceased that were used on mummies, dating from the Egyptian Roman period, circa 31 B.C. to A.D. 300. And prepare to spend some time with the outstanding group of limestone reliefs from the Amarna period, circa 1365–53 B.C. Among them are a fragmentary head of the king Ikhnaton, showing part of his head and shoulders; and a delicate hand, caught in an arrested motion done with an economy of style that no artist through the ages could better.

And good, quiet looking to you.

A Room-by-Room Guide to Nineteenth-Century European Masterpieces

A sparkling survey course in nineteenth-century European art—but a course in which all of the works confront the viewer "live" instead of in the pages of a textbook—awaits the visitor to the André Meyer Galleries at the Metropolitan Museum. Arranged in more than half an acre of viewing space are paintings and sculptures from the century's cool, crisp beginnings in neoclassicism to its exploratory end in Post-Impressionism, a star-studded route that boasts works by such names as David, Ingres, Goya, Turner, Courbet, Constable, Corot, Manet, Monet, Degas, Renoir, Van Gogh, Gauguin, Rodin, Maillol, and Cézanne.

A warning: The route is not easy to travel in the course of one visit. The museum has done wonders in the way of backgrounding, lighting, cleaning, and even reframing to make the works more approachable. Yet the vastness of this collection and its deployment provide a strenuous workout for eyes and feet. Even a casual viewer may want to take it in stages.

NEOCLASSICISM

The best place to start—in fact the only place, since it coincides with the entrance to the galleries—is at the century's beginning, in a room devoted to works of the neoclassical period. The sources of the style were ancient classical, or Greco-Roman; the emphasis was on the figure, ordered composition, and literary subject matter. And the style was central to French art at the turn of the eighteenth century, providing the ideal expression for Napoleonic imperialism and the conservatism of the French Royal Academy. Its best exponent was Jacques Louis David (1748–1825), whose theatrical *The Death of Socrates* is a political allegory of the French Revolution, idealizing the notion of sacrifice for principles.

The room also contains works by David's most illustrious pupil, Jean Auguste Dominique Ingres, whose elegant portraits of Jacques Louis Leblanc and his wife were once owned by Degas, and whose smaller portrait of the French bureaucrat and industrialist Joseph Antoine Moltedo, done in the neoclassical manner but with intense Romantic feeling, is regarded by some as the greatest portrait of the period. A stellar attraction here is a portrait once attributed to David and then to his pupil Constance-Marie Charpentier. Now the work, a beautifully painted, enormously appealing image of a young artist, Charlotte du Val D'Ognes, is again in the process of reattribution, with some scholars opting for Pierre Jeuffrain (1772–1802), who died the year after its exhibition at the Salon of 1801.

The second gallery, titled "The Origins of the Nineteenth Century," is a long one, reserved for Romantic painters whose work had a seminal influence on the century's artistic development. Half the gallery is devoted to ten works by Francisco de Goya (1746–1828). In the rest of the gallery hang important canvases by Eugène Delacroix, J. M. W. Turner, John Constable, and others. Here among other treats are Goya's *Majas on a Balcony,* a pair of nubile maidens attended by two sinister background figures; his people-packed *Bullfight,* and his portraits of two aristocratic juveniles, *Pepito Costa* and *Don Manuel Osorio.*

A famous late canvas by Turner (1775–1851), *The Whale Ship,* gives evidence of his increasingly free handling of light and atmospheric effects that was to influence artists of our own century. And the stagey *The Abduction of Rebecca* by Delacroix (1798–1863) is a fine example of that artist's contribution to the Romantic style, a style in which turbulent emotional expression stands in sharp contrast to the staid restraint of neoclassicism. Out from storage, where they reposed for decades, are *Telemachus and the Nymphs of Calypso,* by the Swiss painter Angelica Kauffmann (1741–1807), and an extraordinary portrait, *The Count of St.-Auffage,* by Théodore Chassériau (1819–1856), a decorative painter in whose oeuvre such a portrait is a rare event. Not to be missed is *Salisbury Cathedral* by Constable (1776–1837), one of the foremost landscapists in art history.

COURBET

The third gallery is devoted to the work of Gustave Courbet (1819–1877), a key figure in the development of Realism who rejected the idealizations of Romanticism and neoclassicism for a naturalistic style of painting in which workers and peasants were frequent subjects. The Courbets on view here represent one of the world's largest holdings of this artist's work. Among them are a generous sampling of Courbet's famous nudes, plus such masterpieces as *Lady in a Riding Habit* and *Source of the Love.*

MILLET AND BARBIZON SCHOOL

Turn left at the end of the Courbet gallery for the first of three rooms hung with paintings of the Barbizon School, named for the small band of pioneer landscapists who clustered in the village of Barbizon near the Forest of Fontainebleau, where they rebelled against neoclassical constraints by painting directly from nature. Noteworthy here are the riverscapes of Charles-François Daubigny (1817–1878), who through Monet directly influenced the Impressionists, and the Dutch-oriented compositions of Théodore Rousseau (1812–1867), nominally the leader of the school.

Another room, to the left, presents works by Jean-Baptiste Camille Corot (1796–1875), an important transitional figure between the century's early neoclassicism and its later Romantic sensibility toward nature. The gamut runs from such masterly figure paintings as the unfinished *Sibylle* through the failed Salon piece *Hagar in the Wilderness* to the filmy landscapes for which the artist is best known today. Straight ahead, in the third Barbizon room, you come on the work of Jean François Millet (1814–1875), and Honoré Daumier (1808–1879), along with lesser lights. Millet's sentimental rendering of peasant figures is seen at its best in *Autumn Landscape with a Flock of Turkeys*, and the satirist Daumier is represented by his famous *The Third-Class Carriage*.

SALON PAINTINGS

Turn right to enter a room that boasts dozens of works by the so-called "Salon" artists, whose academic realism, comprising sentimental subject matter done in a stilted style, won high public favor when exhibited at the conservative, official annual "salons" sponsored by the French Royal Academy. Among the more prominent *salonistes* represented here are Adolphe William Bouguereau (1825–1905), Jean Léon Gerôme (1824–1904), and the sculptor Antoine-Louis Barye (1796–1875), who produced, in what some might consider overgenerous supply, fierce bronzes of animals devouring their prey.

A right turn brings you into another Salon space, containing some of the museum's corniest set pieces, such as the gigantic *Horse Fair*, by Rosa Bonheur (1822–1899); *Salomé* by Henri Ragnault (1843–1871), and *Joan of Arc*, by Jules Bastien-Lepage (1848–1884).

Of particular note in the gallery straight ahead are several paintings by the Russian realists Ilya Repin (1844–1930) and Arkip Kuindji (1842–1910), and one canvas, *City on a Rock*, long attributed to Goya but knocked down not too long ago to that ubiquitous jack-of-all-media, "Unknown."

Farther along in this gallery, and in the gallery to the left, we enter the glamorous, frothy milieu of the Second Empire, where artists such as Franz Xavier Winterhalter

(1805?—1873), Mihaly de Munkacsy (1844–1909), and Jean Beraud (1849–1936) held forth, as attuned to the world of society as to art. Winterhalter's shimmering portrait of the Empress Eugenie in a golden gown is a prime example of the court painter's style, while De Munkacsy's *The Music Room* is a delightful rendering of a period interior, in this case that of the artist's house in Paris.

But the gallery is actually dominated by the work of a sculptor, Jean-Baptiste Carpeaux (1827–1875), represented by a portrait of Napoleon III and a tortuous marble grouping, *Ugolino and His Sons*, that evokes in full measure the agony of *The Divine Comedy*.

SYMBOLISM

Works by the Symbolists, those creative spirits who sought the freer expression of a wild, often morbid fantasy in art, are in somewhat short supply at the Met, but turning right you will encounter them. The chief adornments of the Symbolist room are a pair of borrowed not-very-Symbolist portraits by the Austrian artist Gustave Klimt (1862–1918), and a wall of five paintings by Pierre Puvis de Chavannes (1824–1898), whose friezes of figures in hieratic postures have allegorical significance. Other artists represented are Gustave Moreau (1826–1898), with a sensational rendition of *Oedipus and the Sphinx*, and the English painter Edward Burne-Jones (1833–1898).

RODIN SCULPTURES

A long sculpture gallery follows the Symbolist room, filled mainly with some forty works by Auguste Rodin (1840–1917). The century's most celebrated sculptor is represented in all his media—bronze, marble, terra-cotta, and plaster—and there also are a few works by others: Rodin's pupil Emile-Antoine Bourdelle (1861–1929), Aristide Maillol (1861–1944), whose powerful bronze torso, *Chained Action*, is particularly noteworthy, and Aimé-Jules Dalou (1838–1902). Among the Rodin marbles are *Orpheus and Eurydice*, and a portrait of *Mme. X*, the French poet Anna Elizabeth de Brancovan, Comtesse de Noailles. Bronze works include a small group of figures from the tableau, *The Gates of Hell*. Among the terra-cottas is a magnificent study for Rodin's great *Monument to Balzac*, and the plaster studies, many given by Rodin himself, include a group of hands for *The Burghers of Calais*.

A pair of allegorical paintings by Puvis de Chavannes —the only two-dimensional works in the room—hang on the wall, near Rodin's sculptured head of the painter, and scrutiny will reveal the similarity between the forms created by the painter and the sculptor, who admired each other.

IMPRESSIONISM

From the Rodin room, go left to enter the vast gallery devoted to the cream of the Met's nineteenth-century holdings, Impressionist and Post-Impressionist paintings. The works here are deployed not only along the walls, but also on multi-angled screens that create a more intimate viewing situation. The sensible starting point is on the far side of this gallery, with the work of Edouard Manet (1832–1883), whose reexamination of the Old Masters sparked painting ideas that made him the precursor of Impressionism. The Met's group of eighteen Manets is a great one, allowing a full experience of this artist's work, and its hanging in proximity to Goya makes clear the influence of the earlier artist in such canvases as *Mlle. Victorine in the Costume of an Espada* and *A Boy with a Sword.* Among the other stars of this display are such well-known paintings as *Man with a Guitar, Boating, The Dead Christ,* and *Woman with a Parrot.*

And then we are into the Impressionists themselves, starting on the right with the father of them all, Camille Pissarro (1831–1903), whose lucid early work, *Jallais Hill,* an 1867 landscape with two figures, has been cleaned and beautifully reframed. Nearby is the work of Claude Monet (1840–1926), displayed here in twenty-nine canvases, although the Met owns none of the large, late "Water Lily" paintings that crowned this artist's career. Nevertheless, there is a lot to be grateful for, including such paintings as *The Green Wave,* influenced by Manet, *Morning on the Seine at Giverny,* with its beautiful greens and lilacs, and the famous early work, *La Terrasse à Ste.-Adresse,* for which the museum paid $1.5 million in 1967. And just to prove that even Monet could paint badly, the Met has hung his insipid landscape, *Bordighera,* among the treasures.

A recent acquisition by Henri Fantin-Latour (1836–1904), *Still Life with Flowers and Fruits,* has brought to the Met one of this still-life painter's greatest works. In the center hangs a group of canvases by Vincent van Gogh (1853–1890), a small selection but containing such peerless paintings as *Irises* and *L'Arlésienne,* with its crisp, hard-edged woman's figure on a brilliant yellow ground. Among the seventeen works by the dominant Post-Impressionist figure,

Paul Cézanne (1839–1906), in this vicinity are the strong, stern portrait of the artist's uncle, *Dominique Aubert,* two masterly portraits of Mme. Cézanne, the second of five versions of *The Card Players,* and *View of the Domaine St.-Joseph,* bought by the Met from the Armory Show of 1913.

On the west wall of this vast museum-within-a-museum hang a number of works by Pierre Auguste Renoir (1840–1919). It is not one of the great Renoir holdings because it lacks the artist's important early works. Nevertheless, it boasts the huge *Mme. Charpentier and Her Children,* a handsome commissioned family portrait that made a hit at the Salon of 1878 and marked Renoir's departure from the Impressionists. Among the many other treasures in this gallery, don't miss *La Parade,* by the pointillist painter Georges Seurat (1859–1891), the reframing of which gives it far greater visibility; *The Jetty at Cassis,* by Paul Signac (1863–1935), a Seurat follower; the boldly colored *The Terrace at Vernon,* by Pierre Bonnard (1867–1947), and two breathtaking paintings from the Tahitian period of Paul Gauguin (1848–1903), *Ia Orana Maria* and *Two Tahitian Women.*

DEGAS

From here, reenter the Rodin gallery, and walk left through it for the conclusion of the tour. You'll find yourself in the first of three galleries crammed with some one hundred works by the Impressionist Edgar Degas (1834–1917), certainly one of the greatest Degas installations in the world. A great technical innovator, Degas was at home in a number of media—painting, sculpture, pastel—and the Met's holdings contain fine examples of them all. In painting, there are such masterpieces as *Woman with Chrysanthemums* and the tiny *The Dancing Class*. In sculpture there are bronze castings of almost the complete Degas oeuvre, including the appealing *Little Fourteen-Year-Old Dancer*. An example of his achievements in pastel is *A Woman Having Her Hair Combed*, exhibited at the last Impressionist show in 1886 and described by the artist as presenting a view of the nude "as if you looked through a keyhole."

Fifth Avenue at 82nd Street (212-535-7710). The museum and the galleries are open Tuesday, 9:30 A.M. to 8:45 P.M.; Wednesday through Sunday, 9:30 A.M. to 5:15 P.M. Closed Mondays, Thanksgiving, Christmas, and New Year's Day. Suggested admission: Adults, $4, students and senior citizens, $2, free for children under 12.

CHAPTER 27

....

The Best
Still Lifes
in New York

BY JOHN RUSSELL

If you think that our major museums are just too much for any one human being to cope with, the best way is to break the problem down. If there is more to see than you can bear to look at, you take one kind of picture and follow it through, the way Theseus followed the thread through the labyrinth.

Among the sorts of painting that you could choose, still life would seem to me to be a good idea. The paintings are mostly quite small. But as against their fewness and their smallness, we can set the fact that as often as not they are of very high quality indeed.

Many of them are by Paul Cézanne, for instance. And if the Metropolitan Museum, the Guggenheim Museum, and the Museum of Modern Art have any one thing in common, it is that Cézanne stands out in all of them as one of the greatest painters who ever lived. He has a threefold preeminence—as a painter of the human figure, as a painter of landscape, and as a painter of still life. Moving from one to another of these three museums, we find it hard to believe that he can maintain the same improbably high level of activity. But he does—everywhere, in all his chosen domains and all the time.

Such in particular is the role of still life in Cézanne's total output that it now seems to us almost a historical aberration that the painting of still life was regarded for centuries as one of the humbler forms of art. Of course, it always ranked as an invaluable accessory to more exalted activities—who could forget the passages of still life in Bellini, in Van Eyck, in Dürer, in Rubens, in Vermeer, and in de La Tour?—and it has had a decorative function since the days of Pompeii. There were also occasions—a famous instance is that of Degas's *Woman with Chrysanthemums* at the Met—when we suspect that still life may initially have been meant to play a small role in the painting, only to end by dominating the whole image.

But still life, when unaccompanied, ranked some way below the painting of history and mythology, religion and epic poetry. It was a middle-class, provincial, journeyman activity. There was nothing dishonorable about it, but there was nothing to write home about, either. The idea that a painting of still life could hang in a great picture gallery and be the strongest thing in sight would have seemed merely whimsical. But when we look at Van Gogh's *Irises* in the Met, it momentarily knocks everything else out of mind. Even so, the notion of still life as fundamentally a subordinate form of art seems to have lingered in New York until well into this century. The Metropolitan Museum's collections are, apart from everything else, an index to moneyed New York taste. Looked at with this in mind, the Met's

)

holdings of European paintings could certainly be said to be weak in the area of still life.

Chardin (1699–1779), for instance, is by universal consent one of the great masters of still life. We know exactly what Marcel Proust meant when he wrote as a very young man that thanks to Chardin he saw the everyday disorder of kitchen and dining room in a completely new way. We also know what Proust meant when he wrote of Chardin himself as one of the most touching and sympathetic figures in the whole history of painting. Every great museum in the world would jump at the chance of getting a Chardin.

So it is really odd that the Met should have acquired its first Chardin still life (by purchase) as late as 1959. The painting, *The Silver Tureen*, is an early work, painted about 1725–27. The Met is also relatively weak in Dutch seventeenth-century still life, where lesser museums are often very strong. The little flower piece, dated 1662, by Nicolaes van Veerendael that is now on view at the Met, for instance, could not be said to exhaust the subject any more than the little painting by Jan Bruegel the Younger that hangs next to it can be said to exhaust the potential of Flemish art in a similar vein.

For a glimpse of seventeenth-century Dutch still-life painting at its redoubtable best, we should turn to the *Vanitas Still Life* by Pieter Claesz, which came to the museum in 1949. Not everyone loves paintings of skulls, but this one has the kind of monumentality that Cézanne was later to make his own in that context, together with the tenebrous lighting and spare auxiliary subject matter that Claesz could render to perfection.

Cézanne's apples came straight from the tree, but it was only when the art historian Meyer Schapiro looked at them with fresh eyes that we began to realize their full mythological and psychological significance both for Cézanne and for ourselves. In the same way, we may have looked a hundred times at the painting by Eugène Delacroix of a basket of flowers overturned in the open air, which is one of the glories of the André Meyer galleries at the Met. It looks like an everyday minor mishap in the garden, but when we remember that it dates from the summer of 1848, when all over Europe authority was being overturned—or at any rate called into question—we realize that Delacroix may have had a deeper and wider implication in mind.

For the later history of the still life, we shall do best to turn to the Guggenheim Museum. The Guggenheim has for some time now been shaping up as our alternative museum of modern art; and if you can't for the moment get over to see the Modern's majestic *Still Life with Plaster Head* by Picasso, you can console yourself with the no less majestic still life of 1924 that is the capstone of the Guggenheim's Picasso holding.

Quite apart from that, the Guggenheim can often be counted on for unexpected paintings that enlarge our view of the period in question. As one instance among many, I should like to recommend the Picasso *Flowers in a Vase* of 1906. This is not a large painting, but it manages to encapsulate the past of still-life painting, in the person of Odilon Redon, and the future of still-life painting, in the person of Giorgio Morandi, and yet remain distinctly "a Picasso." For this and for many another surprise, I recommend a visit to the Guggenheim.

CHAPTER 28

....

Musical
New York

BY HAROLD C. SCHONBERG

Ask any musician who plies the international circuit the location of the music capital of the world. The immediate answer, almost a conditioned reflex, will be "New York." Then there is a pause. "Well, maybe London, also."

After that, there is no discussion. No other city approaches them.

"Yes," says Isaac Stern. "There is a great deal of music in London, much of it on the highest international standard. But there is no comparison. London has nowhere near the numbers and quality to be found in New York."

"London is important," says the pianist Gary Graffman. "New York is more important."

"On the grounds of prestigious musical organizations that come and go, New York has the edge," says Jeffrey Tate, the British conductor now at the Metropolitan Opera.

These statements reflect the consensus of most top professionals. There is something very special about appearing in

New York, they say. And when it comes to sheer quantity, New York has the edge.

Even experienced concertgoers may not realize that the weekly offerings at the height of the music season may total more than 150 events.

On a recent weekend alone—which was somewhat slower than usual because of the New Year's holiday—forty-eight events were listed, from the Metropolitan Opera and New York Philharmonic to chamber-music recitals, jazz, events in churches all over the city, a full schedule at the busy Brooklyn Academy of Music, light opera, Baroque, the avant-garde, name it. And the auditoriums in which these are presented descend from the lofty Lincoln Center complex to colleges, museums, lofts, and any room in which musicians can set up stands and invite an audience.

This has been true ever since the turn of the century, though the last two decades have seen a wild intensification. In the early years of the century, the Metropolitan Opera was generally conceded to be the greatest in the world. But more, to foreign artists, New York and—by extension, the United States—was considered El Dorado. Fees were higher. Success paid off with incredible sums. A Paderewski could depart with more than $1 million after an American tour.

New York was undergoing a metamorphosis. It was becoming the financial center of the world. It was attracting numerous immigrants. It was the city with the most newspapers and magazines. Today it is the media center of the world, the art center, the publishing center, and the center of music and music management.

And New York's ethnic mix also puts it alone among the great cities. With such a mixture has come a demand for all kinds of music. Which means that there is no one audience in New York. There are many audiences.

There are also many problems. In Europe, cultural groups enjoy subsidization to a point that makes Americans gasp. New York cultural organizations must struggle to meet annual deficits. There are worries about "elitism" in the arts. But while the city has outgrown its physical plant and sorely needs renovation in many basic areas, it has retained an intellectual life and a cultural vitality unmatched anywhere.

It is true that the repertory is largely traditional. But this is true everywhere. For some twenty years after World War II, composers were busy driving a wedge between themselves and the public. In recent years, though, there has been a change. As the composer Jacob Druckman points out, the audience has expanded beyond a "hard core" of contemporary-music devotees.

"Young people flock to Laurie Anderson and Philip Glass," he says. "These are kids who normally are not interested in contemporary music." Mr. Druckman attributes the increasing interest to the New Romanticism: "I feel strongly that it is not a fad. This is a music that is not doctrinaire and leans toward more intuitive things."

All over the city, groups have been formed to present contemporary music. Prominent among them are Speculum Musicae, the Guild of Composers, the Experimental Intermedia Foundation, the Occasional Singers and Ad Hoc players, the Prism Chamber Orchestra, the Pierrot Consort, the Group for New Music, Parnassus, the Da Capo Players, the American Composers Orchestra, the New Music Ensemble, and a dozen or so others. The music schools and music departments of colleges make a lavish contribution.

Even such establishment groups as the Philharmonic, the

American Symphony, and the Y Chamber Symphony have been giving series of contemporary music. On a recent month alone, the Calendar for New Music, published by the Institute for Arts and Urban Resources, listed more than forty events involving contemporary music in Manhattan.

Ears seem to be more responsive to the new sounds than they used to be. "I find New York audiences very receptive," says Jan DeGaetani, the mezzo-soprano whose repertory ranges from the Renaissance to the latest works of Druckman, Crumb, Davidovky, and Wernick. She says music is in a state of flux. "Young people are trying to solve the problem of reconciling the abstractions of serialism with the New Romanticism," she says, but she is heartened by the great number of groups "busy all over the place" with the new music.

The composer David Del Tredici loves the New York musical scene for its diversity. "In New York, there are violently antagonistic creative groups," he says. "There is a great difference between downtown and uptown. Downtown, I think of experimental mixed-media groups, minimalism. Uptown, I think of Columbia University and a more academic kind of music. Nowhere in the world is there the diversity and experimentation that goes on in New York."

New York is also in the forefront of musical conservatories, the biggest being Juilliard, the Manhattan School, and Mannes College of Music. Each of these, incidentally—as well as the other music schools—offers many performances. A good number are open to the public, and you might catch the next Horowitz, Price, or Stern at one of them.

So in almost all aspects of music, New York remains the beacon, and a musician must conquer the city before being taken seriously as an international star. Such singers as

Sherrill Milnes and Tatiana Troyanos, who have sung in virtually all the major opera houses, confirm the fact that New York is distinctive.

"Audiences are more sophisticated in New York," says Miss Troyanos. "An artist can prepare more creative programs. I say that New York is the center of international musical life. The great artists of the world *must* come to New York. And New York puts more pressure on an artist, more pressure for us to be at our very best."

"Naturally," says Mr. Milnes, "as an American, I am very pro-Met. I think that the Metropolitan turns out more good performances, day in and day out, than any opera house in the world. Every great singer has to come to the Met sooner or later. Without any question, it is more important to sing there than in any one theater in Europe."

By and large, musicians respect New York audiences, and also are greatly concerned about New York reviews. Managers all over the country tend to rely on the New York press for bookings. Harry Dickson, who has been a violinist with the Boston Symphony for some forty years, remembers Serge Koussevitzky saying at a rehearsal, "Gentlemen, maybe it's good enough for Cleveland or Cincinnati, but it's not good enough for New York." Mr. Dickson says that in quoting Koussevitzky he does not mean to knock Cleveland or Cincinnati. "But you know what I mean, and everybody in our orchestra still feels it. Of course, New York is the music capital of the world."

And Joseph Santarlasci, manager of the Philadelphia Orchestra, says, simply: "In my estimation New York is the mecca."

While all musicians say that they try to be at their best wherever they play, they acknowledge that in New York they try to play a little better than their best. Mr. Graffman explains why. His point is that a great success in New York opens doors across the country.

"A career based entirely in America after a smash New York concert is possible," he maintains. "So artists are a little more nervous than they are anywhere else when they walk on a New York stage. They practice harder and take it more seriously, because the stakes are that much higher."

The healthy musical life of London includes five orchestras. But in this regard New York is not a depressed area. In addition to the New York Philharmonic and American Symphony Orchestra concerts, the city is regularly visited by most major American orchestras—the Philadelphia, Boston, Chicago, and Cleveland. And there is the Carnegie Hall Festival of Visiting Orchestras, where American and foreign symphonies present more than fifty concerts a year.

But Seymour Rosen, managing director of Carnegie Hall, says there is one area in which London has it all over New York: recording activity. American orchestras have largely priced themselves out of this market, and records mean a great deal to an international career. Thus Horacio Gutiérrez, who in recent years has ascended to the top echelon of younger pianists, says that in the long run London may be more important to an artist because so much recording is done there.

If New York fails to help an artist through recordings, it has developed another area that has been making reputations—televised opera and concerts. "That's something new," says Mr. Tate, the British conductor, "and it is a phenomenon. The broadcasts from the Met, the 'Live from Lincoln Center' telecasts—things like those are starting to be shown all over Europe. They can have an enormous impact on a career."

There are still things we can learn from musical London, Mr. Tate says. He talks of the much lower ticket prices in London and the high standards of the semiprofessional groups that perform there, especially in the churches. He says there are great conductors who are constantly at Covent Garden and, unaccountably, missing from the Metropolitan—"But the Met was always a singer-oriented house"—and that many more groups in London concentrate on authentic performances of old music than in America.

Mr. Tate also makes a point that Mr. Graffman touched upon, though his pertained to London and Mr. Graffman's to New York. A highly successful London appearance, Mr. Tate says, opens doors on the Continent. European managers may not know much about the New York scene or be very impressed with the findings of the New York critics, but they follow the British press closely. "And don't forget," says Mr. Del Tredici, "that there are so many more newspapers in London than in New York, which means more reviews for an artist or a composer. I also find that the British critics are more hospitable to their composers than the New York ones are to ours."

Yet it is New York that has remained the symbol of bigness and brashness, of intellectual vitality and strength, of ceaseless motion and cultural activity.

As Mr. Stern says, "New York is the dirtiest, largest, ugliest, broken-down city in the world—but it's the only one."

This is recognized, grudgingly or otherwise, everywhere. There is a love-hate relationship between New York and the rest of the country, but New York is unarguably the city that sets the standards, the city in which all who have anything to do with the arts dream of working and succeeding.

Where to Hear Music

Following is a list of the places in New York where music is performed. Telephone calls to some halls and churches will elicit information only about events that they sponsor.

Major Concert Halls
Metropolitan Opera, Lincoln Center (212-362-6000).
New York State Theater, Lincoln Center (212-870-5570).
Avery Fisher Hall, Lincoln Center (212-874-2424).
Alice Tully Hall, Lincoln Center (212-362-1911).
Carnegie Hall, 57th Street at Seventh Avenue (212-247-7800).
Carnegie Recital Hall, 57th Street at Seventh Avenue (212-247-7800).
Merkin Concert Hall, Abraham Goodman House, 129 West 67th Street (212-362-8719).
Grace Rainey Rogers Auditorium, Metropolitan Museum of Art, Fifth Avenue at 82nd Street (212-570-3949).
92nd Street Y, at Lexington Avenue (212-427-4410).
Brooklyn Academy of Music, 30 Lafayette Avenue (718-636-4100).
Town Hall, 123 West 43rd Street (212-840-2824).

Other Halls in Manhattan
Amato Opera, 319 Bowery (212-228-8200).
American Museum of Natural History, Central Park West and 79th Street (212-873-1300).
Alternative Museum, 17 White Street (212-966-4444).
Asia Society, 725 Park Avenue at 70th Street (212-288-6400).
Beacon Theater, Broadway and 74th Street (212-787-1477).

Bloomingdale House of Music, 323 West 108th Street (212-663-6021).

Cami Hall, 165 West 57th Street (212-397-6900).

Casa Italiana, Columbia University, 1161 Amsterdam Avenue at 117th Street (212-280-2306).

Center for Inter-American Relations, 680 Park Avenue at 68th Street (212-249-8950).

City University of New York Graduate Center, Third Floor Studio, 33 West 42nd Street (212-790-4395).

The Cloisters, Fort Tryon Park (212-923-3700).

Paula Cooper Gallery, 155 Wooster Street (212-674-0766).

Cooper Union, East 7th Street, at Third Avenue (212-254-6374).

Dance Theater Workshop, 219 West 19th Street (212-924-0077).

Aaron Davis Hall, Davis Center of Performing Arts, City College, Convent Avenue and West 134th Street (212-690-4100).

Donnell Library Auditorium, 20 West 53rd Street (212-621-0618).

Eastside Playhouse, 334 East 74th Street (212-861-2288).

Ethnic Folk Arts Center, 179 Varick Street (212-675-3741).

Experimental Intermedia Foundation, 224 Centre Street at Grand Street (212-431-5127).

Fashion Institute of Technology, 227 West 27th Street (212-760-7644).

Federal Hall National Memorial, 26 Wall Street (212-264-8711).

Felt Forum at Madison Square Garden, 4 Pennsylvania Plaza (212-563-8000).

Franklin Furnace, 112 Franklin Street (212-925-4671).

Frick Collection, 1 East 70th Street (212-288-0700).

Gramercy Arts Theater, 138 East 27th Street (212-889-2850).

Guggenheim Museum, Fifth Avenue at 89th Street
(212-360-3500).

Henry Street Settlement Arts for Living Center, 466 Grand
Street (212-598-0400).

Hunter College Assembly Hall and Playhouse, Lexington
Avenue and 68th Street (212-772-4869).

Joan of Arc Junior High School, 154 West 93rd Street
(212-678-2902).

Jewish Museum, 1109 Fifth Avenue (212-860-1863).

Juilliard Theater, 66th Street between Broadway and
Amsterdam Avenue (212-799-5000).

Kosciusko Foundation, 15 East 65th Street (212-734-2130).

The Kitchen, 59 Wooster Street (212-925-3615).

La Maison Française, N.Y.U., 16 Washington Mews
(212-598-2161).

Lincoln Center Library-Museum, Bruno Walter
Auditorium, Lincoln Center (212-870-1630).

Liederkranz Foundation, 6 East 87th Street (212-534-0880).

Lillie Blake School Theater, 45 East 81st Street
(212-288-1485).

Loeb Student Center, N.Y.U., 566 La Guardia Place
(212-598-3757).

Madison Square Garden, 34th Street and Broadway
(212-563-8000).

Mannes College of Music, 150 West 85th Street
(212-580-0210).

Manhattan School of Music, Broadway and 122nd Street
(212-749-2802).

Marymount Manhattan Theater, 221 East 71st Street
(212-737-9611).

McMillin Theater, Columbia University, 116th Street and
Broadway (for Columbia University-sponsored events
only: 212-280-2845).

Museum of the City of New York, Fifth Avenue and 103rd
Street (212-534-1672).

Museum of Modern Art, 11 West 53rd Street (212-708-9400).

National Academy of Design, 1083 Fifth Avenue at 89th Street (212-369-4880).

New School Auditorium, 66 West 12th Street (212-741-5689).

New-York Historical Society, 170 Central Park West (212-873-3400).

Public Theater, 425 Lafayette Street (212-598-7150).

Radio City Music Hall, 50th Street and Avenue of the Americas (212-757-3100).

Roulette, 228 West Broadway (212-431-1022).

Soundscape, 500 West 52nd Street (212-581-7032).

Symphony Space, Broadway and 95th Street (212-864-5400).

Theodore Roosevelt Birthplace, 28 East 20th Street (212-260-1616).

Third Street Music School Settlement, 235 East 11th Street (212-777-3240).

TOMI (Theater Opera Music Institute), 23 West 73rd Street (212-787-3980).

Trinity School Auditorium, 101 West 91st Street (212-873-1650).

Uris Auditorium, Metropolitan Museum of Art, Fifth Avenue at 82nd Street (212-879-5500).

Vineyard Theater, 309 East 26th Street (212-683-0696).

Washington Irving High School, Irving Place at 16th Street (212-674-5000).

Whitney Museum, Madison Avenue and 75th Street (212-570-3600).

Whitney Museum at Philip Morris, 120 Park Avenue (212-878-2453).

Other Boroughs

Lehman College, Performing Arts Center, Bedford Park Boulevard West, the Bronx (212-960-8833).

Bargemusic, Ltd., Fulton Ferry Landing, Brooklyn (718-624-4061).

BACA (Brooklyn Arts and Culture Association), 111 Willoughby Street, Brooklyn (718-596-2222).

Brooklyn Center for the Performing Arts, Brooklyn College, Avenue H and Nostrand Avenues (718-434-1900).

Colden Center for the Performing Arts, Queens College, Long Island Expressway and Kissena Boulevard, Flushing (718-793-8080).

Snug Harbor Cultural Center, 914 Richmond Terrace, Staten Island (718-448-2500).

Van Cortlandt Mansion, Van Cortlandt Park, Broadway and 242nd Street, the Bronx (212-543-3344).

Wave Hill, 675 West 252nd Street, the Bronx (212-549-2055 or 212-549-3200).

Churches

Cathedral of St. John the Divine, Amsterdam Avenue and 112th Street (212-678-6922).

Central Presbyterian Church, 593 Park Avenue at 64th Street (212-838-0808).

Christ and St. Stephen's Church, 120 West 69th Street (212-787-2755).

Church of the Epiphany, 1393 York Avenue, at 74th Street (212-737-2720).

Church of the Heavenly Rest, Fifth Avenue at 90th Street
(212-289-3400).

Corpus Christi Church, 529 West 121st Street
(212-666-0675).

Holy Trinity Lutheran Church, Central Park West at 65th
Street (212-877-6815).

Madison Avenue Presbyterian Church at 73rd Street
(212-288-8920).

Riverside Church, Riverside Drive and 122nd Street
(212-222-5900).

St. Bartholomew's Church, Park Avenue and 50th Street
(212-751-1616).

St. Francis of Assisi Church, 135 West 31st Street
(212-736-8500).

St. Ignatius Episcopal Church, West End Avenue at 87th
Street (212-580-3326).

St. Joseph's Church, 371 Avenue of the Americas
(212-741-1274).

St. Michael's Church, Amsterdam Avenue at 99th Street
(212-222-2700).

St. Peter's Church, Lexington Avenue at 54th Street
(212-935-2200).

St. Thomas Church, Fifth Avenue at 53rd Street
(212-757-7013.

Trinity Church, Broadway at Wall Street (212-602-0800).

Church of St. Ann and the Holy Trinity, Clinton and
Montague Streets, Brooklyn Heights (718-834-
8794).

PART 5

....

Manhattan
Explorations

CHAPTER 29

······································

Madison Avenue

BY JOHN DUKA

"We've been on Madison and Sixty-third Street over sixty years, first my father, then I took over," said Robert Christatos, the owner of Christatos & Koster, a florist whose storefront is red with poinsettias and wreaths at Christmas. "We're one of the few stores left from the old days. Just us and M. J. Knoud and Wyler's silver shop and a couple of others.

"We never thought Madison would be like this," he continued. "There are more boutiques here now than ever. All those big names. Madison used to be mom-and-pop stores. Good little dress shops and some of the best food shops in town. There was Wynn & Treanor, the gourmet shop, at Number Seven-twelve. And McNally's drugstore. That was when Madison had a trolley car going in both directions, when the Woolworths used to come for flowers in their Rolls-Royce. When we had a doorman with a top hat."

Few if any doormen wear top hats on Madison Avenue

anymore. Many of the well-heeled but cozy stores of the 1930s and '40s have been replaced by a cluster of international high-fashion clothing and jewelry boutiques and galleries that glitter, well, almost like a tiara.

Still, the heart of Madison Avenue's shopping district above 59th Street has managed to retain some aspects of its character. This is due in part to the avenue's brownstones, a hodgepodge of quaint structures that zoning laws have saved from being sacrificed to make plots large enough for high-rise buildings. Spared the wrecker's ball, they have metamorphosed over the years, but somewhat less radically: They have simply acquired the names of European designers.

The northern reaches of Madison are still quite residential, even with the presence of such monolithic landmarks as the Carlyle Hotel, a thirty-eight-story Art Deco structure that pierces the sky at 76th and Madison. Outside P.S. 6, a red-brick building off Madison on 81st Street, schoolchildren gather, their high-pitched voices an early-morning cacophony. Across the street at the Frank E. Campbell Funeral Chapel, eulogies are said for the famous and the obscure. Farther north, Madison Avenue becomes almost quaint. There is the Buttercake Square bakery, little bigger than a closet, which lures passersby with windows full of tortes and butter cookies. Early on Sunday mornings it is jammed with people, all clutching newspapers and waiting in line for croissants.

But there is no denying change, and what has changed Madison most is the influx of trans-Atlantic stores and restaurants, a Europeanization that, especially in the past three years, has outstripped the collective memory of what Madison used to be.

The change began in 1968, when Yves Saint Laurent opened his Rive Gauche store on Madison Avenue, realizing that Madison attracts an international group of consumers not averse to spending. By the early 1980s Europeans had another reason for coming. Pressed by economic and political changes, they wanted to get their money out of Europe. Investing in stores on Madison Avenue seemed a safe bet.

To the list of such genteel American residents of Madison as the Westbury Hotel, M. J. Knoud Saddlery, and Christatos & Koster can now be added a staggering list of European store names. From France: Daniel Hechter Arche, Fogal, Brigitte Cassegrain, Lanvin, Lancel, Charles Jourdan, and Bruno Dessange. From Italy: Valentino Furla, Tanino Crisci, Santini e Dominici, Verri Uomo, and Pratesi. From the Netherlands: Hans Appenzeller. And from England: Joseph Tricot.

"Madison is a great retail street," said Donald Trump, the real estate developer whose Trump Tower and Grand Hyatt Hotel have altered the face of Manhattan. "The traffic is European, South American, and North American. And the rents are climbing—$250 a square foot. That's less than on Fifth Avenue, but an average store on Madison is still paying about $250,000 a year in rent."

Lifelong residents of Madison watch this evolution with curiosity and some amazement. One of them is Ariane Batterberry, who was raised in the town house now occupied by Didier Aaron, an antiques dealer.

"I have lived on Madison all my life," said Mrs. Batterberry, who, with her husband, Michael, has written books and articles on fashion history and food. "My father, Dr. Simon Ruskin, developed procaine penicillin. My mother used to give New Year's Eve parties for a thousand.

We had the most beautiful staircase, which, I think, was the reason we bought the house in the first place. The staircase was so good for parties.

"Valentina had her *maison de couture* on Sixty-seventh Street," she continued. "The clothes shops were the kinds of places where those who lived on Park and Fifth would shop. Chic, but understated.

"But in the late 1930s and '40s, for those of us who lived here, Madison was the butcher, the baker, and the candlestick maker to the carriage trade. Schaeffer's was the most expensive butcher shop in the world, at least so one was told. They supplied the old Colony restaurant and everyone who lived on Park and Fifth avenues. And there was Kirby Allen, a little upstairs restaurant owned by two little ladies, where the menu would say things like 'Lasagne, A Very Interesting Italian Dish.' Everyone ate there on Thursday night, which was cook's night out. They had cottage pudding, and nobody, I can tell you, does a good cottage pudding today."

Not at Le Relais, anyway. Along with the new European stores that dot Madison like metal studs on a Vuitton trunk, European restaurants with sidewalk tables have sprung up as if transplanted full-grown from French soil. None has quite succeeded like Le Relais at 63rd Street, opened by two Frenchmen, Jean-François Marchand and Albert Hacko, seven years ago. Though it seats only about seventy-five people, it has become a kind of club for those who wear expensive designer clothes and fancy steel-and-gold watches.

"When we opened, the avenue was quiet and much less European," said Philippe Delgrange, the restaurant's manager. "Nobody had opened a place like this before. In the beginning, we got people who didn't look so beautiful, but were very powerful. Now we still get them, and a younger crowd, very beautiful. Sometimes we turn our tables over four times in one night. And some people come at noon and by one in the morning, they're still drinking champagne.''

If turnover is key to the success of Le Relais, it keeps the rest of Madison Avenue jumping as well. No sooner do the older, genteel stores close than they are replaced by the new. Most recently a group of men's and women's clothing stores at the corner of 62nd Street and Madison, including Porter's, Maurice Einat, and Vera Finbert, made way for a Middle Western specialty-store chain. The Limited will open three stores this year in eighteen thousand square feet of space and offer, among other things, the first low-priced collection of Kenzo, a Japanese fashion designer.

This particular change has apparently upset some of the more staid residents of Madison, including Helene Arpels, who sold shoes at 60th Street for the last thirty years. She numbers crowned heads, presidents, prime ministers, and show business people among her clientele. Now she has moved to Park Avenue.

"When we started on Madison, we were the only ones who were fashionable," said André Azria, the manager who started the store with Helene Arpels. "We moved because some discount places are moving onto Madison."

That may be, but most of the residents of Madison seem perfectly content to stay right where they are. And many of the new residents are doing everything they can to keep up with their neighborhoods.

After looking for two years for the right location for his first American boutique, Giorgio Armani decided that Madison Avenue, and not Fifth Avenue, had the kind of customer he wanted. After more searching, he found and

rented a nineteenth-century town house on 68th Street.
Then he spent a few million dollars renovating it.

"I thought, 'So I don't own it,' " he explained. "I still
want the store to be for New Yorkers. In a way, it is like a
gift to them." If it is a gift, it is certainly one that has been
profitable. In August, the store sold $450,000 worth of
clothes. That is a lot of blazers.

CHAPTER 30
....
Riverside Drive

BY PAUL GOLDBERGER

By any reasonable standard, Riverside Drive would be considered the best street in New York. Where else, after all, are there such views—not of a narrow river, as there is across town, but of one of the noblest rivers in the United States? The constant presence of the Hudson is only the beginning of the pleasures of this boulevard. No other street in New York has a park for its entire length, either—when compared with the rambling acreage of Riverside Park, which parallels the drive from 72nd Street to 158th Street, the little grass islands of Park Avenue appear positively mean.

But society has never followed common sense, and thus Riverside Drive has never been able to compete with Fifth Avenue or Park Avenue in social cachet. It flirted briefly with high fashion in the early years of this century, when Charles Schwab, the steel tycoon, erected a vast mansion at the corner of Riverside Drive and 73rd Street and waited for his fellow millionaires to abandon Fifth Avenue and join him. Most declined, and the pleasures of the Drive were thus reserved for the upper middle class—the street grew up more as a place for the *haute bourgeoisie* than for the very rich.

But Riverside Drive grew grand, if not so richly as its physical setting might have suggested, and the street that the rich eschewed remains one of the great boulevards of New York, perfect for strolling on an early autumn weekend afternoon. It is a place that takes as its theme a certain kind of urbanity that the rest of Manhattan rarely sees—its essence is in the mixing of buildings and greenery, the constant interplay of heavy, solid structures and warm, open space. The buildings join together to form an even, coherent grouping that is crucial to any urban setting; the graceful curves of the drive are a welcome counterpoint to the strict Cartesian world of the Manhattan street grid. And the river itself, ever present, ever visible, brings a certain kind of reassurance that few other parts of the city can equal.

This is also a street of monuments, of works of architecture and sculpture of symbolic more than practical purpose, and this, too, sets it apart from so much of the rest of Manhattan. There are many people memorialized on Riverside Drive, but none, surely, more famous for having been so than Ulysses S. Grant, and his resting place—officially the General Grant National Memorial, but known to nearly everyone as Grant's Tomb—is as good a place as any to begin an exploration of the Drive's southern half.

GRANT'S TOMB

Grant's Tomb is at 122nd Street, roughly midway in the Drive's length. It is an immense structure, completed in 1897 to the designs of John H. Duncan; the building is a classical temple modeled loosely on the tomb of Mausoleus at Halicarnassus—the original mausoleum—but it is a drier sort of structure than this style usually yielded. It is more pompous than graceful, but it is imposing, particularly from within, where there is a majestic sequence of spaces leading to a view of the bodies of General and Mrs. Grant lying beneath polished black sarcophagi.

More pleasing than the architecture of the monument itself is the altogether remarkable piece of folk art that surrounds it, a set of benches in mosaic tile created in 1973 by residents of the surrounding community under the guidance of the Cityarts Workshop. The benches are a continuous, free-flowing form, their shape reminiscent of the works of Antonio Gaudí, but their decorations a witty and joyous celebration of city life, with views of the city, people, and automobiles. They are a truly joyful presence and quite respectful, in their way, of the monument; they are far enough back not to compromise its dignity, and they add an exuberant tone that can only make the experience of visiting the General Grant National Memorial more pleasing. It's open, free, 9 A.M. to 5 P.M., Wednesday through Sunday (information: 212-666-1640).

RIVERSIDE CHURCH

This section of the Drive, hard by Columbia University, the Union Theological Seminary, and other institutions, seems appropriate for large-scale monuments, and indeed, just down the block from Grant's Tomb, is the Drive's largest building of all, Riverside Church, which occupies the blocks between 120th and 122nd streets.

The church, a gift of John D. Rockefeller, Jr., was designed by Allen & Collens with Henry C. Pelton and Burnham Hoyt. It is Gothic, of Indiana limestone, and at its top is a 392-foot tower, which visitors can climb and which contains an immense carillon. The building is by no means Manhattan's finest Gothic church; by the time 1930 rolled around, there was a certain tiredness to the Gothic revival, and this church, on the outside at least, has a quality more institutional than ecclesiastical. The building as a work of architecture lacks the passion that the congregation itself, a notable leader in social activism, has shown. But it is worth going inside—there is a cool, serene confidence to the interior that it is difficult not to admire.

GRAND RESIDENCES

South of Riverside Church the biggest buildings are apartment houses, and there are several that are among the city's most appealing. Numbers 454 and 456, known as Oxford Hall and Cambridge Hall, are just below the church; their facades of intricate white terra-cotta ornament gleam in the sun, and they remain an exquisite presence despite the cracks and breaks in the cornices that the years have brought. The architects here were George and Edward Blum. Number 452, next door, by Gaetano Ajello, who designed some of the neighborhood's finest buildings, has white detail at least as delicate.

Number 448 Riverside is notable for the rich cover of ivy that marks its three base floors; together with the lush greenery of Riverside Park across the street, this creates a wonderful illusion of an urban garden. But 440 Riverside, by Schwartz & Gross, at the north corner of 116th Street, is finer architecturally. Here, a handsome, triple-arched porte cochere makes the entrance truly noble.

Across the street from Number 440 is one of the Drive's real apartment-house treasures, the Colosseum, at Number 435. Designed by Schwartz & Gross and completed in 1910, this building turns the corner with a great, sweeping curve, in a single gesture bringing light and a hint of the river view into 116th Street and enhancing the role of 116th Street as a gateway to Columbia University up the hill. Not quite so special, but pleasing nonetheless, is the apartment building a few blocks south at 113th Street, 404 Riverside, long the home of the late Manhattan District Attorney Frank S. Hogan, where a wonderful original iron canopy remains, as do noble five-bowl torch lamps on either side of the entrance.

MONUMENT ROW

The Drive and Riverside Park have long been a repository for monuments smaller and more modest than General Grant's, and these begin to appear frequently at about this point. Samuel J. Tilden is recalled with a statue at 112th Street, a long way indeed from his house at Gramercy Park. Down at 100th Street is an elaborate memorial to firemen lost in the line of duty. At 99th Street is a tiny plaque mourning the early death of John M. Carrère, the architect who, with his partner Thomas Hastings, designed the New York Public Library. And at 93rd Street, an elaborate Gothic base holds a statue of Joan of Arc.

Just as notable as the monuments in this section, however, is the shift in design of the Drive. The layout is simple above 114th Street: There is an even row of buildings facing the Drive, and on the other side is Riverside Park. From 114th Street down to 92nd Street, however, the Drive breaks in two: The main section slips down a bit into the park, and the buildings front on what can only be called a tiny lane. There is thus a sort of parklet between the apartment houses and the busy, traffic-filled Drive.

The architectural standard remains high in this section. There are remnants of the Drive's years as a place of private houses in the twin Beaux-Arts houses with bowed fronts at numbers 352 and 353, between 107th and 108th streets. Number 351, at the north corner of 107th Street, is a particularly ornate, if heavy-handed, free-standing French château, completed in 1909 to the designs of William B. Tuthill.

HISTORIC TOWN HOUSES

But the best block of town houses is just down the street from 105th to 106th streets. It joins with a number of houses on West 105th Street to form the Riverside Drive–West 105th Street Historic District, designated by the Landmarks Preservation Commission in 1973. The district's houses are all French Beaux-Arts town houses, designed between 1899 and 1902 by the firms of Janes & Leo, Mowbray & Uffinger, Hoppin & Koen, and Robert D. Kohn. The graceful Number 331, a Janes & Leo house completed in 1902, was once the home of the actress Marion Davies; along with the new building on the site once occupied by its twin at Number 332, it now forms the headquarters for the New York Buddhist Church and American Buddhist Academy. But the best single facade is on the north side of 105th Street, the spirited front of the church's next-door neighbor, 330 Riverside Drive.

At 104th Street there is an unusual small addition to the cityscape, a canopy of tinted Plexiglas on the front of the apartment house at Number 320. It is quite striking, but it gives the old building something of the feel of a motel, and one hopes it will not be a precedent for the general replacement of canvas with plastic canopies.

TOWER AT 103RD STREET

Worth a longer look is the apartment building at the north corner of 103rd Street, the Master Apartments of 1929 by Helmle, Corbett & Harrison and Sugarman & Berger. This is one of the Drive's only tall towers and among its few Art Deco works; the profile of the tower is splendid, a nicely massed top that can hold its own with many a midtown skyscraper. Unfortunately, the building, an early mixed-use effort, which contains a school and the Equity Library Theater, as well as apartments, is nowhere nearly so handsome close up—it comes off like a dark warehouse to the pedestrian.

MORE NOTABLE BUILDINGS

A pair of notable apartment buildings frame the meeting of 98th Street and the Drive. They are both fairly routine until the top, where they both burst out in an exuberance of decoration. Number 260, on the north corner, has a riot of classically inspired detail, wreaths and cartouches and corbels, while across the street, Number 258 is topped by brilliant blue panels around windows and multicolor brick, set in a crosshatched pattern.

More unusual still is the Cliff Dwellers' Apartments, Number 243, at 96th Street, a thin tower of orange brick that presages the geometric ornament of the Art Deco period two decades later. Cliff Dwellers' has a frieze of animals—mountain lions primarily—rendered in modernistic, Deco-like form. The building, designed by Herman Lee Meader, is topped by an arch and by more Deco-like ornament; it is really one of Manhattan's true, little-known curiosities of apartment-house architecture.

Just to the south of the Cliff Dwellers' is a reminder that the neighborhoods of Riverside Drive have not been immune to social problems in recent years. There had been four ornate bronze lampposts on the bridge that brings the Drive across 96th Street; all four have been vandalized, and are now no more than sparse ruins—sad evidence of the failure of a grand, city-beautiful vision of urban architecture to survive.

BELOW 96TH STREET

The Drive's most expensive section, occupied mostly by co-operative apartments, begins below 96th Street. It starts with a quirk—a lively little seven-story apartment house called the Chatillion, which occupies Number 214 and turns the corner of 94th Street with a pleasing roundness. But what makes this building exceptional is the wild, two-story Ionic portico—an entrance of true grandeur, far too large for the modest building yet appealing nonetheless.

Downtown from here, there is more restraint for the most part, but a lot of architectural quality. Among the best structures is the full-block building between 89th and 90th streets, 173–175 Riverside Drive, designed by J. E. R. Carpenter, which has a concave curve to it that neatly echoes the shape of the Drive at that point and maximizes views from the apartments as well. Similar is 110–118 Riverside Drive, between 83rd and 84th streets, designed by Gronenburg & Leuchtag and completed in 1929.

The Drive's southernmost major work of classicism is just beside 173 Riverside, the Soldiers' and Sailors' Monument at West 89th Street, just inside Riverside Park. Based on the Choragic Monument of Lysicrates in Athens, the columned tower comes off here as a rather appealing folly, blown up to huge urban scale. The design of the monument, completed in 1902, was by Stoughton & Stoughton and Paul Duboy.

And just across the street, slipped between Number 173 and the equally fine apartment house at Number 160, is the mansion built for Isaac L. Rice, an industrial pioneer in electrical storage batteries, surely the finest free-standing house left on the drive. Completed in 1901 to the designs of Herts & Tallent, the house is now occupied by a religious school. The house is at once grand and pleasantly eccentric; its most notable element is the porte cochere on the 89th Street side, half of which is scooped into the mass of the house and half of which projects outward. Below, at the north corner of 86th Street, is the Normandy, an immense building designed by Emery Roth and completed in 1939. It is a late version of Roth's better and more famous Central Park West buildings, the San Remo and the Beresford. Here, however, the architect has begun to accept modernism, and the base of the structure has an Art Deco tone to it. But Roth's preference for Renaissance decorative motifs won out in the end, and he topped the building with a pair of very classical water towers. Across the street, incidentally, is the Clarendon at Number 137, designed by Charles E. Birge and completed in 1907; it was the home for years of William Randolph Hearst, who occupied the top three floors.

THE LOWER REACHES
The lower Eighties and the Seventies are less distinctive—here, restraint seems to have won the day. The buildings below this point are uniformly good, but rarely exceptional—this is the part of the Drive that seems most to want to attract residents from other parts of town, and with the exception of the fanciful French apartment house on the south corner of 79th Street, the buildings here recall the staid and proper structures of West End Avenue more than anything else. Dullest of all is the huge block of 11 Riverside, between 73rd and 74th streets—it is the site once occupied by Charles Schwab's mansion, and now only a banal modern apartment house marks the land once occupied by Riverside Drive's grandest structure.

RIVERSIDE PARK
Of course, if the buildings tire, there is always Riverside Park itself—acres of green running along the river and covering the freight tracks of the old New York Central. The park is not so rich as Central Park, and it is not so capable of providing the pastoral illusion—because Riverside Park is narrow, the city never disappears. But it is a relaxed park, and the band of contrast it provides between the river and the city is splendid.

The park was laid out originally by Frederick Law Olm-

sted, Central Park's creator, in 1873. It was drastically rebuilt in 1937 by Clinton F. Lloyd, working under Robert
Moses. The Moses renovation covered the railroad tracks,
which had prevented the park from fulfilling its function,
but it also brought the six-lane intrusion of the Henry Hudson Parkway, which continues to send automobiles racing
through the park. But even with this unpleasant road, which
cuts the park off from direct contact with the river, the experience of being here is remarkable—from any point in the
park the great river flows on one side, the great wall of buildings holds fast on another, and there is a strong aisle of green
in their midst.

CHAPTER 31

....

Hidden Places

BY PAUL GOLDBERGER

No one, not even the most blindly chauvinistic New Yorker, would call Manhattan's physical landscape intimate. If there is any intimacy at all to this city, it is of an emotional sort, the intimacy that comes from the privacy and solitude city life often entails. The actual physical structure of the city could not be farther from anything intimate—the classic image of Manhattan is of the city of towers, the city of endless streets cutting wide swaths from river to river, the city of landscapes that seem to stretch on to infinity.

But there are places in Manhattan that are not like that. They are not many, but there are nooks and crannies and hideaways that are off the beaten path, that have a certain smallness of scale and eccentricity of detail that make them seem sheltering, warm and intimate in a way that the rest of the city is not. Some of these places are well known; others are less famous. They are all quite handsome, and most have that quality that is so often spoken of as charm. Most important, they all bespeak a certain devotion to the idea of privacy and separation from the rest of city life. For this reason most of these places are places in which people live—it is in the nature of commercial establishments to want to be on the busiest streets in the busiest neighborhoods, and that does not correspond with the notion of a hideaway.

The places discussed below vary in a number of ways. All are old, but some were always unusual; others are remnants of the way the physical landscape of New York once was, and thus seem more striking now that the city around them has changed so drastically. Since most of these nooks and crannies are residential, they are not fully open to the public: Several are best viewed through gates so as not to disturb the privacy of their residents, who came to them, after all, in search of solitude.

DUANE PARK

At the intersection of Duane and Hudson streets, in the Tribeca area of lower Manhattan, is Duane Park. Here, for a start, is a place that is not private at all. It is a tiny public park, and to the extent that it suffers, it is not from too much traffic but from not being well-enough known. Duane Park is, on a literal level, nothing more than the funny little triangle left by the intersection of Duane and Hudson streets. It is like dozens of such intersections all around the city that try so hard to be parks. But this one succeeds where the others fail, for it is surrounded, tightly, by first-rate nineteenth-century buildings that join to form a coherent, handsome, and powerful nineteenth-century landscape.

Stylistically, the buildings are not unified—but in true nineteenth-century fashion, the various historical styles share a certain scale and a sense of compatibility with one another, so there is a sense of variety and order, both at once. Probably the best single building on the square is the red-brick structure at 169 Duane Street, a grand and self-assured mixture of rounded arches, Romanesque and Italianate details, and a mansard roof, designed by Stephen D. Hatch and completed in 1880. But the cast-iron front at 171 Duane Street and the Romanesque brick structure at Number 173 are almost as good. So is the park's one twentieth-century building, the Western Union Building at 63 Hudson Street built by Voorhees, Gmelin & Walker in 1930.

The park itself is not exceptional—just an all-too-tiny spot of green with some benches. But the views of the rest of the city make this little enclave all the more remarkable. From one angle the tower of the Municipal Building is visible to the east, from another, the Woolworth Building pokes up to the south. From almost nowhere in the park can the World Trade Center be seen—so that while the city intrudes just enough to make Duane Park seem real, it does not intrude so much as to break a certain spell.

MACDOUGAL ALLEY

Off Macdougal Street, between West 8th Street and Washington Square, Macdougal Alley is the first of four remarkable residential enclaves in Greenwich Village. In some ways it is the most convincing; it certainly is the one most connected to the realities of city life. Not only are the noises of 8th Street and Washington Square adjacent to these converted carriage houses, so is the huge scale of the new city in the form of the vast apartment house at 2 Fifth Avenue,

which backs up against the alley and closes off its eastern
end. While these presences may destroy the illusion that one
is in a country village, they do not destroy the pleasures of
this ramshackle row; they enhance them by making Macdougal Alley seem stronger by juxtaposition.

WASHINGTON MEWS

Off Fifth Avenue between East 8th Street and Washington
Square, Washington Mews is similar to Macdougal Alley,
but neater. Here the old houses seem to make a more even
line, and the rest of the city stands more at bay, unwilling to
intrude. There is less drama here than at Macdougal Alley,
but more escape. Take your pick.

GROVE COURT

Off Grove Street between Hudson and Bedford streets is
Grove Court. This remarkable group of six generous
Federal-style houses, erected in 1854, is among the most private of all New York residential areas. The houses sit behind
a common V-shaped garden, the entrance to which is
through a gate slipped between the houses at 10 and 12
Grove Street; the overall site plan is a brilliant use of minimum land to maximum effect. The garden provides an extraordinary sense of refuge from city tensions, and this
sense, together with the style and mood of the houses, suggests Cambridge and Boston. There is true serenity here, as
much as is to be found anywhere in Manhattan. Grove Court
is private, however; view it only through the gates on Grove
Street.

PATCHIN PLACE

Off West 10th Street just west of the Avenue of the Americas in Greenwich Village is Patchin Place. This, too, is a very private mews, viewable only through gates on 10th Street or the Avenue of the Americas. It is a collection of small brick houses that seem not so much to be stretched out in line, as houses on streets are, but to huddle together, as if for protection from the rest of the city. There is a sense of plunging into a cave as much as entering a mews; it is somehow not surprising to learn that e. e. cummings lived here, for this place has qualities that are not dissimilar to his poetry—it plays at being charming and is, in fact, almost severe.

RENWICK TRIANGLE

At East 10th Street and Stuyvesant Street, between Second and Third avenues, is Renwick Triangle. This block of Italianate brownstones, erected in 1861 and frequently attributed to the gifted architect James Renwick, lacks the sense of privacy of a mews, but it has a dignity and an elegance that is matched by only a few residential blocks in Manhattan. The houses are discreet and handsome, and the triangular shape of the block adds a certain sense of movement; the point of the triangle heads straight for St. Mark's-in-the-Bowery, the great Federal- and Greek Revival-style church erected in stages in the late eighteenth and early nineteenth centuries, and now undergoing restoration after a disastrous fire in 1978.

STUYVESANT SQUARE

East and west of Second Avenue, between East 15th and East 17th streets, Stuyvesant Square is perhaps the least known of Manhattan's squares. No subway passes through it as at Union Square; it is not celebrated for its charm or its Englishness as is Gramercy Park. But Stuyvesant Square, in its own way, is impressive. It somehow manages to be more tranquil than most city squares, despite the fact that it is bisected by a major avenue and bordered, on its east, by the overpowering Beth Israel Hospital, whose architecture might best be called Miami Beach institutional.

Stuyvesant Square survives these intrusions, perhaps because of the quality of the buildings that line its western side—the Friends Meeting House and Seminary on Rutherford Place (the western boundary), completed in 1860 from the designs of Charles Bunting, and the immense Romanesque brownstone St. George's Church of 1856 by Leopold Eidlitz and Otto Blesch.

SNIFFEN COURT

On East 36th Street between Third and Lexington avenues is Sniffen Court, Murray Hill's real mews, as opposed to the immense apartment tower nearby that calls itself—with not a little audacity—Murray Hill Mews. Sniffen Court consists of ten former carriage houses, roughly Romanesque in style, that have been converted to residences; it is a special kind of hidden pleasure for Murray Hill, a handsome neighborhood that has always seemed to lack a certain kind of inward focus. Sniffen Court provides such a focus, with considerable charm.

AMSTER YARD

At 211–215 East 49th Street, between Second and Third avenues, is Amster Yard. This private court, which can be entered during business hours, is an exception to the rule—it is commercial. Designed by Harold Sterner in 1945 out of the space between a group of houses dating from 1870, it is the territory of the designer James Amster, who keeps his office and residence there and rents the remaining space to other tenants. Across the street, incidentally, is one of Manhattan's greatest private places of all, the absolutely private Turtle Bay Gardens—a remarkable interior landscape between the brownstones of East 49th and East 48th streets, hidden from view and entered only through the houses themselves.

BEEKMAN PLACE

East of First Avenue from East 49th to East 51st streets, the two blocks making up Beekman Place are so well known that they almost do not belong in a list of Manhattan's private, hidden pleasures. But there is a sense of secrecy, of escape from the rest of the city, to Beekman Place that is so intense that it never seems to diminish with familiarity. Beekman Place is a collection of buildings that, while attractive, are not in themselves exceptional—some good town houses, some decent old apartment houses, and some mediocre new ones. What makes it special, beyond the eclectic mixture it represents, is the remarkable sense of enclosure. Beekman Place feels, even on the sidewalk, like being indoors—it seems so cut off from the city that it could be a set for a drawing-room comedy about upper-class life in New York. Also worth visiting, even if it breaks the illusion, is the little park at the end of East 51st Street—it juts out over the F.D.R. Drive for a splendid view of the back of the Beekman Place houses.

RIVERVIEW TERRACE

Off East 58th Street just east of Sutton Place, is Riverview Terrace. This is an enclave of an enclave, so to speak—a private street set overlooking the river, just off Sutton Square, which is itself an impressive group of remodeled brownstones with a common garden along Sutton Place. Riverview Terrace consists of five ivy-covered brownstones that all look out to the river; it is one of the few places in Manhattan that seems to have been built with an understanding of its natural setting. Nearby, and quite pleasant, is the tiny park at the end of East 57th Street: a perch from which to view the river.

HENDERSON PLACE

Off East 86th Street, just west of East End Avenue, is Henderson Place. Its little structures, dating from 1882, were built as houses—no former stables this time. The architects were Lamb & Rich, and the composition was once a coherent group of thirty-two Queen Anne houses of brick. It still hangs together well—the shared architectural elements, such as entryways that serve two houses at once, are especially pleasing—but the construction of the large apartment house on the west side of this enclave, which required the demolition of eight of the houses, has seriously compromised the others.

POMANDER WALK

From West 94th to West 95th streets, between Broadway and West End Avenue, is Pomander Walk. Here on the Upper West Side we find something more fanciful than almost any of the city's other private residential enclaves. Pomander Walk was designed by King & Campbell and erected in 1922; it is an unashamed English stage set, a piece of the English country landscape force-fed into a harsh, densely built section of Manhattan. Time has not treated this little place as kindly as it might have, but the earnestness of Pomander Walk continues to please.

STRIVER'S ROW

The King Model Houses of Striver's Row, on West 138th and West 139th streets, from Seventh to Eighth avenues, are not only the best town houses in Harlem, they are among the finest anywhere in New York. The grouping was built in 1891, commissioned by the developer David King to show that architectural quality and urbanistic harmony could be achieved in speculative row housing for New Yorkers. King hired some of the city's best architects: McKim, Mead & White designed the row on the north side of 139th Street, Bruce Price and Clarence S. Luce designed the rows on the south side of 139th Street and the north side of 138th Street; and James Brown Lord designed the row on the south side of 138th Street.

The results strike just the right balance between variety and unity. McKim, Mead & White produced solid Renaissance palaces of brick; Price and Luce designed lusher, Georgian-influenced houses; and Lord created houses of red brick on brownstone bases. They all work splendidly as blocks in themselves, reminders that town houses can, in fact, be designed as coherent groups, and they work splendidly together, too. Happily, these buildings remain in fine condition.

CONVENT AVENUE

From West 140th to West 144th streets, east of Broadway, Convent Avenue is a serene, quiet street in a remarkable neighborhood just north of City College's main campus. It is a street like many in New York a couple of generations ago— there is a sense of clean, quiet order. The architecture is a wonderful eclectic mixture of styles, with a general Romanesque leaning but a decent helping of Flemish and Tudor elements. The best buildings are the picturesque town houses at numbers 311 to 339, between 143rd and 144th streets, designed by Adolph Hoak and completed in 1890; they exemplify the energetic, eclectic mixture that brought visual variety to these streets at no loss to an overall sense of order. This stretch of Convent Avenue also contains a historic monument of note: Hamilton Grange at 287 Convent Avenue, the country house of Alexander Hamilton and one of the city's earliest Federal houses, built in 1801 and moved here in 1889.

HARLEM RIVER HOUSES

It may seem strange to list Harlem River Houses, a public housing project on West 151st to West 153d streets, east and west of Seventh Avenue, in a group of Manhattan's choice enclaves. But there is something quite special to the design of the project, Manhattan's first piece of large-scale public housing and in many ways still the finest. Designed by a team of architects led by Archibald Manning Brown, with landscaping by Michael Rapuano and completed in 1937, Harlem River Houses consists of four-story brick walk-ups skillfully strung around a large open space in the section west of Seventh Avenue. It is the layout that is so impressive here. It is a mixture of little, sheltered courtyards and large, communal space, and there is always a sense of privacy and ownership, yet a feeling of grandeur as well. There are lessons here in the nature of scale and in what a community consists of that have been understood all too rarely by the architects whose public-housing plans followed this superb work.

HUDSON VIEW GARDENS

At 116 Pinehurst Avenue, between West 183rd and West 185th streets, east of Cabrini Boulevard, is Hudson View Gardens. Designed by George Fred Pelham and completed in 1924, this picturesque group of houses north of the George Washington Bridge comes as close as anything in New York to the feeling of an English country lane. The seven-story buildings, arranged along a U-shaped lane, are massed together like the cottages of a medieval English town, and the entire place is covered with vines—a truly tranquil oasis.

CHAPTER 32

························

The Ladies Mile

BY JENNIFER DUNNING

A century ago, New York's main shopping district ran from 8th Street to 23rd Street, bounded on the east by Broadway, on the west by Sixth Avenue. It was called the Ladies Mile, in the gentler locution of the day, and many of its department stores were sumptuous palaces of commerce.

On a Sunday afternoon, the women who shopped there the other days of the week would likely be enjoying the sleepy ritual of midday family dinner. The mature generations never thought of Sunday shopping, and walking tours might well have alarmed them. But on some weekends the Friends of Cast-Iron Architecture conducts a walking tour along the Ladies Mile, where many of the fine cast-iron store buildings are still intact, though the emporiums of old are long gone.

The nearly two-hour tour usually begins at the delicate and fashionable Grace Episcopal Church on Broadway and

11th Street. Further information may be obtained by calling (212) 427-2488.

An early example of the Gothic Revival architecture, Grace Church was designed by a very young James Renwick, Jr., and built in 1845. With a parting glance at the fine iron fence enclosing the church's garden, the site of Fleischmann's Vienna Model Baker, a popular meeting place of the day, the tour sets off under the direction of a group of volunteer guides. They are all architects and architectural historians, and one of them might be Margot Gayle, director of the Friends of Cast-Iron Architecture. As the tour parties proceed up Broadway, guides are likely to give a little of the history of the group, an international association founded in 1970 to preserve a form of architecture unique to the United States.

Pointers will also be given on the identification of cast-iron buildings. (Miss Gayle suggests the city walker always carry a magnet to apply to possible iron building fronts.) With between 250 and 300 iron-front buildings in Manhattan and two or three in Brooklyn, New York has more cast-iron architecture than any other American city.

Cast iron was often used for commercial establishments, and the view up the Ladies Mile must have been spectacular on a sunny day; shimmering white, often exuberantly sculptured fronts, and colorful awnings to shade the large display windows and the fashionable passersby.

Cast iron, molded in many local foundries that existed at the end of the nineteenth century, was used for facades and only occasionally for interiors. Interior cast iron took the form of elegant slender columns that supported the floors and permitted an unusual amount of open space inside the building. Occasional stair elements were built in iron as fireproofing, and a few large iron buildings had primitive iron framework that foretold the steel skyscrapers that were to come. The exterior facades were made of many small parts bolted together to create an unbroken surface and then often painted to look like stone.

"We try to evoke how grand the work on iron was then," Miss Gayle explains. "The industry developed great skill and craftsmanship. Thousands of items were cast and then carted by dray horses over cobblestone streets—what a clatter that must have made!—to be lifted up and bolted into place. Little cornice brackets might have five separate parts, they were so detailed."

STEWART'S AND McCREERY

A block south of Grace Church is the site of A. T. Stewart's Department Store, at Broadway and 10th Street, built in 1862. The first department store to be built on the Ladies Mile, it had a typical central rotunda, a double staircase and continuous organ music. In 1902, a still standing iron extension was built just south and was long the headquarters of Wanamaker's department store.

A block north, at 801 Broadway, is the cast-iron building that once housed the James McCreery & Company store, and though it is now an apartment house, its exterior has been preserved, and the colonnade of high columns on the facade, with its Corinthian capitals and cornice decorations, illustrates one of cast iron's most dramatic features: the ability to be reproduced in even fine detail.

The Friends of Cast-Iron's enthusiasm does not limit itself entirely to their specialty. Interesting stone buildings will also be pointed out along the way.

Near the corner of the Avenue of the Americas and 14th Street, a tall thin building perches incongruously. Its sign is almost too faded to read, but it is the Beaux-Arts extension of the original Macy's, the first store to move out of the Ladies Mile and uptown, in 1902.

B. ALTMAN & COMPANY

Turning up the Avenue of the Americas, the tour passes a particularly fine red cast-iron fire alarm box on 17th Street. From 18th to 23rd streets, Sixth Avenue, as it was then called, with its fiery wooden elevated trains and the 23rd Street ferry that brought customers over from New Jersey, was a commercial center of vast department stores and small specialty shops, theaters, and hotels.

It was perhaps not entirely so elegant an area as its counterpart on Broadway, but B. Altman & Company certainly compared with the best Broadway had to offer. The store's original cast-iron building, designed by David and John Jardine and built in 1876 (an extension by William Hume was added in 1887), still stands on the west side of the avenue from 18th to 19th streets, with its symmetrically detailed facade and stylized, incised ornamentation.

The best stores had their own delivery service, and west of Sixth Avenue were Benjamin Altman's stables, where the merchant kept the five hundred horses he himself had selected to be hitched in matched pairs to his shining delivery carts. B. Altman's was the first store to build on Sixth Avenue, and the glass-dome light court rising six floors through the store's center was a celebrated interior feature.

Across the avenue stood the brick-and-terra-cotta home of a chief competitor, Siegel-Cooper & Company. Henry Siegel might be said to have been the P. T. Barnum of the trade, for though the store's facade is ornate enough, the interior was even more lavish. A reproduction of Daniel Chester French's sculpture *Republic*, made for the Chicago World Trade Fair of 1893, stood in the center of a fountain just past the columned entrance to the store, and "Meet you at the fountain" became a popular expression of the day. The store's opening in 1896 attracted a crowd of 150,000.

O'NEILL AND ADAMS

The Ladies Mile section of the Avenue of the Americas takes on the look of a vast canyon of imposing iron monuments to mercantilism, and the Hugh O'Neill store, occupying the block from 20th to 21st streets on the west side of the avenue, is one of the most imposing. Its somber, formal look of today belies its flamboyant role in serving yesteryear's working-class clientele. The enormous domes at each end are gone, but the round end towers remain, and the forthright letters spelling the name of the store in the big triangular cornice are a ghostly reminder of the area's prominence. In the later Beaux-Arts style, Adams Dry Goods Store, just to the north, is a good example of the integration of cast iron into a masonry front, with fluted columns and cast-iron arches. So rich was the trade here that none of the Adams merchandise was sullied with price tags.

Turning right into 23rd Street and continuing east, the tour passes the former Flint & Horner Furniture Company. It has a sculptured facade and a hierarchical arrangement of windows, ranging from simple high ones at the bottom to ornate little ones at the top. Although the store was built by a leading cast-iron architect of the day, it was designed not so much for esthetics as to provide maximum light and space.

Across 23rd Street, on the south side, at numbers 32–46, stands the former Stern Brothers Department Store. It catered to both the rich and the working class, and was the largest store in the area in the 1880s. Doormen in top hats presided over the entrance, but inside, Isaac Stern often greeted his customers by their names.

Now the home of the New York Merchandise Company, this is one of the best preserved cast-iron facades in the city. Its handsome white front gleams in the sunlight, and the free-standing colonnettes are decorated with leaves, berries, vines, and rosettes, like an Italian palazzo wedding cake.

Miss Gayle cites it as a particular example of enlightened preservation. "Buildings like this don't have anything going for them except the owners, because this isn't an historical district like SoHo," she says.

Walking east toward Fifth Avenue, the tour passes several cast-iron-front buildings of some historical interest. On an airless July evening in 1870, Benjamin Nathan was beaten to death in the still unsolved "23rd Street murder" at Number 16, and at Number 14, Edith Wharton was born in 1862.

LORD & TAYLOR

The Lord & Taylor building, 901 Broadway, at 20th Street, designed by James H. Giles and erected in 1869, is now an apartment house. Its endlessly fascinating front has been preserved by the present owner, but little of its history or decoration are revealed to the casual, everyday glance. It was the fourth location in forty-three years for Lord & Taylor, as the store followed the residential and commercial drift north. But this building, which Miss Gayle refers to as a "cast-iron palace" and a "French Second Empire extravaganza," was by far its most ornate headquarters.

Much of the iron frontage along Broadway is gone now, but over what was the arched entrance to the store a pyramidal tower remains, its mansard roof topped with lacy metalwork and decorated with balustrades and a dormer window. The corner is cut flat across the surface facing the intersection to give more interest.

Along the 20th Street facade of a building that once reached to Fifth Avenue may be found waves of freestanding columns, which together with the deep-set windows and richly sculptured surfaces, create that absorbing play of light and shade achieved by the best of the sculptured iron facades.

Inside, one of the first steam elevators ran up and down the store's five floors and was such a popular attraction that a divan was added along with the carpeted floor and gas chandeliers.

The fashionably dressed woman of 1881 might wear a "suit of colored silk" trimmed with a scarf "finished with jet balls," made to order for $28. Her boots might have been Prunella or Curaçao-kid, and her cloak an ulster or dragoon jacket in Satin-de-Lyon, satin surah, or silk grenadine. There were bonnets and lace jabots, muslin, merino, or silk underwear, and formidable corsets for matrons and their daughters.

Babies were dressed in French cambric or nainsook, and "it is considered the best taste to use no color for children under a year old," an 1881 catalogue advises. Gentlemen might buy only their accessories at Lord & Taylor, but their sons could be outfitted in suits ranging from the elegant long-trousered "Metropolitan" to the "Clarence," a two-piece kilt suit. And for the home there were awnings and linoleum, horse blankets and crumb cloths to be had.

ARNOLD CONSTABLE

South, on the west side of Broadway and 19th Street, a former Arnold Constable's rises solidly from the street, a froth of iron grillwork at the top its only frivolous touch. In 1868, the architect Griffith Thomas designed the store's Broadway facade in white marble, the only material Aaron Arnold considered suitable for a prosperous emporium, but the 19th Street facade is in cast iron, the material preferred by James Constable, Mr. Arnold's forward-looking son-in-law. And in the store's final expansion in 1877, the Fifth Avenue facade was a cast-iron copy of the first Broadway facade.

W. J. Sloan's, outfitters to rajahs and sailing ships in the 1880s, when it stood across the street from Arnold Constable's, is brick and terra-cotta on the Broadway side. But around the corner, walking east on 19th Street, the tour will see thick molded iron columns with palm fronds, asters, and twisting daisies.

The north side of Union Square was once marked with an iron trellis set with flagpoles and decorated with incandescent electric lights, then the newest thing. The same gaiety is visible in an intricate Moorish filigreed iron building at 33 Union Square West nearby. And then, turning south, the tour ends, going past the statues of Washington, Lafayette, and Lincoln that people Union Square Park, with its echoes of long-ago strolling families outfitted in the best from the Ladies Mile.

CHAPTER 33

····································

Earliest
New York

BY JENNIFER DUNNING

Weekdays, New York City's financial district bustles with
activity. Its streets are rivers of rushing humanity, its air is
thick with the sounds of traffic. The bustle may approxi-
mate the climate of life of an earlier era, but in the hubbub
the district's historical secrets and architectural jewels can
easily go unheeded. On some weekends, however, New
Yorkers have a chance to walk into the past when the Museum of the City of New York presents "The World of Wall
Street: Tycoons and Tickertape," a walking tour down
Broadway from City Hall. For information, call (212)
534-1672.

"The tour should take about two hours, but really it
could go on for days," Arthur Marks, the museum's natty,
irrepressible, singing head tour guide, said the other day.
"There's so much to see and talk about."

The first stop will be City Hall and the complex of municipal buildings surrounding it. Built between 1802 and 1811,

317

this City Hall, the third in New York's history, was designed by Joseph François Mangin, a designer of the stately Place de la Concorde in Paris, and John McComb, Jr., in the Federal style with French Renaissance detail. The interior, with its big domed central rotunda and twisting, self-supporting marble stairs, is not always on view during the tour, but the exterior has the same sense of formal balance and grandeur. Its facade is in handsome Alabama veined limestone.

"The back was just brownstone from Newark," Mr. Marks said. "There wasn't anything north of City Hall in those days, so who would ever see it?"

After a walk across pleasant City Hall Park, which was a common pasture during the early Dutch days, then the site of almshouses and later a British jail for captured American prisoners and a public execution square, the tour reaches the Woolworth Building at 233 Broadway. When Mr. Marks has finished singing "I Found a Million-Dollar Baby in the 5 & 10 Cent Store," the tour enters this Gothic Revival "cathedral of commerce." Designed by Cass Gilbert and erected between 1911 and 1913, the lacy white building rises 729 feet, which made it the "highest in the world" until the Chrysler Building was finished in 1930.

With its Gothic and Tudor arches and flying buttresses and the faces of the world's peoples—a popular motif at the time—the building repays close scrutiny. The facade and interior are also decorated with an oak-and-acorn motif. "This was a fortune that grew from nickels and dimes," Mr. Marks explained. "Mighty oaks from little acorns." Frank W. Woolworth, the founder, who paid $15.5 million in cash for the building's construction, is immortalized in a detail in the entranceway, as is Mr. Gilbert. The three-story lobby, with its vaulted gold and turquoise mosaic ceiling, stained-glass skylight, and walls of Grecian golden-marble slabs, does have the air of a cathedral, though details like the letter-box caduceus give the space a fanciful human touch.

Back on Broadway, Mr. Marks will point out a sweeping cityscape of wildly different architectural styles to the east. Then it's on to St. Paul's Chapel—said to be the oldest church and public building in Manhattan—a plainspoken pre-Revolutionary structure designed by Thomas McBean and modeled after St. Martin's-in-the-Fields in London. After a ritual cleaning of the feet on the handsome footscraper, installed when the city's streets were a sea of garbage and animals, tour members enter the church, an oasis of serenity decorated in cool pink, blue, and mauve with fourteen Waterford crystal chandeliers, a "very, very Baroque" reredos, and the pew where George Washington worshiped.

After pausing for a peek at the awesome, ghostly colonnaded lobby of the American Telephone and Telegraph Building just to the south, the group will make a detour west to gaze up at the dizzying towers of the World Trade Center. Then it's back on Broadway, and a jaunt south past the sleek headquarters of the brokerage house of Merrill, Lynch, Pierce, Fenner & Smith. Mr. Marks shook his head a bit wistfully as he looked into the sunken entrance to the building, designed, as were many of the newer office buildings around it, by Skidmore, Owings & Merrill.

"You notice that a lot of the buildings down here no longer have the impressive entranceways that told you you were entering the chambers of commerce," he said. "Here people are reduced to ants scurrying through."

The Equitable Building, at 120 Broadway, elicits another wistful nod. Designed by Ernest R. Graham, the building

sprawled so high and wide that its construction in 1915 led
to the enactment of the city's first zoning laws. Passing narrow, dark Thames Street to the south, tour members will get
a glimpse of what the city might have become without those
zoning laws. The Federal Hall National Memorial on Wall
Street, the next stop, will be opened specially for the group
to view the historical exhibitions in its rotunda. At the back
of this Greek Revival-style building, designed by Town &
Davis and completed in 1842, one can stand between the
massive columns and imagine the scene when Washington
took his Presidential oath of office in 1789.

"Wall Street was named that because of the wall erected
in 1653 that bound New Amsterdam, as New York was
called then—a wall that kept the Dutch in and the Indians
out," Mr. Marks said. "People worked and lived here. The
area was full of tiny houses. Alexander Hamilton lived in
one from 1787 to 1790, in fact, at what is now Thirty-three
Wall Street."

At the head of Wall Street stands Trinity Church. The
third Trinity Church on that site, it was rebuilt in 1846 after
designs by Richard Upjohn. The scale and detail of this
Gothic Revival-style church have an intimate charm that is
likely to draw Mr. Mark's most enthusiastic comments,
though he promises not to break into "Nearer My God to
Thee." There will be time to wander through the interior,
to scrutinize the detailed bas reliefs on the three bronze
doors designed by Richard Morris Hunt and donated by
William Waldorf Astor, and to look into the church's pretty
cemetery, crammed with historical monuments and graves
(including Hamilton's).

The site of 39–41 Broadway, where George Washington
once lived, is now home to exponents of twentieth-century

enterprise. But 26 Broadway, formerly the Standard Oil Building, is much as it was in the days when Rockefellers in their morning coats and cutaways passed through its imposing marble lobby, days that will be commemorated by Mr. Marks in song, specifically "Puttin' on the Ritz." After a glance at the bulky whimsy of the egg-shaped clock that sprouts from the doorway of 28 Broadway, tour members will be directed to the graceful curve of the facade of Number 26, designed by Carrère & Hastings and erected in 1922, its tower designed to harmonize with the roofscape around it.

Tour participants can next inspect the handsome Renaissance facade of the Cunard Building just across Broadway, which the historian Henry Hope Reed, who began the Museum of the City of New York tour program, describes as "great art." Tired participants will have a chance to rest on the benches in nearby Bowling Green, which was once rented by Colonial bowlers from the British for a peppercorn a year. While they listen to tales of pre-Revolutionary War squabbles, tour members can feast their eyes on the grandeur of the United States Custom House to the south, a Beaux-Arts monument designed by Cass Gilbert and erected in 1907.

The facade's limestone statues by Daniel Chester French represent the continents of Asia, the Americas, Europe, and Africa. The cartouche, which Mr. Marks describes simply as "spectacular," the statues of famous navigators and symbols of the maritime nations, and the copper flashing topped by Neptune's tritons, combine to make this a rich architectural experience.

The row of handsome town houses that gave the street on the south side of Bowling Green the name "Nobs' Hill" in

1815, before those houses became the shipping offices that renamed it "Steamship Row," have long since vanished, though a room from one of those houses has been preserved in the Museum of the City of New York. But Castle Clinton is still to be seen at the Battery after its evolution from an 1807 fort to Castle Garden, the domed pleasure palace overlooking the Battery promenade, to a clearing house for millions of immigrants and finally to an aquarium, before its rehabilitation as a National Historic Monument in 1946. There the tour will end with a view across the harbor to the Statue of Liberty, an 1886 gift from the children of France that was considered one of the wonders of the world. The voice of Jenny Lind, the "Swedish Nightingale," who made her American debut at Castle Garden, is no more, but Mr. Marks will sing a number from the Broadway musical *Miss Liberty*, the final serenade of "The World of Wall Street: Tycoons and Tickertapes."

CHAPTER 34

....

Critics' Holiday Choices

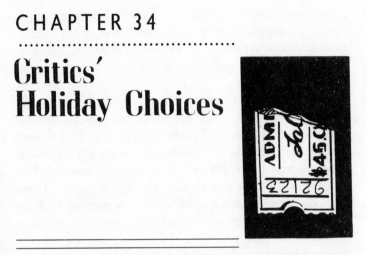

Simply for the fun of it, seven *New York Times* experts offer their Christmastime suggestions—from the crèche at the Metropolitan Museum to video art at SoHo's Kitchen.

Peek at a Rehearsal

BY DONAL HENAHAN
MUSIC CRITIC

It is in the nature of the human animal to enjoy snooping. The urge is ignoble, perhaps, but who can resist it? Even the illusion of being unobserved, like the Invisible Man, can be titillating. That is why attending an orchestra rehearsal is so appealing. Not only is it one of the least harmful forms of voyeurism, it is also socially sanctioned and widely practiced. The snoopee is fully aware of being watched, and may

323

even enjoy it. However, and this is the titillating part, both snoopee and snooper are also fully aware that something traditionally sacrosanct is being revealed to outsiders, that mistakes may be witnessed, that professional secrets may be exposed.

Did you know, dear snooper, that on Thursday mornings, at 9:45, most New York Philharmonic concerts are rehearsed in the presence of paying eavesdroppers? You may want to join them. Sometimes audiences are not allowed at these rehearsals. The Philharmonic offers its guest conductors and soloists the option of rehearsing in private. However, during the concert season, from September to May, there are many rehearsals that are open to the public for a fee.

Beyond the lure of snooping, Philharmonic rehearsals are enticing for a number of reasons. They appeal to visitors to New York who are determined to pack both day and night with music and theater, and to suburbanites who want to spend the day in town but do not want to head home in the dark after an evening concert. Students and others on tight budgets find the three-dollar ticket price quite attractive.

But take a peek at the schedule and make your own choices. At three dollars a snoop, what can the compulsive eavesdropper lose?

New York Philharmonic

Avery Fisher Hall, Lincoln Center, Broadway at 65th Street, New York, N.Y. 10023 (212-874-2424). Mail orders are accepted when they are accompanied by a check made out to Avery Fisher Hall Box Office and a stamped, self-addressed envelope. Box office open Monday through Saturday, 10 A.M. to 6 P.M.; Sunday, noon to 6 P.M.

The Neapolitan Crèche

BY JOHN RUSSELL
ART CRITIC

On December 1 of every year, as punctually as a Swiss express train, the Neapolitan crèche moves into the Metropolitan Museum, thereby making a great many people think better of the world, and of themselves. Some of the curatorial staff think of it as an unwarranted intrusion, but "children of all ages" clap their hands, and they are very much in the majority.

The crèche in question is not, as it happens, altogether out of place in the Met. The tree is a tree, and the candles are candles, and no one has ever maintained that these are works of art. But the angels, the cherubs, the Holy Family, the Three Kings with their exotic entourage, the shepherds with their sheep, the multitudinous townspeople with their gifts of flowers and fruit and vegetables—all these were made in Naples in the eighteenth century and early nineteenth century, at a time when many a gifted artist found in the crèche a form of expression that gave him considerable scope.

Visitors to eighteenth-century Naples were of one mind on this point. Nothing was prettier, they said, than the Neapolitan crèches. According to Olga Raggio, chairman of European sculpture and decorative arts at the museum, legend has it that even King Charles III, the Bourbon king of Naples, was not too proud to take an active part in the royal crèche, rearranging the arms and the legs of its many little figures, modeling and baking tiny cakes of clay, and working with effects of perspective and light as if he thought himself a stage director of genius. As for his queen, she had been sewing costumes for the figures all year long and could hardly wait to see them put to use. Today the task of preparing the little figures for their annual display is handled by Johanna Hecht, associate curator of European sculpture and decorative arts.

Although not of royal heritage, the Metropolitan's crèche is in every way fit for a king, consisting of close to two hundred figures in all, with an architectural background that is closer to Rome than to what we know of the historical Bethlehem. It was given to the Met in 1964 by Loretta Hines Howard, a painter who collected eighteenth-century Neapolitan religious art. Many of its figures have been attributed to the foremost Neapolitan crèche-makers of the day, and they have in common a breadth of fancy, a command of physiognomy, and a variety of costume that repay sustained examination.

Naples at that time was a great city, but it was a great city that stood in an unflawed countryside. Many of the figures are quite clearly portraits of individual country people. Their dress, their bearing, their facial expressions all point that way. We are reminded that theater of all kinds had burgeoned in Naples, from the Italian comedy in its purest and most vivacious form to the puppet plays that were the talk of the informed traveler right up to the outbreak of World War II. There is in the Met crèche a note of wonder and awe that is just right for the august events with which it deals. But we also detect in it a sense of the human comedy and a delight in dramatic situations that have not yet been played out to a finish. A small, complete world is set before us in the Metropolitan crèche, without pomposity or pretense.

Neapolitan Crèche

Metropolitan Museum of Art, Fifth Avenue at 82nd Street. (Recorded schedule of events, 212-535-7710. For further information, 212-879-5500.) The crèche is on view from December 1 through January 6. Museum hours: Tuesday, 9:30 A.M. to 8:45 P.M.; Wednesday through Sunday, 9:30 A.M. to 5:15 P.M. Closed Mondays, Thanksgiving Day, Christmas, and New Year's Day. Suggested admission: adults $4, students and senior citizens $2, free for children under 12.

Behind the Stage Door

BY FRANK RICH
DRAMA CRITIC

The pleasures of New York theater are not confined to the best plays and musicals. There is colorful, serendipitous theatrical entertainment to be had watching theater people and their hangers-on offstage, at haunts before and after work.

By day, many young actors making the audition rounds can often be found at the major theatrical bookstores such as the Drama Bookshop and the Theater Arts Bookshop, or sometimes at the Library and Museum of the Performing Arts at Lincoln Center.

After the final curtain, Broadway performers, producers, directors, and backstage personnel often repair for hamburgers and drinks to Joe Allen, Charlie's, and Jimmy Ray's. Though illustrious stars and producers can still be spotted at the venerable Sardi's, they are just as likely to turn up at other recently fashionable restaurants, such as Carolina, Orso, and Wally's and Joseph's. Downtown the number one off-Broadway hangout is still Phebe's, though La Rousse is the place to gawk when visiting Theater Row, the burgeoning off-Broadway district on 42nd Street west of Ninth Avenue.

If there's any one place where theater lovers are likely to congregate during an afternoon or early evening, it is the discount ticket booth, known as TKTS, at Duffy Square. As the bargain hunters wait to buy half-price tickets to that day's Broadway and off-Broadway shows, friendships are formed and debates are waged about the merits of the season's productions. Officially or not, nearly everyone in line seems to be a critic.

CAROLINA, 355 West 46th Street (212-245-0058).

CHARLIE'S, 263 West 45th Street (212-354-2911).

DRAMA BOOKSHOP, 723 Seventh Avenue between 48th and 49th streets (212-944-0595).

JIMMY RAY'S, 729 Eighth Avenue between 45th and 46th streets (212-246-8562).

JOE ALLEN, 326 West 46th Street (212-581-6464).

LA ROUSSE, 414 West 42nd Street (212-736-4913).

LIBRARY AND MUSEUM OF THE PERFORMING ARTS, lower floors, 111 Amsterdam Avenue between 64th and 65th streets (212-870-1630).

ORSO, 322 West 46th Street (212-489-7212).

PHEBE'S, 361 Bowery at East 4th Street (212-473-9008).

SARDI'S, 234 West 44th Street (212-221-8440).

THEATER ARTS BOOKSHOP, 405 West 42nd Street (212-564-0402).

TKTS, Duffy Square at 47th Street and Broadway (212-354-5800). Opens Monday through Saturday at 3 P.M.; for matinees, 1 P.M. Wednesday and Saturday; 12 P.M. Sunday. TKTS closes one hour before curtain time. Other TKTS outlets are in the lower mezzanine lobby of 2 World Trade Center and the Fulton Mall at Dekalb Avenue, Brooklyn. Both are open daily from 11 A.M. to 5:30 P.M.

WALLY'S AND JOSEPH'S, 249 West 49th Street (212-582-0460).

Strangers in the Dark

BY VINCENT CANBY
MOVIE CRITIC

Every Manhattan movie theater has a way of imposing its own personality on the people who go to it. The same well-dressed young people who stand patiently in line discussing the latest three-star French restaurants and the fate of the earth while waiting to see a Woody Allen comedy at the Beekman, become rowdy popcorn-stuffed Pepsi-guzzlers when watching the latest Steven Spielberg or Ivan Reitman film at their neighborhood RKO or Loews theater.

At the extremely elegant Cinema 3 in the Plaza Hotel, where even the walls are upholstered and where it is possible to reserve seats in advance, the atmosphere is so refined that even very young children keep quiet. Inside a 42nd Street theater, it is always one A.M., no matter what time of day it may be outside. Tempers are always short, snores are loud, and money belts are advisable.

The movie audiences at New York's fine repertory theaters—the Regency, among others—are, perhaps, the most serious and best behaved in the city. These people don't casually fall off the street into their seats; they have made a conscious effort to get to the theater to see some beloved chestnut or a recognized classic.

The most devoted New York audiences are those obsessed, enthusiastic, monomaniacal nighthawks who attend the special midnight shows at theaters such as Greenwich Village's Waverly and the Eighth Street Playhouse. Theater 80 St. Marks screens classics at midnight each weekend. The movies can be just about any old thing: a sentimental valentine like *King of Hearts*, *a* camp exposé like *Reefer Madness*, a horror film like *Night of the Living Dead* or *The Texas Chainsaw Massacre*, or a cult extravaganza like *The Rocky Horror Picture Show*.

The point is that, for whatever their reasons, New York audiences not only love the films, they know them word for word, so that moviegoing, usually thought of as a passive experience, becomes a participatory sport. Members of the audience speak the lines with the actors on the screen, adding another dimension to film that no 3-D process has ever achieved. With audiences like these, who needs polarized plastic glasses?

BEEKMAN THEATER, 1254 Second Avenue at 66th
Street (212-737-2622).

CINEMA 3, 2 West 59th Street (212-752-5959).

METRO CINEMA, 2626 Broadway at 99th Street
(212-222-1200).

EIGHTH STREET PLAYHOUSE, 52 West 8th Street
(212-674-6515).

REGENCY THEATER, 1987 Broadway at 67th Street
(212-724-3700).

THEATER 80 ST. MARKS, 80 St. Marks Place
(212-254-7400).

WAVERLY TWIN, 323 Sixth Avenue at West 3rd Street
(212-929-8037).

Sitting with the Gods

BY ANNA KISSELGOFF
DANCE CRITIC

The homing instinct among most dancegoers is for the best seat in the house—and this they rightly think is the one from which you don't need a telescope to see the dancers onstage. As an experiment, however, it might prove worthwhile and fascinating to see your favorite ballet at least once from the last row in the top balcony. The result certainly makes for a different show from the one on orchestra level. Anyone who saw *The Red Shoes* knows that "the gods," as the top galleries are known in Europe, are identified with the aficionados.

Out of choice or economic necessity, those who frequent these cheaper seats have the benefit of the bird's-eye view to which dance is especially congenial. This is particularly true of ballets that emphasize formal patterns such as George Balanchine's. Balanchine choreography seen from on high is breathtaking at Lincoln Center's New York State Theater. Other places recommended for balcony-hopping are the Brooklyn Academy of Music and the City Center Theater.

Everything you ever wanted to know about dance seemingly can be found at the world's premier dance research library, the Dance Collection in the New York Public Library's Performing Arts Research Center. The Dance Collection is a joy for the tourist and a must for the scholar and any dance lover. A key attraction is the film and videotape archive. A hand viewer allows you to stop a film and gaze at your favorite dancer undisturbed. The thousands of clippings, books, manuscripts, and photographs in the collection demonstrate why this library is an international magnet for all concerned with dance. It is not unusual to see a famous ballerina perusing the material, holding in her hands a score of a ballet that was actually performed at Louis XV's court.

Rare dance books turn up with regularity at the Ballet Shop, the city's major dance bookshop, and, of course, current dance books and magazines are on sale, too. Customers stop in for T-shirts, video cassettes, autographs, memorabilia, fan photos, and even for the dance gossip.

BALLET SHOP, 1887 Broadway at 63rd Street (212-581-7990).
BROOKLYN ACADEMY OF MUSIC, 30 Lafayette Avenue, Brooklyn (718-636-4100).
CITY CENTER THEATER, 130 West 56th Street (212-246-8989).
DANCE COLLECTION, New York Public Library Performing Arts Research Center, 111 Amsterdam Avenue at 65th Street (212-870-1657).
NEW YORK STATE THEATER, Lincoln Center, Broadway at 65th Street (212-877-4700).

Adeste Video

BY JOHN J. O'CONNOR
TELEVISION CRITIC

Television in New York these days is leaping off the home screen and popping up in a wide variety of nooks and auditoriums all over town. Just as movies in the 1950s began to be screened in film clubs and museums, indicating that the popular entertainment form was at last ready to be taken seriously, television is now maneuvering for what it hopes will be serious attention. No major museum would be caught napping without a television and video department of some sort. There is even one prestigious center specializing solely in television and radio archives, the Museum of Broadcasting.

Two of the city's oldest video spaces, in operation for more than a decade, can be found in SoHo. The Kitchen Center for Video, Music, Dance, Performance, and Film is dedicated in large part to the work of video artists, the kind of material that still has a hard time getting on commercial or public television. Global Village, on the other hand, focuses on the documentary form. With John Reilly and Julie Gustafson as codirectors, the group has had five of its own works shown on national television and produced a public-television series called *Other Visions, Other Voices*. Founded and still thriving in an old loft building, Global Village has been exploring and exhibiting possible alternatives to standard broadcast television. A seventy-five-seat public room on the second floor is used for screenings and panel discussions, often revolving around the plight of independent documentarians. The mix can range from relatively unknown video makers to Bill Moyers, who participated in a retrospective of his own work last spring. Whatever the event, the content is usually lively and provocative.

GLOBAL VILLAGE, 454 Broome Street (212-966-7526).
  Admission charge: $3.
THE KITCHEN, 59 Wooster Street (212-925-3615). Free.
MUSEUM OF BROADCASTING, 1 East 53rd Street
  (212-752-7684). Contribution: adults, $3; students, $2;
  children under 13 and senior citizens, $1.50. Open
  Tuesday, noon to 8 P.M.; Wednesday through Saturday,
  noon to 5 P.M.

Literary Lodestars

BY CHRISTOPHER LEHMANN-HAUPT
BOOK CRITIC

For a New York City bibliophile, the cup is either half full
or half empty. The pessimist notes that Brentano's has
closed; the ranks of independently owned bookstores have
dwindled, and the chains, with their supermarket merchan-
dising techniques, continue to elbow aside what competition
is left. But the optimist responds that stately Scribner's still
exists, and so does doughty Doubleday, and farther up the
East Side there is Books & Company, with its eclectic stock,
including poetry and a large collection of African fiction,
and its sponsorship of readings from old works, new works,
and works in progress.

The pessimist moans that the secondhand bookstores that
used to thrive on lower Broadway have all but disappeared,
to which the optimist rejoins, "Wise men still fish" at the
Gotham Book Mart on West 47th Street. Nearby, there is a
magnificent brownstone where H. P. Kraus will be glad to

sell you an illuminated medieval manuscript or an incunabulum or two.

Lovers of books do not require crowds and action, however. Reading is solitary; all that is needed is a place to do it and a supply. For one professionally devoted to books—a reviewer, for example—the supply beats a path to one's doorstep. In a book reviewer's office, as Gertrude Stein once said of Oakland, "there's no there there." There's only a pile of books.

Still, it never hurts to stay in touch with reality—reality being the places where New York's bibliophiles go to pick out what they feel like reading. For this booklover, reality is a place in the Bronx called Paperbacks Plus, where, to judge from the window full of hardcover books, the emphasis is very much on the plus. One of the borough's few remaining trade bookstores, Paperbacks Plus did surprisingly well during its first decade, despite being located up a flight of stairs. In fact, it did so well that the landlord refused to renew the lease and spoke of starting his own bookstore there. Paperbacks Plus responded by reopening three doors away at street level and doing even better. To think of them fighting over readers: It was a caution! But the landlord got cold feet and opened a toy store instead.

Paperbacks Plus is a true community bookstore. At different times during the year, you find local high school students consulting their assignment lists or older residents preparing for summer at the beach. Almost every day there are piles of telephone orders on the counter that let you know what readers are particularly avid to get. You are reminded that plenty of people pay good money to read books. For eight to twelve hours of fun or intellectual stimulation, a twenty-dollar book is still a considerable bargain.

BOOKS & COMPANY, 939 Madison Avenue between 74th
and 75th streets (212-737-1450).

DOUBLEDAY BOOKSHOP, 724 Fifth Avenue between
56th and 57th streets (212-397-0550). Other branches
throughout Manhattan.

GOTHAM BOOK MART AND GALLERY, 41 West 47th
Street (212-719-4448).

H. P. KRAUS, 16 East 46th Street (212-687-4808).

PAPERBACKS PLUS, 3721 Riverdale Avenue between
West 236th and 238th streets, Bronx (212-796-3119).

THE SCRIBNER BOOKSTORE, 597 Fifth Avenue at 48th
Street (212-758-9797).

PART 6

Feasting

CHAPTER 35

....

Confessions of a Deli Addict

BY NORA EPHRON

On Sunday mornings, we would get into the car, my father and I, and drive to the delicatessen—Linny's Delicatessen on Beverly Drive in Beverly Hills. We would take a number and wait our turn. My father would talk with the other men waiting at the counter, half of them dressed for tennis, half of them dressed for golf, all of them tanned to a shade I always thought of as Naugahyde. I would stare at the food. Sometimes I would chew on a miniature salami called a *schtickel* (there was a sign at Linny's that read: "A nickel a schtickel is a rhyme, now a nickel a schtickel is a dime") and press my nose against the glass case as the counterman sliced the Nova on the diagonal and laid it on sheets of waxed paper. It was my idea of rapture. I used to spend hours daydreaming about how wonderful it would be to be locked overnight in Linny's so I could taste everything, including the sturgeon, which we never bought.

Finally, our turn would come. A half-pound of Nova, six

bagels, a package of cream cheese, and two butterfish for my mother if they had butterfish. This was our weekly ritual, and I took part in it throughout my childhood knowing on some level that it was a ritual performed in exile, an exercise in ethnic memory, a pale imitation of the real thing, which had been left behind.

"You don't have any water bagels today, do you?" my father would ask, knowing the answer would be no, but asking nevertheless. No, they did not. Water bagels were New York bagels. What we got in Los Angeles in the 1950s were called egg bagels; they were yellow and a little sweet. My mother made a face at them every time she opened the bag. It seems to me, looking back, that whatever sense I had of the Diaspora had nothing to do with the serious meaning of the term and everything to do with the sense that there were hundreds of thousands of Jews scattered across America who were forced to make do with second-rate appetizing.

Years later, when I moved to New York, I came upon the New York delicatessen with the same feeling of awe that Arabs who have spent years in the desert must feel when they arrive at Mecca. I don't mean to trivialize the Moslem religious experience by that comparison, but only to elevate my own. After all those years of praying toward the East, here I was, at the source: at Russ & Daughters on East Houston, the most authentic and beautiful of all delicatessens, with its barrels of pickles and crates of herring; at Murray's Sturgeon Shop on Broadway on the Upper West Side, the purest and most sacrosanct of all delicatessens, a shrine to smoked fish and immaculate fish-handlers; and, of course, at Zabar's, nine blocks south, the most rambunctious and chaotic of all delicatessens, with one foot in the

Old World and the other in the vanguard of every fast-breaking food move in the city.

I want to write here about delicatessens in general; I want to write about the New York delicatessen as institution and amusement park; I want to avoid focusing on any one particular delicatessen. But I can't do it. Although I love all New York delicatessens, although I feel enormous affection for Russ & Daughters (the delicatessen I would choose if I had to be married in a delicatessen) and have great respect for Murray's (the delicatessen I would choose if I had to have open-heart surgery in a delicatessen), I am preoccupied with Zabar's.

For the past five years, I have lived a block from Zabar's, so I go there five or six times a week. I go during the off-hours, and I go when it's crowded. I think about Zabar's all the time. I think about Murray Klein, the only one of the three owners who is not a Zabar, standing at the entrance most of the day, making sure that no one with a stroller gets past the fruit section when the No Strollers Today sign is on the door; I think about Steve Hart, the assistant manager, whose hair is the color of rye bread, lurking behind the cash registers initialing credit card slips. I have a proprietary feeling about Zabar's price war with Macy's—although to me it would be more fitting if it were a war with Bloomingdale's—and I felt proud the day Zabar's cut Norwegian smoked salmon to $9.95 a pound. On Sundays, around closing time, when Saul Zabar gets on the loudspeaker to announce that the price of croissants is "dropping fast, get them now, hot croissants," I get giddy with excitement.

Zabar's is the ultimate West Side institution. It is messy and middle-class; it gives the impression of disorganization without being disorganized; it gives the appearance of warmth without being truly friendly. But more important—and I suppose this is the primary reason I remain obsessed with it year after year—Zabar's perfectly embodies New York's most basic emotion: unrequited love. I love Zabar's more than Zabar's loves me. I'm not complaining, just stating a fact.

Zabar's cares about its customers, of course; I'm not saying it doesn't. But if you are looking for the store to return your affection and loyalty, forget it. Zabar's is too busy and too involved in its own metamorphosis. In recent years, it has grown from the long sliver of a one-story store it once was to a two-story establishment four times as large. And every time you blink, it expands even more. Or its floor plan is rearranged. The dried fruits end up in the window, a candy counter suddenly appears, the fresh pasta arrives with a fanfare only to be relegated to the back within seconds by the chocolate-chip cookies. The croissant-baked-on-the-premises is introduced; a few days later, the scone-baked-on-the-premises bumps it from the limelight, followed by the bran-muffin-baked-on-the-premises. Fall in love with the corned beef sandwich, and they will stop making it. Fall in love with the blintzes, and they will start using the blintz machine for knishes. The store, like the city of which it is a part, never quits on you. And the only solace you can take in its mistakes—such as the tendency of the meat department to wrap virtually everything in phyllo—is that eventually the mistakes will be superseded by new ones.

I never daydream about being locked overnight in Zabar's, because the last thing I want is to taste everything they have got crammed in there, especially the stuff wrapped in phyllo. But I do have a Zabar's fantasy. Sometimes I imagine I am a Zabar. I imagine that we Zabars all live together in a West Side apartment with pots and pans hanging from the living room ceiling. I imagine that every night those of us who have worked at the store that day bring home six kinds of bread and the week's smoked salmon special and the latest Italian cheese and the Virginia peanuts. I imagine that we sit around blindfolded conducting taste tests on the relative merits of, say, the beluga and the sevruga, and I imagine that we have bitter fights about how to eliminate the congestion at the cash registers and how to get the space into which we plan to expand to look as cluttered and discombobulated as the rest of the store. In my mind's eye, on the outskirts of all this, Zabar children scamper around, nibbling chocolate croissants.

The fantasy goes on and on. For a while I thought I created it because to me the Zabars represent a kind of Jewish royalty, and the idea of being one a schmaltzy version of the old fairy-tale-princess fantasy. But the truth is I like to imagine I am a Zabar because I think of myself as family, and since Zabar's doesn't treat me as family, I have to do it unilaterally.

So I go to Zabar's—mostly on weekday mornings, when the store is almost empty, and I can pick up the current sensation: the long, thin loaves of sourdough bread baked for Zabar's by younger brother Eli Zabar, who runs his own gourmet deli, E.A.T., across town. But sometimes I go with my children on Sundays. They stand at the counter, staring at the smoked fish, and we wait our turn. I ask for a half-pound of Nova, six bagels, fresh cream cheese, and two butterfish if they have butterfish, although they haven't had any in over a year. We never buy sturgeon. And so it goes.

CHAPTER 36

····································

Lochs and Bagels

BY ISRAEL SHENKER

When my wife, Mary, and I left New York five years ago to live in Scotland, Abe Lebewohl wondered why.

"What will you find to eat?" he asked.

Mr. Lebewohl owns the Second Ave. Kosher Delicatessen & Restaurant, at the corner of 10th Street, and austerity is not his line. He has pursued the good life throughout Western Europe and Israel, and once almost succeeded in catching a waiter's eye in Russia. Never having been to Scotland, he tried to visualize our setting: "It's like a *shtetl?*" he suggested. "Between one house and the next, it's a half a mile?" For him, our move to Scotland spelled ethnic starvation.

So he began shipping pastrami. The first parcel arrived like manna from heaven, and we ate as if our lives depended on it. Our home is in the Trossachs, an area of rural splendor and deli deprivation. The closest Jewish restaurant is in Glasgow, forty-five miles away. Last winter, we were

snowed in for three weeks. At the height of a raging bliz-
zard, the postman struggled to the door bearing a heavy parcel. Inside, we found a brief note from Mr. Lebewohl and a
vast expanse of pastrami.

My wife, moved by the sight of lambs at the window, has
renounced eating meat, her abstinence reinforced by the
spectacle of pastrami on the hoof—lovely Highland cattle,
unpickled, unspiced, unsmoked. Obedient to her master's
choice, however, she prepared the pastrami, while the Saint
Bernard went onto the ice floes with a rush order for mustard and sour pickles.

Day after day, I feasted on pastrami. Eventually, keen on
the scent, local friends arrived to lend a few hands and hear
wondrous accounts of this and other exotic delicacies.

When I returned to New York for a visit in April, Mr.
Lebewohl gave me a menu to nourish nostalgia on long
winter evenings. Now, between pangs of heartburn and pastrami deliveries that continue to arrive by mail or by an occasional itinerant customer pressed into service by Mr.
Lebewohl, rise visions of charms remote and inaccessible:
boiled beef flanken, potato knishes, noodle pudding, gefilte
fish, Yankee bean soup, and the penitential half sandwich at
half price after buying a whole one at full price.

As I nibble à la carte, my wife labors in the kitchen, indul-
gently permitting the lambs to trample our shrubs while she
bakes shortbread and oatcakes to ship to the Second Ave.
Deli, just to show Mr. Lebewohl that ethnicity bites both
ways.

CHAPTER 37

Eat-In Delis

BY CRAIG CLAIBORNE

The New York restaurants that specialize in deli food are as much hallmarks of city life as the Empire State Building and the Metropolitan Museum of Art. With a few exceptions, there is a certain sameness in the quality of the food and the atmosphere. The coleslaw, always a trifle sweet, varies from one place to another mostly in liquidity; the new pickles—cucumber or tomato—vary mostly in texture, and the borschts vary mostly in garnishes. Decor typically is banal and largely uninspired.

With respect to pastrami, corned beef, and brisket of beef (my standard choices at delis), there is one important fact to note: If you order the meat lean, the counterman will probably cut away all the surface fat. But, to be honest, it is the marbling—the calorie-laden fat in the meat—that makes the difference between a dry-tasting sandwich and one that is melting and rich. You just do not discuss diet and deli in the same breath.

My apartment is in the Carnegie Hall–West 57th Street neighborhood; the delis I most frequently patronize are nearby. All are open seven days a week, and all serve beer, wine, and cocktails, except Carnegie, which offers only beer.

My Favorites

Carnegie Delicatessen and Restaurant, 854 Seventh Avenue (212-757-2245). Owned by the personable, dedicated, and enthusiastic Leo Steiner, the Carnegie is, to my taste, the finest delicatessen in the city. The tables are pushed together and the chairs almost touch, making it elbow-to-elbow dining. The meats are of the finest quality, and sandwich fillings are piled extraordinarily high. One of the great soups of the city is the cold borscht with, if you request, chopped vegetables, a splendid blend of beet juice, chopped scallions, chopped cucumbers, radishes, tomatoes, and sour cream. The barley soup, however, is a bit pasty. Sandwich prices range from $5.75 for "The Egg and Oy" (that's what the menu says), made with sliced eggs, tomatoes, and chicken salad, to $12.75 for "Nova on Sunday," made with Nova Scotia salmon, lake sturgeon, olives, cream cheese, lettuce, tomato, and sliced Bermuda onion.

Kaplan's at the Delmonico, 59 East 59th Street (212-755-5959). This deli is a bit gaudy. The tables have gold-flecked, resin-coated tops, and the deli cases that display meats and salads at the entrance remind me of food counters at airports. The food is very good, although the generously apportioned sandwich meats—such as pastrami and corned beef—are a bit on the dry side. I have heard customers praise the barley and mushroom soup, but I found it somewhat dark and pasty. The smoked sturgeon has a delicate flavor and texture. Sandwich prices range from about $3.75 for a half-pound beefburger to $10.95 for the Volga Boatman: cream cheese, Nova Scotia salmon, and sturgeon on a bagel. The house wine ($4.50 a half carafe, $8 a carafe) has a nice balance and is recommended.

Stage Delicatessen Restaurant, 834 Seventh Avenue (212-245-7850). This establishment is considered by many to be one of the finest delicatessens in the city, and with that evaluation I heartily agree. One dish I particularly admire is the kasha varnishkas, a rich, nutty-flavored combination of cooked kasha, bow-tie pasta, onions, mushrooms, and brown sauce. Our good-natured, talkative waitress assures me that it is "very healthy and just like my Russian grand-mother prepared it." The borscht (hot or cold) with sour cream is top flight, and the corned beef, pastrami, and brisket—even when ordered lean—have a melting goodness. The decor is theatrical, as the restaurant's name implies, and sandwiches are named for show-business celebrities: You can have a "Warren Beatty" triple-decker of egg salad, anchovies, lettuce, and tomato for $7.05; or a "Raquel Welch," made of corned beef, pastrami, coleslaw, and Russian dressing for $8.65. (As is often the case in show business, the ingredients usually remain constant, but the names change with the times and the reviews.)

Wolf's Sixth Avenue Delicatessen and Restaurant, 101 West 57th Street (212-586-1110). A fellow diner remarked recently that eating at Wolf's is a bit like eating in the packed dining car of a passenger train. The corned beef and pastrami sandwiches are high-piled New York fare, with the meat on the lean side. The sturgeon is of excellent quality, hand-sliced and delicate in flavor. Combination sandwiches range from $6.15 for corned beef with pastrami to $10.25 for sturgeon with Nova Scotia salmon. Full meals—salad platters and so on—are also available.

Where to Buy Salmon

Following is a list of shops at which salmon is sold:

Balducci's, 424 Avenue of the Americas between 9th and
   10th streets (212-673-2600).

Barney Greengrass, 541 Amsterdam Avenue at 86th Street
   (212-724-4707).

Dean & DeLuca, 121 Prince Street (212-431-1691).

E.A.T., 1064 Madison Avenue at 79th Street
   (212-879-4017).

Fairway, 2127 Broadway between 74th and 75th streets
   (212-595-1888).

Food Emporium, various locations.

Fraser Morris, 931 Madison Avenue at 74th Street
   (212-968-6700).

Macy's, Herald Square (212-695-4400).

Maison Glass, 52 East 58th Street (212-755-3316).

Murray's Sturgeon Shop, 2429 Broadway at 89th Street
   (212-724-2650).

Petak's Appetizers and Caterers, 1244 Madison Avenue at
   89th Street (212-722-7711).

Petrossian, in Bloomingdale's, Lexington Avenue at 59th
   Street (212-705-3176).

Russ & Daughters, 179 East Houston Street between
   Orchard and Allen streets (212-475-4880).

Todaro Brothers, 555 Second Avenue at 31st Street
   (212-532-0633).

William Poll, 1051 Lexington Avenue between 74th and
   75th streets (212-288-0501).

Zabar's, 2245 Broadway at 80th Street (212-787-2000).

CHAPTER 38

....

Wine Capital of the World

BY FRANK J. PRIAL

Wine is made all over the world, but wine excitement is made in New York. When a Bordeaux Rothschild wants to sell his wine, he doesn't go to Paris; he comes to Manhattan. When Italy decides it is time to create a great modern showcase for its wines, does it build in Rome? Or Milan? No, the Italian Wine Center is at Park Avenue and 59th Street. And where would Beaujolais nouveau be today if New York had not made a fad of it a dozen years ago?

Californians are responsible for 90 percent of all the wine made in this country, and they sell most of it to other Californians. But when they want to congratulate themselves in style, they come to New York. For more than a decade, the California wine industry's most significant party, the Annual California Vintners' Barrel Tasting Dinner, has been held at Park Avenue and 52nd Street, at the Four Seasons restaurant.

Paris may be the capital of the most famous wine-making

nation, but wine makers and buyers rarely stop there, at least not to do business. They meet in the wine country, or they meet in New York. The average Bordeaux shipper would rather do business in the bar at the "21" Club than anyplace in France. "We go to Paris to battle the bureaucracy," said Philippe Cottin, president of La Bergerie, the wine-marketing division of Baron Philippe de Rothschild's empire. "We come to New York to do business."

The New York metropolitan area is easily the biggest, wealthiest, most enthusiastic wine market anywhere. It has the importers, the distributors, the money, the shops, and, most of all, New York has the wine. A modest wine store in Brooklyn or the Bronx will have a wider selection of good bottles than the grandest wine merchant in Paris. Hediard and the Caves de la Madeleine and other sophisticated Paris shops will stock a few California wines at staggering prices and consider themselves exceptionally broad-minded; Italian, Spanish, and German wines are even rarer. Neighborhood shops in New York will have a German wine section, an American section, French and Italian sections, and a special area for jug and other inexpensive wines. There are also retailers who specialize: Goldstar, in Queens, for example, is one of the great repositories of Italian wines. There are no wine supermarkets yet, as there are in Paris, London, and Los Angeles, but those will come.

By the count of *Beverage Media*, a trade publication, there are more than 260 American still wines available in New York, 90 brands of American sparkling wines, and well over 2,000 different imported wines that originate anywhere from New Zealand to Lebanon. No city in the world can match that.

So New York wine drinkers are spoiled: It is easy to buy

good wine here, for $2 a bottle or $2,000. Bordeaux wine prices determine the market for most other imports, and, many importers will agree, Bordeaux prices are now set in New York and not in France. According to one industry estimate, 35 percent of all classified Bordeaux wines, the hundred or so top names, are sold in the United States, and up to 40 percent of that total is sold in the New York area. For first-growth Bordeaux—the term applied to vintages from the top five châteaus—Latour, Haut-Brion, Margaux, Mouton-Rothschild, and Lafite-Rothschild—the ratios are even higher; some 45 percent is sold in this country and better than half of that total is sold in and around New York.

One important reason for New York's preeminence in the wine world is its open-mindedness. Almost any kind of wine, from any part of the world, will get a trial here. Tell a New Yorker to pay $15 for a California chardonnay and he or she will shrug and buy a Meursault for $11. Should the third-string Bordeaux take on airs and go to $10, a New Yorker will pick up a good Spanish rioja for $5. New Yorkers tend to be very skeptical about West Coast Rieslings and Gewürztraminers, because they see the German and Alsatian versions on their merchants' shelves at extremely favorable prices. And when the French lose their heads again, as inevitably they will, and send their prices through the roof, New Yorkers will simply content themselves with the extraordinary variety of other wines available to them. Above all, New Yorkers are trend-setters. If Italian merlot or Spanish sparkling wine catches on in New York, it will sweep across the country.

Of course, the key to the New York wine scene is its wine merchants. The best of them, in the European tradition, are educated, articulate, sophisticated men, totally absorbed in their métier. They not only sell wine, they love it. There are New Yorkers, it's probably safe to say, who choose their wine merchant more carefully than their psychiatrist.

Sam Aaron, at seventy-five, is the doyen of New York wine retailers. Three years ago he celebrated his fiftieth year at the helm of Sherry-Lehmann Wine & Spirits Merchants, probably the best-known wine shop in the world. Mr. Aaron does not hesitate to say that he has shaped the wine tastes of the nation over the past fifty years, and most of his competitors will admit that a *Who's Who* of the wine trade would include a significant number of executives and even wine writers who started out behind the counter at Sherry-Lehmann.

There are other great retail shops. Morrell & Company is as large, as attractive, and as well stocked, and not even Sam Aaron is always as well versed in wine knowledge as Peter Morrell. Lee Iacucci at Goldstar Wines & Spirits is the acknowledged maestro of Italian wines, not only in New York but anywhere in the country. For bargains, it would be hard to beat the Surrey Liquor Shop or Garnet Wine & Liquor. But even people who don't shop there will readily acknowledge that Sherry-Lehmann contributes to New York's stature as a wine center of the world.

Over the years, before age slowed him down a bit, Sam Aaron's trips to Europe became wine events. He held court at least once a year at the Hotel Crillon in Paris. Wine makers and exporters from every corner of France came to pay homage—and try to sell a few cases of wine. They knew, and they still know, that Sherry-Lehmann is the retailer that sets the pattern for wine shops all over the country. They know that a couple of inches of shelf space at 679 Madison Avenue is the best possible foothold in the American wine market.

Sam Aaron's buying trips may be over, but he has not been forgotten in France. Last year he was honored at a week of parties in Bordeaux, Burgundy, Beaujolais, and Champagne. All the legendary figures of the French wine trade turned out to celebrate his fifty years in the business, which, of course, coincide with the fifty years of French wine sales in the United States since the end of Prohibition.

Like most wine-and-spirits operations that started up right after Repeal, Sherry-Lehmann had its roots in Prohibition. Jules Endler, a colorful figure from the era of bathtub gin, opened Sherry Wine & Spirits in 1934 in the old Louis Sherry Building at 62nd Street and Madison Avenue. But Jules Endler wasn't truly interested in the retail trade in New York and decided to sell. The buyer he chose was Jack Aaron, a friend from the Prohibition years and a drinking companion at the epoch's most famous speakeasy, The Red Head.

There were three Aaron brothers, Jack, Sam, and Charles, the sons of Harris Aaron, a Russian immigrant who came to Brooklyn at the end of the last century. Sam never planned to be a merchant—he had a master's degree in educational psychology—but there were no jobs in 1934, so he went in with Jack, and they took over Sherry Wine & Spirits. Jack paid himself $125 a week and Sam took $75, along with the title of president.

As Sam Aaron tells it, Sherry Wine & Spirits was just another liquor store until the day a man walked in who would change not only the shop but Sam Aaron's life. He was the late Frank Schoonmaker, a former writer for *The New Yorker* magazine who had become a wine importer. The two hit it off.

"I was in the liquor business, but I didn't know anything

about wine," Sam said of those days. "Frank changed all that." In 1937, Sam made his first trip to the wine country—Frank Schoonmaker knew how to get an enthusiastic retailer hooked on wine.

During World War II, while Jack Aaron ran the store, Sam went into the army and became chief psychologist at Mason General Hospital (now Pilgrim State) on Long Island. "For a time, I thought of staying with psychology," he said, "but someone convinced me I'd spend my life working for psychiatrists."

So he rejoined his brother just after the war, and they opened a small gourmet shop, called Alanberry, next door to the liquor store. To operate it, they hired a sometime actor and avid food enthusiast named James Beard. In 1948, however, Mr. Beard moved on to begin his writing career, and Alanberry was closed. The Aarons had decided to stick to what they did best.

Those were the years when Sam Aaron was developing his flair for advertising copy. A sample come-on from one of his early catalogues:

"Savigny-Les-Beaune 1949, Estate Bottled, M. Doudet. The little town of Savigny-les-Beaune, in a fold of the hills between Beaune and Corton, produces what are perhaps the pleasantest medium-priced Burgundies of the whole Côte d'Or. This 1949, fine, not too heavy and now ready, is an exceptional wine of its class." Addicts of the current Sherry-Lehmann catalogues will easily recognize the Aaron style.

Around 1960, the store manager of Sherry Wine & Spirits, Joseph Stricks, announced to the Aarons that he had come into some money through marriage and wanted to buy the store. When they demurred, he walked five blocks up the avenue and bought M. Lehmann Inc.

"It was a strange situation," Sam Aaron said. "Our chief competitor was now owned by our former manager." But in 1965 the Aarons bought the Lehmann name and inventory, forming Sherry-Lehmann Wine & Spirits Merchants.

Jack Aaron died suddenly in 1967, and Joseph Stricks, who had come back into the business, died in 1971. Jack's place was filled by his son, Michael, who had done his apprenticeship in California wineries and vineyards in France. Gradually, Michael has assumed more and more of the daily management of Sherry-Lehmann, and is now president, while Sam has assumed the mantle of elder statesman and expert emeritus. In 1968, he and James Beard wrote *How to Eat Better for Less Money*. In 1970, he edited the *Wines and Spirits* volume in a Time-Life series on food. *The Joys of Wine*, a big, splashy compendium of wine facts and fancy he compiled with Clifton Fadiman in 1976, still sells moderately well.

The wine business can be mercurial, and not even successful Sherry-Lehmann is immune to economic difficulty. In the euphoria of the early 1970s, the Aarons invested heavily in 1971 and 1972 Bordeaux. The market collapsed in 1974 with the arrival of the huge 1973 vintage, which was both superior and cheaper. Retailers who had invested early, like the Aarons, had to sell below their own costs to compete. In the blackest days there were half-hearted discussions about selling Sherry-Lehmann, but the storm passed and the Aarons still control their business. They even own their building on Madison Avenue.

These days, when he isn't loafing in East Hampton or conjuring up elegant dinners with Craig Claiborne, an old friend, the elder Aaron holds court on the awninged deck behind his store or at his table at the Perigord Park, a favor-

The Best Deals in Town

Acker, Merrall & Condit Company, 2373 Broadway
between 86th and 87th streets (212-787-1700). For the wine
to go with whatever you just bought at Zabar's, down the
street.

Astor Wines & Spirits Inc., 12 Astor Place, at Lafayette
and 8th streets (212-674-7500). The nearest thing to a wine
supermarket in New York. Get a cart and wander up and
down the aisles.

Garnet Wine & Liquor, 929 Lexington Avenue between
68th and 69th streets (212-772-3211). A bit chaotic, but
arguably the best bargains in town.

Goldstar Wines & Spirits, 103–05 Queens Boulevard
between 68th Road and 68th Drive, Forest Hills, Queens
(718-459-0200). If it's an Italian wine and Goldstar doesn't
have it, it probably isn't worth drinking.

Morrell & Company Wine and Spirit Merchants, 307
East 53rd Street (212-688-9370). Encyclopedic. A landmark

ite restaurant. He likes to tell about the time he and Frank
Schoonmaker practically cornered the market in 1953
Petrus and persuaded Henri Soulé to feature it at his
restaurant, Le Pavillon. Or how he missed making a million
on 1961 Lafite. "My stories have three things in common,"
Sam Aaron says. "They are all about wine, they are all about
me, and they could only happen in New York."

on the East Side where the clerks actually like to help. House wines always excellent.

Quality House, 2 Park Avenue between 32nd and 33rd streets (212-532-2944). Unprepossessing outside; enormous expertise and matching stocks inside.

Sherry-Lehmann Wine & Spirits Merchants, 679 Madison Avenue between 61st and 62nd streets (212-838-7500). Alpha and omega. Whatever happens in wine in New York starts or ends here. Their catalogue is social history.

67 Wine & Spirits Merchants, 179 Columbus Avenue at 68th Street (212-724-6767). The wine shop of the West Side intelligentsia. The staff is knowledgeable, which helps because the intelligentsia don't know any more about wine than the rest of us.

D. Sokolin, Wine Merchants Ltd., 178 Madison Avenue between 33rd and 34th streets (212-532-5893). Bill Sokolin is the P. T. Barnum of wine retailers. Step into his refrigerated front window.

Surrey Liquor Shop Inc., 19 East 69th Street (212-744-1946). These are the people who showed Garnet how it's done. Frank Small, the house guru, deserves landmark status.

Vintage Sources

New Yorkers profit from what may be the most competitive wine market in the world. But even current low prices pale in comparison with what they were in the late 1940s. Here are examples from the 1948 Sherry-Lehmann catalogue.

Red Bordeaux wines were listed in three classes: below $2, from $2 to $3, and "rare old clarets." Regional bottlings, such as the 1943 Medoc and Margaux, sold for $1.39 each. A 1937 Château Pontet-Canet was $2.59, and the now legendary 1945 first growths, châteaus Haut-Brion, Margaux, Lafite-Rothschild, and Latour, sold for $2.99 each. Among those "rare old clarets," the 1937 Latour was $3.79, the 1934 Lafite was $3.98, the 1928 Cheval Blanc, $4.98, and the 1918 Latour, $6.95. Prices are higher now; but there are still bargains around. Here are a few of the places to seek them out.

CHAPTER 39

Restaurants: Festive Dining

Which places to choose for that special Christmas holiday treat? Eight food and wine writers confide their favorites.

Blessed Are the Blinis

BY CRAIG CLAIBORNE
FOOD EDITOR OF *THE NEW YORK TIMES*

Restaurant-going can be a form of theater. When diners enter, they become members of the cast. The lavishness of the show varies from one establishment to another, and, to my mind, one of the most colorful stage sets is the celebrity-filled dining room of the Russian Tea Room, where, 365 days of the year, the *mise en scène* happens to be Christmas.

The chandeliers are always festooned with gold tinsel and sparkling red Christmas tree balls. The polished brass wall sconces, the samovar, the red banquettes, the mirror in the rear that reflects the holiday mood, all add up to a joyous happening. And where can you find a finer selection of fellow actors and actresses, and directors, writers, and composers, for that matter? At a recent lunch at the Russian Tea Room I was surrounded at various tables by Peter Stone, Robin Williams, Anthony Perkins, and John Kander.

Fine Russian cooking is undeniably festive to my palate, and the menu of the Russian Tea Room is a celebration. The caviar, ruby-red or stygian-black, is always joyous, and the blinis with which it is served are masterfully made. (Butter and sour cream are added at the table, the caviar is used as a filling, and the pancakes then rolled.) The cold matjes herring, delectably sweet, tender, and moist, with red onion rings and sour cream, is a personal favorite, and so is the pepper-flavored Russian vodka (just one of sixteen vodkas available). The soups range from a decent but not exceptional borscht with cabbage to a superb cream of spinach soup listed on the menu as *schi*. (It is sometimes spelled *schchi* or *schchii*.) All the soups are served with an outrageously good *pirojok*—ground meat baked in high-puffed, golden-brown pastry triangles.

The *côtelette à la Kiev*—a skinless, boneless, plump breast of chicken—is stuffed with what appears to be no less than half a cup of clarified butter that, when the chicken is sliced, spurts out generously onto a bed of excellent rice. It is delectable, but the real unadulterated triumph of a recent meal was the costly *karsky shashlik*, a magnificent marinated saddle of spring lamb broiled to pink perfection along with pieces of lamb kidney.

There is a special Christmas menu, mostly all-American, that changes from year to year. The main dish is generally roast turkey. Make mine *shashlik!*

Let Us Eat Cake

BY JULIA CHILD
COOKBOOK AUTHOR AND TELEVISION HOST

The Four Seasons is such a jolly place at holiday time. I enjoy it and my husband, Paul, likes it particularly, so we go often. The people who work there make you feel welcome and they're so professional. They really know how to put on a big splash. I especially enjoy the oysters during the holidays, and if there is any caviar on the menu, I have that, too. The special chocolate-covered cake is marvelous. It's a lovely thing, so ribboned and entwined and garlanded with sheets of chocolate that it looks like a fancy hat.

I once had the opportunity to see how they make the cake. I was working in the kitchen, preparing a quail tart with the late Albert Stöckli, the Four Seasons's first chef, when I saw some cooks standing around what looked like an old-fashioned clothes wringer with marble rollers. They passed the chocolate back and forth through it until it softened into malleable, thin strands. It was wonderful.

I prefer to be in the Pool Room next to the bubbling pool, but the whole place has a special elegance about it. The people at the Four Seasons try very hard to do everything well, and I think that they have succeeded over the years.

For Kids from 1 to 92

BY MARIAN BURROS
FOOD COLUMNIST OF *THE NEW YORK TIMES*

My parents brought me to New York only once during the Christmas holidays when I was a young girl. They took me to see the skaters and the Christmas tree at Rockefeller Center and treated me to hot chocolate at the Promenade Café. Ever since, all other Christmas trees have paled by comparison. When I had children of my own, I treated them to the same hot-chocolate-warmed view.

The lower plaza café at Rockefeller Center is gone now, but three new restaurants have taken its place. The most delightful of them is the American Festival Café, a snug spot from which to view the skaters and the tree. The restaurant is home to many enchanting pieces of Americana, part of a rotating exhibit from the Museum of American Folk Art.

Most children will be too enthralled by the sights and sounds to think about food, but the restaurant plans to cater to them at weekend breakfasts and brunches, with children's menus and visits from Santa. With the holiday traffic jams and crushes of people, probably only those New Yorkers who are unabashed lovers of the city would choose to visit Rockefeller Center between Thanksgiving and New Year's Eve. But I don't see why we should turn this cherished landmark over to out-of-towners. We should reclaim some of its joy for ourselves.

Two Evergreens

BY JAMES BEARD
COOKBOOK AUTHOR AND TEACHER

For years I have made a habit of going to the Coach House on Christmas Eve if I am in New York. It has an especially warm, neighborly feeling at that time of year. On the dessert table there is always a steaming plum pudding bubbling away. A certain group of people have made it a tradition to gather there for dinner on Christmas Eve, so I often bump into someone I know. It is a very convivial group.

Once in a while the Coach House has a remarkable Greek tripe soup for the holiday season. It takes about three days to put this concoction of tripe, veal, and calves' feet together. If you like gelatinous textures, it is really something to try. It is served as an appetizer, but it is quite rich. The last time I had it, I ordered two bowls and did not eat anything else.

La Tulipe is another place with a good, homey feeling at Christmas. Sally and John Darr, the owners, sometimes invite friends and fellow restaurateurs over late at night to celebrate and enjoy two of Mrs. Darr'a holiday specialties, a classic French head cheese with pistachios and her excellent pastries.

Camaraderie at the Clubhouse

BY FRANK J. PRIAL
WINE COLUMNIST OF *THE NEW YORK TIMES*

Perhaps the most persistent of holiday myths is the one that says Christmas is for children. It is, of course, but even more, it is a time for grown-ups to act like children. And nowhere do grown-ups do that with greater style or more élan than at the "21" Club.

Isn't the bar at "21," its ceiling hung with airplane models and toy trucks and old footballs, all supplied by captains of commerce and media superstars, more like a teen-ager's bedroom than a famous restaurant? Someone once called the "21" bar a perpetual fraternity party. At this time of year, it is the frat house, the country club, and the ski lodge, all in one.

There is an elegant holiday style in New York. There is also a chic holiday style, a frenzied holiday style, and, New York being New York, a tacky holiday style as well. "21" is none of these. Never has been. The barroom can be noisy and boozy, and now and then a bit sophomoric, but there is a sense of warmth and well-being and tradition at "21," especially at this time of year, that brings to mind an earlier, more innocent time in this city.

It won't be exactly like the old days. Nothing ever is. Old regulars such as John O'Hara won't return from the shades. Neither will Papa Hemingway or Lucius Beebe or Bob Benchley—except perhaps as ghosts of "21" Club's Christmases past.

But there will be a Kriendler and a Berns, just as there were sixty years ago when the place was Jack and Charlie's, and New York was strenuously ignoring Prohibition. Jack Kriendler and Charlie Berns are gone, but younger brothers, Pete Kriendler and Jerry Berns, will be there, proving, as ever, that nepotism is not always bad.

The biggest days of the holiday season at 21 West 52nd Street are those days in December when, honoring another "21" custom, a Salvation Army band performs in the bar and dining room, accompanied by a full chorus and as many of the regulars as can cram themselves into the low-vaulted room. The caroling is not exactly angelic, but, to the Salvation Army's spiritual joy, "21" revelers are known to make up for their tin ears with fat checks.

A British Banquet

BY PIERRE FRANEY
FOOD COLUMNIST OF *THE NEW YORK TIMES*,
CHEF AND AUTHOR

I like to go to Tavern on the Green around the holidays. With poinsettias and twinkling lights everywhere, it really seems like a storybook Christmas place. Last year I took my four little granddaughters there as a treat. We sat in the big, glass-enclosed garden room, filled with trees and lights and wreaths. Outside, the trees were coated with ice, sending out shards of light in various directions.

During the holidays Kay LeRoy, the British wife of the owner, Warner LeRoy, supervises the menu and all the details for the holiday celebration. It's a traditional English offering of roast goose, wassail, *buche de Noël*, fresh roast turkey, eggnog, and, of course, plum pudding with hard sauce. We tried everything. The girls had a ball.

Glamour and Sentiment

BY PAULA WOLFERT
COOKBOOK AUTHOR

Since I don't have a Christmas tree at home, I love the holiday glitter at Maxwell's Plum. In many ways, the place may be too glitzy, but it is just the opposite of my reserved self, and I love it. Maxwell's makes me feel like it really is Christmas.

I tend to get quite sentimental at this time of year when I go to certain places. The reception you get at a restaurant is important. There are a couple of restaurants in town where I know the owners and they make me feel especially welcome. Le Cherche-Midi is one of them. Sally Scoville, the owner, is like family to me, and the restaurant is such a homey place.

When you think about it, we are all strangers in New York, and we tend to seek out those few places where we feel loved and cared for. My feeling is that all of us should find restaurants we like and patronize them. That way we'll have a home away from home any time—but especially at Christmas.

An Italian Interlude

BY BRYAN MILLER
RESTAURANT CRITIC OF *THE NEW YORK TIMES*

The holidays are more a matter of attitude than ambience. For me the magic of the season is in the special conviviality it brings out in certain restaurateurs. When I am looking for a blue-plate special of Christmas cheer, I often go to Nanni Al Valletto.

Nanni Al Valletto—*valletto* means footman—is an expensive East Side restaurant where the food is usually exceptional. What makes it special, though, is the staff. They are starched and efficient but they are warm and friendly, too, never brusque or obsequious.

My reception starts at the small front bar where Dante, the rotund and risible bartender, offers a big smile—and probably a lame joke. This time of year, he may be wearing a bow tie with flashing lights or a silly New Year's Eve paper hat.

Luigi Nanni, who can be Napoleonic in temperament and bearing when he chooses, appears in stiff kitchen whites and suggests a special pasta. Perhaps homemade ravioli stuffed with fresh vegetables or a pasta topped with fragrant porcini mushrooms imported from Italy. I always go along with his recommendations.

There are two dining areas, each with its own charm: an intimate area up front with creamy beige banquettes and about five tables, and a majestic main room with gold-striped beige silk walls and a stunning fifteenth-century Venetian tapestry.

Nico, the maître d', and Antonio, one of the captains,

Holiday Fare

American Festival Café, 20 West 50th Street
(212-246-6699). Open for breakfast, lunch, dinner, and late
supper Monday through Friday, for brunch and dinner
Saturday and Sunday. Open Christmas Eve and Christmas.
All major credit cards.

Coach House, 110 Waverly Place (212-777-0303). Open
for dinner Tuesday through Sunday. Open Christmas Eve.
All major credit cards.

Four Seasons, 99 East 52nd Street (212-754-9494). Open
Monday through Saturday for lunch, dinner, and late
supper. Closed Christmas Eve and Christmas. All major
credit cards.

La Tulipe, 104 West 13th Street (212-691-8860). Open
Tuesday through Sunday for dinner. Closed Christmas Eve
and Christmas Day. All major credit cards.

Le Cherche-Midi, 936 First Avenue between 51st and
52nd streets (212-355-4499). Open for lunch Monday
through Friday and for dinner Monday through Saturday.

provide impeccable service. If you are in their hands, the
menu is superfluous. "Just talk to me," Antonio will say.
"Tell me what you want and we'll make it."

Stay late some evening when there is a special party. You
just might see one of the other waiters put down his tray and
sing Italian love songs in a romantic tenor voice. If that is not
the holiday spirit, what is?

Closed Christmas Eve and Christmas. VISA and MasterCard.

Maxwell's Plum, 1181 First Avenue at 64th Street (212-628-2102). Open daily for lunch, dinner, and late supper. Open Christmas Eve and Christmas. All major credit cards.

Nanni Al Valletto. 133 East 61st Street (212-838-3939). Open for lunch Monday through Friday and for dinner Monday through Saturday. Closed Christmas Eve and Christmas. All major credit cards.

Russian Tea Room, 150 West 57th Street (212-265-0947). Open daily for lunch, dinner, and late supper. Open Christmas Eve and Christmas. All major credit cards.

Tavern on the Green, Central Park West and 67th Street (212-873-3200). Open daily for lunch, dinner, and late supper. Open Christmas Eve and Christmas. All major credit cards.

"21" Club, 21 West 52nd Street (212-582-7200). Open Monday through Saturday for lunch and dinner. Open Christmas Eve, closed December 23 and 25. All major credit cards.

PART 7

The Outer Boroughs

CHAPTER 40

....

Utopia in the Outer Boroughs

BY PAUL GOLDBERGER

New Yorkers sometimes say that Middle America begins at the East River, that once you get outside Manhattan the rest of New York starts to look, if not quite like other places, a lot more ordinary, a lot more mundane, a lot more like Trenton or Hartford or Erie, Pennsylvania, than like the most intense city in the world. Hardly. While it is true that the voltage level drops noticeably in Brooklyn and Queens and the Bronx, and descends to almost nothing in Staten Island, the tranquility is deceptive. The outer boroughs, as they are forever destined to be called (even by their own residents, who persist in describing trips to Manhattan as "going to the city"), are as characteristic of New York, in their way, as the skyscrapers of Madison Avenue.

While they may no longer be beacons of prosperity, and in more than a few cases they contain poverty more devastating than anything on Manhattan Island, it is not the slums of Brooklyn and the Bronx that I am talking about. It is the concept of the city that these places represent, as ambitious as midtown, aspiring to all the grandeur and nobility of any city in the United States.

The boroughs are not a unified place, of course, but several dozen disparate neighborhoods. Not only is Brooklyn different from the Bronx, so is the Grand Concourse different from Grand Army Plaza, Sunnyside Gardens different from Forest Hills Gardens. They grew up at different times and in different ways; these places did not look alike when they were new, and they do not look alike now. What ties them all together is that sense of aspiration; for more than anything else, the outer boroughs embody the dreams of the middle class, and the way in which those dreams were translated into concrete reality.

It is not very fashionable any longer to think of cities in terms of hope. They seem to represent satisfaction to those who have arrived and despair to those who have not, with little room for those who fall in between. But the outer boroughs are where the hopes of New York, for generations, have been focused.

And it was in the outer boroughs that this country came as close as it has ever come to making a truly noble city for the middle class. Monuments, parks, boulevards, planned communities, and grand vistas exist elsewhere, but nowhere else on this scale and in this quantity. The Grand Concourse in the Bronx, Eastern Parkway and Ocean Parkway and Grand Army Plaza in Brooklyn, Forest Hills Gardens in Queens— they are among the grandest urban gestures in this country. There is nothing in Manhattan to compare with them.

Collectively, these places constitute a true public realm. In the great era of New York as a middle-class city, a time that ran from the late nineteenth century to around the end of World War II, the city of the middle class was not merely one of rows and rows of little houses and little yards, each set apart from the other. Neither was it rows of brownstones squeezed tightly together. There were plenty of those, and there still are, but there were also open spaces: stately avenues and squares among the individual buildings, a commitment to a kind of shared grandeur. In the end, it is the belief in some sort of public realm that distinguishes a city from the suburbs, and it was the commitment to a genuine and noble public realm that made New York's outer boroughs so different from other places.

Take, for example, the Grand Concourse in the Bronx. The name itself resonates with bourgeois respectability: The very words call to mind the dreams of the middle class, for whom the boulevard constituted, in the 1920s, an escape from the slums of Manhattan, a confirmation that one was no longer poor but solidly established. Here, in fact, is the whole story—the ambitious beginnings, success, decline, and, quite recently, as a kind of coda to the main drama, some glimmers of renewed hope. It is an ongoing story, as much as anything in Manhattan; but for now, look at the past.

The original name was more ambitious still—the Grand Boulevard and Concourse is what the engineer Louis Risse called it in the 1890s, when he proposed a wide road to connect Manhattan with the city's newly acquired parkland in the Bronx. Inspired by the boulevards of Baron Georges Haussmann in Paris, Risse envisioned a "speedway," a protohighway that would run more than four miles along one of the high ridges that remind us that the Bronx is the beginning of upstate New York, with bridges leaping across breaks in the ridge and local streets passing below.

The eight-lane Concourse opened in 1909, when the Bronx was still semirural, so in its first years it was as much a scenic highway as anything else. But in the building boom after World War I, the West Bronx sprawled and the Concourse was its spine. Six-story apartment buildings lined the wide street, the earliest vaguely classical in style and the later ones, by the end of the 1920s, Art Deco. It was not great architecture (despite its current vogue), but the streamlined Art Deco buildings did seem to epitomize the sense of freshness, of newness, that the Concourse represented. It was big and wide and open and full of light, and if you came from Hester Street or Rivington Street on the Lower East Side, you felt that you had moved into another world.

Now the Grand Concourse exudes something less than prosperity, something more than despair—while it is hardly a slum to escape from, it is no longer the haven immigrants struggle to escape to. The windows tell us everything: There are some Art Deco apartment houses with their original casement windows still intact, but they are the deteriorated buildings; there are others with new, double-hung windows, an architectural aberration but a sign of renewal nonetheless; and there is a handful of buildings with no windows at all but with the mock-window decals the city has been using to mask abandonment. The whole range is there, from remnants of things as they were to total decay to the beginnings of resurgence.

The mood is more so even on Ocean Parkway, one of the two great boulevards in Brooklyn laid out by Frederick Law Olmsted and Calvert Vaux, the designers of Central Park and that vast Brooklyn oasis they considered superior to it, Prospect Park. Ocean Parkway runs from Prospect Park to

Coney Island. It is wide, sumptuous, and full of trees. As on the Grand Concourse, there is a main central roadway, wide side islands, and side service lanes. Here, too, the architecture is commonplace, but the well-kept buildings come together to create a strong and self-assured public space.

Better still, at least as a work of urban design, is Olmsted and Vaux's Eastern Parkway, which runs from Grand Army Plaza across Crown Heights and on into the slums of East New York. The architecture is better: imposing public buildings like McKim, Mead & White's Brooklyn Museum at the beginning, a few medium-size apartment houses gaining in grandeur from their presence on this boulevard and, best of all, block after block of nineteenth-century row houses with rounded front bays. Much of Eastern Parkway—sociologically a curious mix of West Indian, black, and Hasidic communities—is sadly deteriorated, but the underlying sumptuousness of the place is overpoweringly evident. At its best, this street ranks with Commonwealth Avenue in Boston, and it makes Park Avenue in Manhattan seem almost mean and dark.

It was also Olmsted and Vaux who laid out the greatest public square in Brooklyn, perhaps in the city: Grand Army Plaza, the main entrance to Prospect Park. Here the expansive vistas denied by Manhattan's squeezed landscape become possible. At the hub of a huge oval stands the monumental Soldiers' and Sailors' Memorial Arch. Completed in 1892, the arch was the work of John H. Duncan, designer of Grant's Tomb; the sculpture around and atop it was done by Frederick MacMonnies, better remembered as the creator of the statue of *Civic Virtue* for City Hall, a male nude that so offended the public that it was banished to Queens, where it now stands about a block from Borough

Hall. The classical temples, pavilions, railings, and urns that edge the park itself were designed by Stanford White.

It is not the Arc de Triomphe, to be sure, but that is less because of the arch itself than because the buildings surrounding it do not come together to make as tightly woven an urban fabric as the buildings around the Place de l'Étoile in Paris: The monument itself is the greatest classical grouping in New York City, capable of anchoring Park Avenue better than Grand Central Terminal does, but here, surrounded by largely indifferent structures of varying sizes, the arch is an anchor in shifting sands.

Its power, though, still holds when it is approached from Flatbush Avenue, pulling the eye up and toward the park. From there, it stands as a reminder of nineteenth-century Brooklyn's certainty that it would become—indeed, already was—a noble city. So, too, with the great neo-Gothic gateway to Green-Wood Cemetery on Fifth Avenue at 25th Street, Richard Upjohn's exclamation point in stone that is surely the triumph of the nineteenth-century Gothic revival in New York City.

It was not just Brooklyn that managed to create individual monuments of such significance (though Brooklyn also has the Dime Savings Bank at Fleet and DeKalb and the Williamsburg Savings Bank on Broadway, two of the most splendid places anyone has ever had to stash his pennies).

The largesse of the late nineteenth and early twentieth centuries went far beyond Brooklyn's borders. The Bronx, for example, has the prancing glass forms of the Enid A. Haupt Conservatory in the New York Botanical Garden, a building that is New York's most monumental greenhouse, handsomely restored by the architect Edward Larrabee Barnes in 1978. It has the overpowering brick mass of

Kingsbridge Armory, said to be the world's largest, a galumphing pile of masonry that, like the conservatory, has an amiability unexpected in buildings of that size. And it has the embracing curve of Orchard Beach, a man-made shoreline in the eastern reaches of the Bronx that has proved to be one of Robert Moses's unquestioned achievements as New York City Parks Commissioner.

Also in the Bronx are Stanford White's buildings for New York University's uptown campus (now Bronx Community College), a set of classical temples overlooking the Harlem River that brings to vivid reality turn-of-the-century visions of civic grandeur. The central building, Gould Memorial Library, is a kind of pantheon, surrounded by the long, curving colonnade of one of the most remarkable places in New York, the Hall of Fame for Great Americans. It is a place of almost touching earnestness. Between classical columns, busts of Henry Clay, James Greenleaf Whittier, Harriet Beecher Stowe, and other celebrated Americans survey the vista across the Harlem River. They sit quietly and invisibly, for the colonnade is now inaccessible to the public; signs say Closed for Reconstruction, though the easygoing guard says he knows of no reconstruction, and there is no evidence of work in progress. Still, it is hard to think of another site where inspiration for the middle class has been made more literal than in this acropolis of great visages.

The plazas, arcades, and boulevards that embody the public realm were intended as points of relief from the denser, tighter cityscape of brownstones and row houses, though in some ways the most potent public spaces in the outer boroughs have always been the streets themselves, the stoops and steps and the curbs that line up along them. But the living spaces inside the old brownstones and tenements have never been the most civilized, and there is a long history of attempts to create alternatives.

Some of the best model housing (complexes designed to demonstrate the feasibility of other approaches) anywhere in the United States was built in the outer boroughs, and most of it still exists. In Sunnyside Gardens in Queens, for example, three of the greatest names in twentieth-century utopian housing, architects Clarence Stein and Henry Wright and socially conscious developer Alexander Bing, joined forces to create a twelve-hundred-unit apartment complex intended to test the garden-city theories of Sir Ebenezer Howard, the English city planner. Completed in 1924, Sunnyside has a simple and direct plan. It groups apartment units closely together as a means of freeing land for common use. The low-rise brick buildings are plain, almost dreary, but the sober face they turn toward the street is altogether in contrast to the lush, landscaped courtyards inside each block. The courts are large and parklike, with most of the space given over to central communal areas, although in the late 1970s, when fifty-year covenants on the open space expired, some residents of Sunnyside decided to turn parts of it into more conventional private backyards.

While there is not much architectural distinction to Sunnyside, there is a balance between the individual and the community, between the private and the public, that is altogether magnificent. Just as good on that score, and better as architecture, is a complex just a few blocks away, also designed by Clarence Stein: Phipps Garden Apartments, a sort of Art Moderne château in red brick with an intricate, richly landscaped inner courtyard that is truly one of New York's hidden wonders.

Much more suburban than Sunnyside Gardens and

Phipps, but every bit as uplifting, are two early communities of detached houses: Prospect Park South in Flatbush, Brooklyn, and Forest Hills Gardens in Queens. Prospect Park South is one of the great surprises of the New York cityscape—fifteen blocks of gracious, rambling turn-of-the-century houses on wide, tree-lined streets, just yards from the harsher streets of central Brooklyn. To enter it is to move in one step from urban tensions to an almost rural sense of ease.

It was planned in 1889 by Dean Alvord, a developer who envisioned it as a place in which "people of intelligence and good breeding" might find comfortable, esthetically pleasing homes reasonably close to downtown Brooklyn and Manhattan. Alvord laid out Prospect Park South with wide streets, in some cases with malls down the middle; he ordered trees planted at the property line just inside the sidewalk, creating the illusion that the streets were as wide as boulevards. He put all utility lines into the ground before the houses were built, a dramatic advance for his time, and he ordained a series of design guidelines to assure that the houses of Prospect Park South were compatible with one another.

The result was, and remains, an unusually serene, restful place. Within the gateposts that mark the entrances to the community lie a number of first-rate houses, most of which remain in superb condition. Among the best are the stately colonnaded mansions of Albemarle Road, those northern, urban versions of Tara. But there is considerable stylistic variation, from Queen Anne to the Shingle Style to a house with a vaguely Japanese motif.

There is frequently some sort of angel behind utopian communities; rare is the case in which a profit-minded de-

veloper, such as Dean Alvord, creates an ideal project within
the confines of the real estate market. Yet Forest Hills Gardens had a philanthropic backer committed to improving
the physical environment of the masses. The Russell Sage
Foundation purchased a large plot of land and in 1913 began
to build what it thought would be housing for the working
classes. Grosvenor Atterbury, designer of the John S.
Phipps house in Manhattan, was hired as architect, and
Frederick Law Olmsted, Jr., and John Charles Olmsted as
landscape architects.

The foundation's plan did not work, for the reason that it
worked too well: Atterbury and the Olmsted firm created a
garden suburb of such quality that Forest Hills Gardens
quickly developed into one of the city's choicest residential
enclaves, and so it remains today. Loosely English Tudor in
style, this epitome of the garden suburb is built around a
central square that is tied into the Forest Hills station of the
Long Island Railroad. The square is a wonderful example of
picturesque American eclecticism. It has brick paving and
an arched bridge over one of the streets leading into it, as
well as a handsome, roundtopped tower to serve as a symbol
of the entire project. It is almost a storybook version of an
English village—but good enough so that it never appears
precious or cute.

What about the present? Sunnyside Gardens is more than
half a century old. Forest Hills Gardens older still. Prospect
Park South and the Brooklyn parkways go back to the nineteenth century. Is there anything now being made in the
outer boroughs that equals these achievements in scope?

There is, and it is on Staten Island, the quietest, most
isolated borough. Always the least dense section of the
city, Staten Island grew rapidly after the opening of the

Verrazano-Narrows Bridge in 1964 tied it to the rest of the city. Most of the growth was a disaster from the standpoint of planning—cheaply built, garish houses, hastily erected on what had been forest land, brought Staten Island in one step from rural tranquility to the worst of suburbia. A decade ago it looked as though the entire borough would be paved over with flat, treeless streets, or with six-lane expressways, like the one that was planned to slice right through the remaining forested open space in the island's heart. High-rise apartment towers were almost built on the site of an old Girl Scout camp adjacent to Ohrbach Lake, a tranquil treasure that could be in the midst of the Adirondacks. Now that old camp is High Rock Park Conservation Center, a seventy-two-acre city park containing a swamp, forests, streams, and hiking trails. The expressway was stopped abruptly at the edge of the forest. And the city, through a series of legal provisions, is establishing the Staten Island Greenbelt, a set of loosely connected open spaces that is to remain either undeveloped or lightly developed in perpetuity.

The Greenbelt will be a mixture of city- and state-owned lands and private property that will remain private but will have sharp restrictions placed on its development. The proposed Greenbelt will include Latourette Park, Staten Island's largest; the now abandoned Farm Colony, where the poor were once housed in landmark-quality buildings; as well as the grounds of Seaview Hospital and Home, Willowbrook Park, Kaufmann Camp, and the former estate of the architect Ernest Flagg, where a developer is now constructing a small suburban subdivision superbly designed by the architect Robert A. M. Stern. The setting aside of these portions of Staten Island as the Greenbelt—already thirteen hundred acres, and which may someday total as much as six thousand—is a major political and social triumph, not only for the cause of open space and guided development, but also for the extension into our time of the impulses that inspired the design of Prospect Park, Central Park, and the Grand Concourse. It stands a reminder that the city cannot exist solely as a series of separate, disconnected private worlds.

The dream of the public realm is not as vivid now as it was seventy-five or a hundred years ago, when the noblest public gestures in the outer boroughs were made; the financial realities of this strapped city are but one reason its brightness has dimmed. But the dream has not vanished altogether. We are realizing again that there is a need for a public life. It took very little, once, to give the city a sense of grandeur and permanence—more than money, it took a belief in the future. And that is what, in the last few years, the city is beginning to have once again.

A Walking Tour of Park Slope

With its fine collection of brownstones and row houses, Park Slope may be New York City's most beautiful neighborhood. There is a consistency and a level of quality rarely matched in Manhattan brownstones—here the houses go on for block after block, visually varied so there is never a sense of monotony, yet similar enough to create a sense of unity, a sense of place.

Park Slope is also one of the great recent success stories of the outer boroughs, an urban neighborhood that acquired a solid, family-oriented, middle-class identity in the late 1960s and early 1970s and has managed to hold on to that identity in the decade since. It has not become an enclave of the rich, as so many parts of the Upper West Side of Manhattan have done, but neither has its economic base slipped away. While gentrification is never without its price, in Park Slope the cost seems to have been lower than in many other parts of the city and the benefits greater.

Park Slope was an upper-middle-class neighborhood in its first incarnation, in the late 1880s and early 1890s. That was more or less the time the Upper West Side of Manhattan was developing as well, and there are recognizable similarities between the two areas; both are certainly among the city's showcases for row-house architecture.

It was a great time to build this kind of urban neighborhood. There existed a commitment not only to quality in the design of individual houses, but also to the concept of a noble public environment, particularly in Brooklyn, where even a century ago there was a greater sense of available space than in Manhattan. At the edge of Prospect Park and Grand Army Plaza, the Park Slope neighborhood is an almost perfect blend of private elegance and public grandeur—and most of it survives intact.

Begin your walk—and it should be a walk, even if you choose to travel to Park Slope by car (many of these are one-way streets)—at the entrance to the IRT Grand Army Plaza subway station at the intersection of Flatbush Avenue and Plaza Street West. There is a large newsstand right at the corner to mark the spot. Note that Plaza Street encircles Grand Army Plaza (there seems something particularly Brooklyn-like about the plainness of its name; it could have been Plaza Circle or Plaza Crescent, but instead it is just good old, workaday Plaza Street).

From this corner, when the trees are bare, you can see in

the plaza the noble Soldiers' and Sailors' Memorial Arch, designed by John H. Duncan and completed in 1892, with a Frederick MacMonnies sculpture atop it and Stanford White columns around it. The monument is large in scale, although not, in fact, large enough to anchor the long vista up wide Flatbush Avenue and the huge size of Grand Army Plaza itself. In the foreground, as you look toward the memorial, part of the elaborate classical composition around the arch is the city's only official memorial to John F. Kennedy, dating from 1965. It consists of a bust of the late president by Neil Estern in a modest setting by Morris Ketchum, Jr., rather too small for this grandiose plaza. There is also a fountain from 1932 designed by Edgerton Swarthwout with sculpture by Eugene Savage. (If you choose to inspect these monuments at closer range, it is safest to walk along Plaza Street West to the intersection with Union Street and cross the busy traffic circle at the signal, then retrace your steps to the newsstand.)

To begin the architectural tour, walk into Park Slope along Plaza Street West, away from Flatbush Avenue. It is an atypical introduction to this intense concentration of brownstones, for the first town houses you will see are not brownstones at all but limestone-fronted houses, the group of four at 5–11 Plaza Street. In the distance, around the curve of Plaza Street, you can see some of the few Brooklyn apartment buildings that resemble those built in Manhattan in the 1920s.

The first apartment house you will see, however, is a mediocre six-story structure hardly worthy of its Plaza Street address. Ignore it, and look instead at one of Brooklyn's greatest architectural treasures, on the near corner of Plaza Street and Lincoln Place. The Montauk Club is a Venetian

Gothic palazzo by Francis H. Kimball, completed in 1891. It fronts on Eighth Avenue, but a generous, swooping bay faces you on Plaza Street, richly ornamented in terra-cotta. The model for the Montauk Club was the Ca' d'Oro in Venice, but here the motifs recall the Montauk Indians, a Long Island tribe.

Turn right on Lincoln Place and walk down to Eighth Avenue to see the Montauk Club's more formal facade; this is truly a building you like better and better the more you see of it. Then turn left on Eighth Avenue. Now you are in real Park Slope brownstone territory: tree-lined streets with splendid houses, many of them with four full stories atop a high ground floor, and most of them in superb condition with original stoops. Most, but not all, of the houses have projecting bays, rounded or three-sided, an architectural device that served not only to increase space within the house, but also to enliven the streetscape by providing a continuous rhythm and avoiding the flatness of so many Manhattan brownstone streets.

Walk south on Eighth Avenue past numbers 64 and 66, between Berkeley Place and Union Street, a pair of houses designed by Parfitt Brothers and built in 1889. Their rich, swirling ornamentation recalls the designs of Louis Sullivan. The next block, between Union and President Streets, has given way to apartments on its west side, but fine, high brownstones still hold the entire block on the east. In most cases the houses are set back behind small front gardens, a further anomaly to eyes accustomed to the tightness of space on Manhattan row-house blocks.

Continue beyond President Street to Carroll Street, past the neoclassical mansion at 105 Eighth Avenue that is now the Montessori Academy (Helme & Huberty, 1916); it has a bit less grace than that style usually produced, but the mock portico, actually a huge front bay with classical columns and entablature, is unusual.

Turn left at Carroll Street. Immediately on your left is 117 Eighth Avenue, one of the city's richest and most picturesque late-nineteenth-century houses. The architect was C. P. H. Gilbert, the year 1888, the client Thomas Adams, Jr., the Chiclets chewing gum magnate. The architecture is best described as Louis Sullivan meeting Henry Hobson Richardson with a nod to Queen Anne. The entry is through a Sullivanesque arch cut into the rough-hewn brownstone base, the corner is marked by a round mass that turns into a multisided turret as it rises, and the house culminates in a frontal gable with a burst of ornamentation.

Continue up Carroll. This is very much C. P. H. Gilbert's street. He was an active Manhattan architect who designed the Felix M. Warburg Mansion on Fifth Avenue (now the Jewish Museum), among other projects. But his work elsewhere never achieved the degree of success it did in Park Slope, where he, more than any other single figure, gave the neighborhood its picturesque quality. Number 838 is a Gilbert house, and so are 842 and 846 Carroll Street; they are all variations on the Romanesque theme, consistently inventive. If you doubt Gilbert's skill, look for comparison at the houses at 856 and 858 Carroll Street. They are surprisingly flat and dull; the entry arches here do not pull you into a deep space, but seem merely to be two-dimensional openings poked through a thin wall. But Gilbert's massive, cavelike Romanesque is not the only approach. Look at Stanley M. Holden's 1892 buildings at 855 and 861 Carroll. These houses are lighter and thinner, with exquisite, layered arches of brick.

At the top of Carroll Street, where it intersects Prospect Park West, look far to the left for the best view of all of the great arch: The MacMonnies sculpture group looks from here as if it is about to march right into the park. There are two fine classical houses just to your left, 16 and 17 Prospect Park West. Note the curious detail at the front entrance of Number 16: a pair of Ionic columns stop short of the heavy lintel above the door, leaving a space to be filled in with extra ornamental pieces.

Turn back, away from the arch, and walk along Prospect Park West past another pair of limestone-fronted classical houses, numbers 18 and 19, built in 1898 and designed by Montrose W. Morris. Number 18 has a particularly fine half-spherical canopy of bronze and glass and a handsome three-part Palladian window; and the pattern of rustication in the stone, a set of angled, parallel lines, is particularly unusual.

Turn right at the next block, Montgomery Place, past 27 Prospect Park West, a fine 1920s apartment building with a marble lobby to equal almost any in Manhattan. Montgomery Place was created mainly by C. P. H. Gilbert, working with a real estate developer, Harvey Murdock, who envisioned an especially picturesque street. Worth particular note are Number 47 (R. L. Daus, 1890), a rich reddish brownstone, and a long row from Number 36 to Number 46 by Gilbert. Number 46 is a likably eccentric composition in Roman brick; numbers 40, 42, and 44 have ornamental brickwork recesses yielding an unusual staccato effect. Numbers 32 to 34 (Robert Dixon, 1896) are similar architecturally to many of the other houses, but the materials—white brick and white terra-cotta—make for a dramatically differ-

If You Go

The Brooklyn Museum, 200 Eastern Parkway at Washington Avenue (718-638-5000). Hours: Monday, Wednesday through Friday, 10 A.M. to 5 P.M.; Saturday, 11 A.M. to 6 P.M.; Sunday, 1 P.M. to 6 P.M. Suggested contribution: adults, $2, students and senior citizens, $1. (Children under twelve, free.) The outdoor sculpture garden features permanent installations of architectural remnants from various periods of New York history.

Brooklyn Botanic Garden, 1000 Washington Avenue (718-622-4433). Hours: April 1 to September 30, Tuesday through Friday, 8 A.M. to 6 P.M.; Saturday, Sunday, and holidays, 10 A.M. to 6 P.M.; October 1 to March 31, Tuesday through Friday, 8 A.M. to 4:30 P.M.; Saturday, Sunday, and holidays, 10 A.M. to 4:30 P.M. Grounds and conservatory open Thanksgiving, Christmas, and New Year's Day. Free Admission. Tour of the gardens Sunday at 1 P.M. except the Sunday following Thanksgiving.

The Park Slope establishments listed on the opposite page offer food and drink.

ent effect. And be sure to note Number 18, another Gilbert house, with a splendid stepped-back gable at the top.

Montgomery Place ends at Eighth Avenue opposite one of Park Slope's few Art Deco apartment houses, this one of an orange brick that joins it neatly to the Romanesque houses around it. Turn right on Eighth Avenue and left again on Carroll Street to see one of the most unified blocks anywhere in the city—a long array of three-story brownstones with

Charlie's, 350 Flatbush Avenue between Sterling Place and Eighth Avenue (718-857-4585). Opens at 4 P.M. daily; 11:30 A.M. to 3:30 P.M. Sunday for brunch.

J. T. McFeely's, 847 Union Street off Seventh Avenue (718-638-0099). Opens 5 P.M. daily; 11:30 A.M. to 3 P.M. Sunday for brunch.

Le Parc Gourmet, 743 Carroll Street at Seventh Avenue (718-857-2600). Open daily 11 A.M. to 11 P.M.

Minsky's, 222 Seventh Avenue at 3rd Street (718-499-2311). Open Sunday through Thursday, 11:30 A.M. to midnight; Friday and Saturday, 11:30 A.M. to 1 A.M.

New Prospect Café, 393 Flatbush at Eighth Avenue (718-638-2148). Opens at 5 P.M. Monday; 11:30 A.M. Tuesday through Saturday; 10:30 A.M. Sunday.

Raintree's, 142 Prospect Park West at 9th Street (718-768-3723). Opens at 5 P.M. daily; 11:30 A.M. to 3:30 P.M. Sunday for brunch.

Snooky's Pub, 140 Seventh Avenue between Carroll Street and Garfield Place (718-788-3245). Opens at 11 A.M. every day.

stoops, absolutely unbroken, which create a perfect nine-teenth-century street rhythm. The houses are a slight bit more modest here than in the block east of Eighth Avenue, but not by much, and their unity is remarkable. This is truly the urban street, as a whole vastly greater than the sum of its parts.

You can continue along Carroll Street for the rest of the block to the neighborhood's main commercial street, Seventh Avenue, which has numerous restaurants and cafés. Or take Eighth Avenue back to the subway at Grand Army Plaza. Or travel by subway or on foot (through the park or around Grand Army Plaza, past the streamlined Beaux-Arts mass of the Brooklyn Public Library at the intersection of Flatbush Avenue and Eastern Parkway) to two of Brooklyn's great cultural attractions, the Brooklyn Museum and the Brooklyn Botanic Garden.

CHAPTER 41

································

Brooklyn's "Little Odessa"

BY BRYAN MILLER

There aren't many beaches this side of the Baltic Sea where sunbathers can cool off at a boardwalk food stand with a chilled bowl of beet-red borscht and sour cream. In the Brighton Beach section of Brooklyn, not only can bathers do that, at a takeout lunch stand called Gastronom Moscow, but they can also walk a block away to restaurants that serve such Russian specialties as Caucasian lamb casserole, grilled chicken with walnut sauce, Ukrainian dumplings, mutton soup, *piroshki*, and, of course, caviar and iced vodka.

Brighton Beach is one of the newer patches in New York City's colorful ethnic quilt, a home for an estimated twenty-five thousand Russian immigrants, most of whom are Jewish and have arrived in the past few years. They have brought to this once-fading seaside neighborhood of older Jewish couples and younger Hispanic families their exotic alphabet, uplifting music, and megacaloric foods.

Once referred to as the Nice of New York because of its

broad urban beach, the area's new nickname, "Little Odessa," is now more appropriate. Many of the immigrants come from that Ukrainian city on the Black Sea, which they say in some ways resembles this seaside neighborhood. The feel of this corner of the city can best be experienced on a stroll along Brighton Beach Avenue, where most of the Russian-owned stores can be found.

One of the more bustling spots is M. & I. International Food on Brighton Beach Avenue, sort of the Ukrainian version of Zabar's. It is a two-level store that stocks a wide variety of Russian- and American-style smoked fish, sausages, cold cuts, canned goods, breads, pastries, and candies.

On a recent afternoon the downstairs meat counter was thick with animated Russian women calling orders to a half-dozen employees behind the counter. Except for the bountifully stocked display counters and some boxes of American breakfast cereal, the shop could be a scene in Odessa or Kiev. Virtually all the food signs are in Russian without English subtitles, and not a word of English could be heard. The store was doing a brisk business in Russian-style rolled shoulder of veal seasoned with garlic and black pepper as well as spicy homemade kielbasa and black bread. The phone rang behind the counter, and a woman left her meat slicer to answer. "Sofia, Sofia!" she shouted to Sofia Vinokurov, one of the owners, in a tone suggesting some sort of emergency. "English, English! I am not understanding."

Mrs. Vinokurov, an Odessa native who has been in this country ten years and who speaks English, runs the International as well as a nearby nightclub, the National, which is open on weekends. The businesses are a family affair run by her husband, Naum, her brother, Mark, and other relatives.

Mrs. Vinokurov worked in a factory before coming to this country; her brother was an engineer.

Since most immigrants in Brighton Beach come from the southern Ukraine or Georgia, food in shops and restaurants leans heavily toward those cuisines. There is a strong Middle Eastern influence readily seen in the abundance of lamb shish kebabs as well as dishes with nuts, cumin, and fresh coriander.

"People from Odessa have certain preferences, especially fish," Mrs. Vinokurov explained. "But we have a few things from all over because Russian people come here from all parts of New York City."

Upstairs at the International is devoted to pastries and candies—thick, dense versions of napoleons, meringue balls on cookie bottoms, pastry cones filled with cream, thin chocolate-dipped waffles, and walnuts in sugar syrup. An American's attempt to elicit an explanation for one intriguing-looking dessert—stubby chocolate fingers with little candy decorations—illustrates the frustration non-Russian-speaking customers can face.

"Patata, patata," replied the saleswoman matter-of-factly when asked what they were. "You mean they are made from potatoes?" "Patata, yes, patata." Further research revealed that they were marzipan potatoes, a popular pastry named for their potato shape. A few blocks down Brighton Beach Avenue is a handsome store called Fish Town, owned by Gregory and Raisa Fishilevich. Fish Town specializes in smoked fish prepared Russian style. American smoked fish is "hot smoked," that is, smoked at a temperature of over 110 degrees, which cooks it; Russians prefer "cold-smoked" fish, in which no heat accompanies the smoke, leaving the flesh moister, in some cases almost raw tasting.

The degree of smokiness and saltiness varies, depending on the process. Russians in general prefer less salt than Americans and a light smoky flavor.

Fish Town straddles both sides of the ethnic fence that runs through this community; the front of the shop stocks American-style hot-smoked whitefish, mackerel, and chub, while the back features cold-smoked sturgeon from the Caspian Sea, *kopchonka* (cold-smoked whitefish), Russian lox (cold-smoked salmon trout), and little dried whole fish about the size of perch that Ukrainians peel and eat as a snack.

"It is good with beer, like potato chips," Mr. Fishilevich said. Fish Town is a bargain basement for lovers of fine caviar. Iranian, American, and Russian brands are carried, but it is the Russian varieties—beluga, osetra, and sevruga—that offer the best buys. For example, a four-ounce jar of Russian beluga caviar in Manhattan generally costs $75 or more; here it costs $57.80.

Russian restaurants on the avenue offer comparable bargains. At Primorski, a Georgian-owned establishment, diners can have a three-course lunch for $3.99. It begins with a salad followed by *kharcho*, a robust mutton and rice soup flavored with celery, onions, and fresh coriander. Entrees include poached chicken in a walnut sauce, a staple of Georgian cuisine; *pelmeni*, dumplings filled with ground mutton and onions; *solyanka*, a sprightly lamb stew with green peppers, tomato, onion, and fresh dill; or *shashlik*, skewered lamb or mutton cubes served over sliced white onions and sprinkled with fresh dill.

At Kavkas the specialty is lamb chops on skewers. The tender, flavorful lamb goes well with red bean salad, which is flavored with walnuts, onions, fresh coriander, and vinegar.

Ukrainian-style borscht here is a vegetable and beef soup, served with a dollop of sour cream. Stuffed cabbage, filled with mutton, rice, parsley, and coriander, is also a popular dish. One of the best vegetable preparations is fried eggplant with garlic and coriander. Stolichnaya vodka is served in little cruets.

Nearly all of the Russian restaurants in Brighton Beach share the same décor—stark, almost fortresslike exteriors with few or no windows, and inside, a discothèque atmosphere with lots of mirrors, glittering mirrored balls, and a dance floor.

On a recent weeknight a Russian crooner, who was also a one-man band, sang native songs while patrons of all ages got up and twirled on the dance floor while holding their right hands high over their heads.

Longtime residents of Brighton Beach say they haven't seen this kind of night life in decades. "The Russians have been very good for this area; they have livened things up," said Martin Snyder, a fifty-year resident. "Before they arrived, there was nobody on the street after sundown."

Proponents of Brighton Beach contend the Russian residents suffer an image problem resulting from news reports about the so-called "Russian Mafia." They counter that relatively few immigrants are troublemakers, that the typical Russian-American is an industrious citizen who obeys the law and has helped improve the area. Mr. Snyder points out that in the late 1970s Brighton Beach Avenue was blighted with boarded-up stores; today there are no vacancies.

For the real flavor of big-time Russian entertainment, American style, a visitor must go to one of the weekend nightclubs, like the National. At nine P.M. on a Friday the cavernous hall was filling up with families, teen-agers, and children wearing their evening best.

Each table overflowed with enough food for the Soviet Olympic squad—fifteen plates heaping with *piroshkis*, pickled herring, fried fish, potatoes with dill, tongue and smoked pork, prunes, golden caviar, Georgian chicken casserole, pickled cabbage, an assortment of relishes, and more. A five-piece Russian band warmed up the crowd with pop and traditional songs, followed by two sisters in gold-spangled jump suits who strutted and sang until after midnight.

Throughout the evening more food arrived—three types of shish kebabs, chicken Kiev, varieties of stuffed chicken—and plenty of vodka.

A man who was watching the singers and clapping his hands to the music explained that in his hometown, near Odessa, he was a construction engineer. Since he immigrated to the United States two years ago, he has been working as an elevator operator on Manhattan's West Side.

"In Russia you do not even have control over the type of music you hear at a nightclub," he said, obviously enjoying the sisters' gyrations. "It is difficult sometimes coming to a new place, but, believe me, this is a great country!"

Recipes

The following recipes have been adapted for home use from traditional dishes served in the Brighton Beach neighborhood.

PAN-FRIED EGGPLANTS WITH WALNUT SAUCE

THE SAUCE:

1 cup walnuts
1 tablespoon walnut oil
1 tablespoon white wine
   vinegar
½ onion, coarsely chopped
1 clove garlic, diced

¾ cup chicken stock
Salt and freshly ground pepper
   to taste
1 tablespoon minced fresh dill
1 teaspoon minced fresh
   coriander

THE EGGPLANTS:

2 large eggplants
Coarse kosher salt for draining
   eggplants
¼ cup vegetable oil

3 cloves garlic, minced
1 tablespoon minced fresh
   coriander

1. In a food processor or blender, puree the walnuts until they form a coarse paste. Add the walnut oil, vinegar, onion, garlic, and chicken stock, and process another 30 seconds or until mixture is smooth.

2. Pour the sauce into a mixing bowl. Add salt and pepper to taste. Add dill and coriander, stir well, and chill.

3. Halve the eggplants lengthwise. Sprinkle cut sides with kosher salt, and let them drain for 1 hour. Wipe off the salt with paper towels before cooking.

4. Heat the vegetable oil in a large skillet over medium-high heat. Place eggplants in the skillet, cut side down; reduce heat immediately to low. Cook, covered, for 6 to 8 minutes, or until the cut surfaces of the eggplants are golden brown. Flip the eggplants, and make a deep slash down the center of each. Sprinkle the garlic and coriander evenly into the slashes.

5. Cover and cook for another 8 minutes or until very

soft. Check occasionally to make sure the eggplants do not burn. Gently remove from the skillet to a plate, and let the eggplants cool. Serve at room temperature with the walnut sauce.

Yield: 4 servings.

Note: The sauce can also accompany cold chicken or other vegetables. The recipe yields about 2 cups.

LAMB SHASHLIK
(Grilled marinated lamb)

½ large onion, diced
2 tablespoons minced fresh dill
2 tablespoons minced fresh coriander
1 tablespoon lemon juice
2 tablespoons vegetable oil

Salt and freshly ground pepper to taste
2 cloves garlic, crushed
3 pounds lamb from the leg, cut into large cubes

1. Combine all ingredients for the marinade in a bowl. Add lamb, toss well, and refrigerate overnight.
2. Place lamb cubes on skewers and cook over a charcoal fire until done to taste, 5 to 8 minutes.

Yield: 6 to 8 servings.

PELMENI
(Russian dumplings)

THE DOUGH:

1 egg

¼ cup water

2 cups all-purpose flour

THE FILLING:

1 tablespoon vegetable oil

2 cloves garlic, minced

½ onion, minced

½ pound lean ground lamb

1 tablespoon chopped parsley

2 teaspoons minced fresh dill

½ teaspoon salt

Freshly ground pepper to taste

½ teaspoon paprika

1 cup sour cream

1 tablespoon minced fresh dill

Salt and freshly ground pepper to taste

1. In a mixing bowl, beat the egg with the water. Place the flour in another mixing bowl and make a well in the center. Pour the water-egg mixture into the well, and slowly incorporate with your hands. Knead the dough until smooth, adding water if necessary. It should be soft and not sticky. Cover with plastic wrap, and refrigerate for 1 hour.

2. Heat the oil in a sauté pan over medium-low heat. Add garlic and onion, and cook, stirring often, until they are soft, about 8 minutes. In a bowl, combine the ground lamb, parsley, dill, salt, pepper, paprika, and the onion-garlic mixture. Mix well.

3. Divide the dumpling dough in half; refrigerate one portion. Roll out half on a lightly floured surface, forming a circle about 16 inches in diamter. The dough should be as thin as possible without breaking. Repeat with the other half. Using a cookie cutter or other device, cut out circles about 2½ inches in diameter. You should have about 60 circles.

4. Place about ¼ teaspoon of dumpling filling in the center of each circle. Fold over the dough to form a crescent, and press the edges to seal with your fingers. Fold the two corners of the dumplings so they meet, and secure with your fingers. Place prepared dumplings on a platter, covered, as you go along.

5. Bring a large pot of salted water to a boil. Drop in the dumplings, five or six at a time, and cook until they float to the surface, about 2 to 3 minutes. Remove with a slotted spoon.

6. Combine the sour cream with a tablespoon of fresh minced dill; add salt and pepper to taste. Serve the dumplings warm, accompanied by a dollop of the dill-cream mixture.

Yield: about 60 dumplings (4 to 6 dumplings per serving).

MARZIPAN POTATOES

(Adapted from *The Russian Tea Room Cookbook*, by Faith Stewart-Gordon and Nika Hazelton, Marek, 1981)

THE CHOCOLATE CAKE:

1 cup sifted cake flour
1 cup sugar
¼ teaspoon baking powder
½ teaspoon baking soda
½ teaspoon salt
½ cup water

*2 ounces unsweetened baking
    chocolate*
¼ cup buttermilk
1 egg
½ teaspoon vanilla extract

THE MARZIPAN POTATOES:

5 cups chocolate cake crumbs
  (recipe above)
1 cup finely chopped walnuts
1 tablespoon rum or brandy

½ cup apricot preserves
2 8-ounce cans of almond paste
  at room temperature
½ cup sifted cocoa

1. Preheat oven to 350 degrees.

2. Butter and dust with flour an 8-inch-diameter circular cake pan. In a large bowl, sift together flour, sugar, baking powder, baking soda, and salt.

3. Bring the water to a boil in a saucepan. Chop the chocolate coarsely and add it to the water. Lower the heat and melt the chocolate, stirring constantly. Let it cool for several minutes.

4. Add chocolate to the dry ingredients. Using an electric beater, mix for 1 minute or until well blended.

5. In another mixing bowl, combine egg, buttermilk, and vanilla. Add to the chocolate mixture. Beat again for a minute until smooth. Pour the batter in the cake pan, and bake for 30 to 35 minutes, or until a knife inserted in center comes out clean and the cake pulls away from the sides of the pan. Remove from heat and cool for 10 minutes. Remove from the pan; cool thoroughly on a rack.

6. When the cake is at room temperature, break it up into small pieces. If you have a food processor, place it in the bowl and pulverize it to the texture of fine bread crumbs. This can by done by hand by placing cake pieces in a plastic bag and running over them with a rolling pin.

7. In a third bowl, combine cake crumbs, walnuts, rum, and preserves. Stir with a wooden spoon or your hands and blend thoroughly.

8. Form a ball with ¼ cup of the mixture. You should be able to make about 12 balls. Set aside.

9. Cut the almond paste into 12 pieces. Roll each piece into a little ball.

10. Place one ball of the almond paste between two sheets of wax paper. Roll out each to a 5-inch diameter. Wrap the rounds of almond paste around the chocolate balls. Roll the balls into a roughly oval shape, somewhat like a potato.

11. Place the ovals on a baking sheet, and refrigerate for 40 to 60 minutes to firm up the paste. Roll each oval in cocoa, shaking off excess, and serve at room temperature. You may poke little holes in each oval with a skewer to simulate potato eyes.

Yield: 12 marzipan potatoes.

CHAPTER 42

....

In Queens, a Medley of Latin Flavors

BY BRYAN MILLER

It is six o'clock on a balmy evening, and Jackson Heights is jumping. All along Roosevelt Avenue, in the shadow of the elevated train tracks, the end of another school and workday in Queens is being celebrated with characteristic Latin élan. Salsa music seems to cascade from every other storefront, and a half-dozen strutting teen-agers, infected by the beat as they pass by, break into a whirl of loose-limbed dancing. A moment later, they calmly resume their stroll toward the next sidewalk ballroom.

Over at Cali Viejo, a Colombian restaurant about the size of a Volkswagen van, early diners are drifting in, some of them lured by the powerful scents of onions, garlic, and frying sweet plantains that swirl under the front door and set up a roadblock on 73rd Street.

In an apartment a few blocks away, Tulia Maria Caicedo is soaking oxtail in a deep pot and chopping fresh coriander

409

while preparing a traditional Colombian soup called *san-cocho*.

On 37th Avenue, in a small, narrow butcher shop called El Tata ("Big Daddy"), the owner, Pedro Tatarian, a Uruguayan whose girth testifies to his enthusiasm for the larder on display, is flipping blood-red *chorizo* sausages and plump sweetbreads over a gas grill in the front window. Men from the neighborhood stop by, laugh, and chat with El Tata in machine-gun Spanish, then sit down to dinner at spindly Formica tables crowded against the wall. A black-and-white television set perched above the meat counter broadcasts a soccer match from Madrid, and the diners, who are drinking beer, hoist the cans and hoot every time a team scores.

To a visitor, certain streets in Jackson Heights are nearly indistinguishable from commercial neighborhoods in Bogotá, Lima, Quito, or Buenos Aires. One can walk for blocks without hearing a word of English, and the signs in many retail shops and restaurants make only token concessions to the Anglo tongue. A fish shop on 37th Avenue advertises *bacalao* (cod), *cangrejo* (crab), and *langosta* (phonetically identified as "labster"); produce stands display all sorts of exotic-looking provisions such as the bumpy green vegetable chayote, the dark and fibrous yuca roots, mounds of bright green plantains, yellow-green papayas, and red-tinged mangoes. This neighborhood, which is roughly framed by Junction Boulevard on the east, the Brooklyn-Queens Expressway on the west, Roosevelt Avenue on the south, and the Grand Central Parkway on north, is one of New York City's most culturally diverse (some would say confounding) areas. Tides of ethnic migration have washed over this urban cove so often—first the Irish, Italians, and Jews, then Indians and Orientals, and most recently immigrants from the Caribbean and Central and South America—that the result is a polyglot landscape where a local shopping excursion can expose a visitor to more cultures than a month of nonstop touring abroad.

For the moment, at least, the dominant flavor of Jackson Heights is Latin, an impression that can best be savored through the exotic and colorful foods the residents enjoy. Latin American residents of Jackson Heights are proud of their culinary heritage and eager to introduce it to newcomers. They lament that most outsiders, if they know Jackson Heights at all, associate it with news stories about cocaine arrests and drug-related shoot-outs. The reality, they say, is that of a middle-class neighborhood with its share of urban woes but also with many positive sides that inspire community pride.

"This is a major commercial center for people from all over Central and South America," said Mrs. Caicedo, a native of Cali in southwestern Colombia who has lived in Queens for eighteen years. She commutes to work in Manhattan and in her spare time serves as director of *Via*, a magazine for the Colombian community in New York that is published in Jackson Heights.

While Spanish-speaking residents of the neighborhood come from virtually every country in Central and South America, those from Colombia are most numerous and appear to own the majority of groceries and restaurants in the area. "Colombians are aggressive business people," Mrs. Caicedo said. "They like to own their own places rather than work for someone else."

One evening Mrs. Caicedo invited some Colombian friends over to her apartment for a traditional meal that included *sancocho*, the spicy beef, oxtail, and yuca soup that is seasoned with fresh coriander and scallions; *papas chor-readas*, boiled red potatoes with a sauce of tomatoes and *queso blanco* (Colombian white cheese); coconut-raisin cake, and white cheese with brown-sugar syrup.

"In Cali we never put potatoes in the *sancocho*, but in Bogotá they always do," Mrs. Caicedo explained as she stirred her potatoless soup. *Sancocho* often serves as a main course, perhaps combined with rice and accompanied by a vegetable dish and some cheese.

At Mrs. Caicedo's dinner, a side dish, *papas chorreadas*, provided a simple and tasty counterpoint to the fiery soup. "Whenever you go to a restaurant in Bogotá you get *papas chorreadas*," said Mariella Vega, one of the guests. In Colombia the dish is usually made with an indigenous dark-fleshed potato that is not available in the United States; red potatoes are the closest thing here. They are simply boiled and served with a warm sauce combining chopped ripe tomatoes and diced *queso blanco*. The meal ended with Mrs. Caicedo's raisin-coconut cake flavored with sherry as well as *caspiroletas*, little pastry thimbles filled with homemade syrup.

The first stop on a gastronomic tour of Jackson Heights was Las Americas Bakery on 37th Avenue near 93rd Street, a twenty-year-old family operation that specializes in all sorts of Colombian pastries and breads. Every morning residents on their way to work stop there to pick up a pastry, a cup of coffee, and the morning newspaper. At Las Americas, however, the pastry may be a *buñuelo*, a round cheese, corn, and egg fritter, the coffee is strictly 40-weight Colombian crude, and the newspapers are *El Espectador* from Bogotá, *El Colombiano* from Medellín, and *El Pais* from Cali.

Another specialty at Las Americas is *ponque,* a dark, moist cake made with diced fruit and raisins that have been soaked several weeks in vermouth, eggs, butter, and flour. The *ponque* is moderately sweet, with a strangely pleasant burnt-sugar edge to it. "We cook the sugar until it is dark, but not really burned, to give the cake that color and flavor," explained Hernan Ochoa, one of the owners.

The store does a brisk trade in all varieties of Colombian breads, including *pan de queso,* small, chewy rounds made with white cheese and yuca starch; *almojabanas,* similar to *pan de queso* but with the addition of some rice flour; *pan uva,* sweet bread with raisins; *roscon,* large, doughnut-shaped pastries filled with sweet guava jelly; and *arepas,* the Colombian version of tortillas made with coarse white-corn flour.

Colombian cuisine, like American or French cuisine, is a varied platter that changes dramatically depending on the region of the country. If there are certain common denominators in Colombian food, indeed Latin American food, they are *empanadas* and *tamales.* Some of the best around are at the two Cali Viego restaurants, operated by the same family. At both, the *empanadas,* which are small corn-dough pockets filled with a combination of shredded meat, onions, cumin, and other spices, are deep-fried to greaseless, crispy perfection. They are superb when dipped in some *ají pique,* a sinus-clearing combination of chilies, garlic, fresh coriander, scallions, oil, and vinegar.

The two Cali Viejo restaurants also turn out first-rate *envueltos de maíz* (crispy, honey-sweetened corn and cheese fritters) and *tamales* in the style of southwestern Colombia. While native Colombians may debate endlessly about which style of *tamale* is best—with rice, without rice, with chicken, with pork—to a Yankee novice's taste the Cali version is flawless. This style calls for making a dough with corn flour and potato starch, filling it with peas, chunks of pork, and various spices, then wrapping it in large leaves of plantains. The *tamales* are tied securely and then boiled until the filling is firm.

"Whenever Americans come in and try them, they love them," said Alba Bastidas, one of the owners. At El Kiosco, a restaurant at 89–05 Northern Boulevard, some estimable *tamales* are made with the addition of rice, according to the style of Tolima, the mountainous area southwest of Bogotá. Ruth Romero, a native of Tolima who owns El Kiosco with her husband, Jorge, got the idea for opening a restaurant after making homemade *tamales* for private parties in the neighborhood.

"People started calling me and asking for more and more," said Mrs. Romero, a congenial, enthusiastic woman. "They said, 'Why don't you open a restaurant?' so I did!"

Mrs. Romero makes another savory specialty called *sobrebarriga a la brasa*, flank steak that is tenderized by braising it in water and beer with scallions, garlic, cumin, and pepper, then finishing it over a charcoal grill. The meat is surprisingly tender and flavorful, with a wonderful smoky veneer imparted by the grilling.

When Colombian cooks entertain a crowd, they may serve a dish called *picada*, sort of a Latin smorgasbord combining grilled *morcilla* (blood sausage), *chorizo*, steak, plantains, and deep-fried yuca. Yuca, a tropical root vegetable also known as sweet cassava or sweet manioc, is a staple in the cuisine of many Latin American countries and finds its way into dozens of Colombian dishes.

Frozen yuca often is used by home cooks, Mrs. Romero

explained, because it is so much easier to work with and yields good results. The yuca is cut into strips the size of thick french fries and deep-fried. Served with a sprinkling of salt, they are lighter than french fries and more flavorful.

Aside from certain specialty items like the dark native potatoes, most fruits and vegetables available to Colombians in their home country can be found in Jackson Heights.

"My parents still call me from Colombia all the time and say, 'Can we send you some food from here?' " said Mrs. Romero. "I say, 'Mother, don't bother, we have everything here.' "

Recipes

AJÍ PIQUE
(Hot sauce)

7 scallions, white parts only,
   minced
¼ cup minced fresh coriander
1 tomato, peeled, seeded, and
   minced
1 tablespoon minced hot red or
   green chilies (or to taste)

¼ cup white wine vinegar
¼ cup water
1 tablespoon vegetable
   oil
Salt to taste

Combine all ingredients in a small bowl, and stir well.
Prepare at least a half hour before serving. This sauce will
keep for more than a week tightly covered in the refrigerator.

Yield: about 1½ cups.

SANCOCHO
(Colombian beef and plantain soup)

1½ pounds oxtail, usually sold
   in 2-inch-long pieces
5 scallions
6 large cloves garlic, peeled
   and crushed
10 sprigs fresh coriander
2 tablespoons coarse salt

Paprika to taste
Freshly ground pepper to taste
6 quarts water
1½ pounds lean stew beef, cut
   into bite-size cubes
3 green plantains
1½ pounds frozen yuca

1. Remove all excess fat from the oxtail. In a deep soup
pot, place the oxtail, scallions, garlic, coriander, salt, pep-

per, and paprika. Cover with water, and let stand for 10 minutes.

2. Bring liquid to a rolling boil, and cook for 10 minutes, skimming off the fat. Lower heat, cover, and simmer for 45 minutes.

3. Return soup to a boil, and add the stew beef. Cook for 5 minutes at a low boil while skimming off fat. Return to a simmer, and cook 45 additional minutes.

4. Peel the plantains. Cut them into 2-inch pieces. Add the plantains and the yuca to the soup, one piece at a time, making sure the soup continues to simmer as you add them. Simmer for another 45 minutes. Serve with *ají pique;* diners can add the sauce to the soup to taste. If desired, white rice can be added to the soup at the table.

Yield: 6 to 8 servings.

Note: Frozen yuca can be found in many Spanish groceries.

YUCA FRITA
(Deep-fried yuca)

3 pounds frozen yuca
Salt to taste

3 cups (approximately)
vegetable oil for frying

1. Place the frozen yuca pieces in a large, deep pot. Cover with salted water, bring to a boil, and cook for 15 minutes at a low boil.

2. Carefully remove yuca from the pot, and place the pieces on a large plate. Set aside to cool.

3. When the yuca pieces are cool enough to handle, cut them into strips roughly the size of thick steak fries.

4. Heat about 3 cups of oil in a deep pot or a wok to about 380 degrees. Carefully drop in the yuca pieces, a few at a time, and fry them until they are golden—about 4 minutes. Drain on a paper towel, sprinkle with salt, and serve immediately.

Yield: 6 servings.

PAPAS CHORREADAS
(Potatoes with tomato and cheese sauce)

6 medium-size red potatoes
Salt to taste
1 tablespoon vegetable oil
1 medium-size onion, chopped
1 tomato, peeled, seeded, and
  chopped

Freshly ground pepper to
  taste
1 teaspoon paprika
¼ pound queso blanco (white
  cheese), crumbled

1. Boil the potatoes in lightly salted water for about 20 minutes.

2. Heat the oil in a skillet over medium-high heat, and sauté the onion and tomato, stirring often, for 15 minutes, or until the onion is soft. Season with paprika and pepper.

3. Add crumbled cheese; stir well. Halve the potatoes; serve with sauce.

Yield: 4 to 6 servings.

Note: Queso blanco, a firm, slightly salty white cheese, is sold in many Spanish groceries.

SOBREBARRIGA A LA BRASA
(Flank steak Colombian style)

¾ cup beer
1 onion, chopped
1 teaspoon ground cumin
Salt to taste
¼ teaspoon cayenne pepper

½ green serrano or jalapeño
  pepper, chopped
1 cup water
2 pounds lean flank steak

1. In a large pot, combine beer, onion, cumin, salt, cayenne pepper, and green pepper. Add the water, and bring to a boil. Add the meat, lower heat, cover, and braise the meat until it is very soft and tender—about 1½ to 2 hours, depending on thickness.

2. Drain the meat well, and grill it over a charcoal fire or under a broiler just to heat it and impart a crispy texture. Serve with *ají pique* on the side.

Yield: 4 servings.

TORTA DE COCO
(Coconut cake)

1⅓ cups sweet sherry
9 ounces raisins
2 cups sugar
3 cups water
2 cinnamon sticks
7 ounces unsweetened
    shredded coconut

1 pound cake (recipe below)
10 eggs, separated
2 teaspoons ground cinnamon
Butter for greasing cake
    pan

1. Soak the raisins in sherry. Preheat oven to 375 degrees.

2. In a saucepan, combine sugar, water, and cinnamon sticks. Cook over medium heat until the mixture forms a thick syrup. Add coconut, stir well, and cook over medium heat for 3 minutes, stirring occasionally. Remove from heat and let cool. Remove the cinnamon sticks.

3. Grate the pound cake into a large mixing bowl. Beat the egg yolks, and add them to the pound cake along with the coconut mixture, the raisins and sherry, and the ground cinnamon.

4. Butter a 10-inch-diameter springform cake pan.

5. Beat the egg whites until they form stiff peaks. Fold them into the batter. Pour the batter into the pan, and bake for about 1 hour or until a knife inserted in the center comes out clean.

Yield: 10 to 12 servings.

POUND CAKE

2 cups (1 pound) sweet butter
   at room temperature, plus
   butter for greasing cake pan
1½ cups sugar
9 eggs, separated

2 tablespoons brandy
1 teaspoon vanilla
4½ cups cake flour, sifted
½ teaspoon salt

1. Preheat oven to 325 degrees.

2. With an electric mixer, cream the butter with the sugar until it is fluffy. Add egg yolks one at a time while mixing at medium-high speed; blend well. Stir in brandy and vanilla.

3. Mix the flour and salt. Sift this into the butter-egg mixture, and blend well.

4. Beat egg whites until stiff. Fold whites into the batter with a rubber spatula. Pour this into a buttered 10-inch cake pan, or two smaller ones.

5. Bake for 1 hour, or until a knife inserted in center comes out clean and the cake pulls away from the sides of the pan. Cool on a rack.

Yield: one 10-inch cake.

EMPANADAS

THE FILLING:

½ bay leaf
1 clove garlic, crushed
¼ pound skinless, boneless chicken
1 medium-size potato
1 large onion, chopped
1 tomato, peeled, seeded, and chopped

3 cloves garlic, minced
1 teaspoon ground cumin
¼ teaspoon paprika
Salt and freshly ground pepper to taste
3 tablespoons vegetable oil

1. In a deep pot, place enough water to cover the chicken, and add the bay leaf and crushed garlic. Bring the water to a boil, add chicken, reduce heat, and poach for 15 minutes. Remove the chicken, drain, and set aside.

2. Boil the potato in lightly salted water for about 20 minutes. Remove and set aside.

3. When the potato is cool enough to handle, peel it and cut it into small cubes. Cut up the chicken in the same manner.

4. In a large skillet over medium-high heat, sauté the onion, tomato, minced garlic, cumin, paprika, salt, and pepper in the oil for about 10 minutes. Stir often. Add the diced meat and potato, stir well, heating thoroughly. Set aside.

THE EMPANADA DOUGH:

3 cups (approximately) vegetable oil
2 cups water
2 cups precooked white cornmeal
½ teaspoon salt

1 teaspoon butter at room temperature
1 tablespoon cornstarch or yuca starch
1 teaspoon bijol (optional, see Note)

1. Preheat oil to about 380 degrees in a deep pot or a wok.

2. Boil the water in a saucepan. Place the cornmeal in a large mixing bowl. Pour the boiling water over the meal, and stir vigorously. Add salt, butter, cornstarch, and *bijol,* if desired, and continue mixing until it forms a firm, rubbery dough.

3. When the dough is cool enough to handle, form it into a large ball. Pull away a Ping-Pong-ball-size piece of dough. If the dough seems crumbly, add a splash of water, and work it in with your hands.

4. Place the ball on a layer of plastic wrap over a flat surface. Add another layer of plastic wrap on top. Using a flat plate, press the ball into a thin round approximately 5 inches in diameter. Remove upper layer of plastic wrap. Place about one teaspoon of filling in the center of the round, and fold the dough in half, forming a crescent, by lifting one side of the plastic wrap. It is easier to handle the plastic wrap than the dough itself. Press the edges of the dough gently through the plastic wrap. Seal the *empanada* by running a blunt instrument, such as a butter knife or a spoon, around the curved edge, cutting off excess dough.

5. Gently remove the plastic wrap, and drop the *empanada* into the hot oil. Cook for 2 to 3 minutes, or until the *empanada* is golden brown and crispy. Drain on paper towels, and serve immediately with *ají pique,* the hot sauce.

Yield: 15 to 20 *empanadas.*

Note: Precooked white cornmeal, which is available in many Spanish groceries, is distributed by companies such as Goya, Iberia, and La Venezolana. *Bijol* is a Spanish condiment, usually sold in powdered form, that is also used as a food coloring. It, too, can be found in many Spanish groceries.

CHAPTER 43

Astoria: "Little Greece"

BY FRED FERRETTI

What you notice first in the rectangle of Astoria that has come to be known as "Little Greece" are the signs. Taverna Vraka reads one, Omonoia II another, and Kostas, Olympus, Thessaloniki, Nea Hellas, Aegean, Agrinion, Kalamata, Kiryakos, Ikos Efkerias, Athens, and Zaxaroplasteion, the last a wonderfully convoluted word that is Greek for pastry shop.

The music of the bouzouki and the mournful songs of men come at you from the tavernas and the coffee shops, called *kaffenion,* until the early hours of the morning. You can smell the aromas of rich olive oil and thick, pureelike coffee, of bitter, pungent olives, and sharply salted Halloumi cheeses, of garlic-laced potatoes called *skordalia* and spit-roasted lambs, of *souvlaki* and honey-drenched *baklava.*

This section of western Queens is one of the few places in New York City where you can find a *hypovrychio,* literally a "submarine," a humorous name the Greeks have for a sweet that involves placing a spoonful of sugary mastic resin in a glass of water, then eating and drinking it.

Nowhere else in the city is a morning-after *patsa* available; an eye-opener made from beef tripe, calves' feet, and garlic, boiled together into a soupy stew. "It absorbs everything," says Jerry Haritos, owner of the K & T Meat Market, 37–11 Broadway, Astoria, from which five hundred whole lambs are sold each week. "*Patsa* cures everything."

Little Greece is where Greek and Cypriot immigrants from all over the metropolitan area go for lamb, for that special barbecued preparation of lamb innards called *kokoretsi*, for black olives from the old country, and Gruyère-like *graviera* cheese. Fish markets like Matthew Vrasidas's Hunter of the Sea, at 22–78 31st Street, pile up red mullet and smelts and porgies, fish the Greeks call *barbuni*, *marides*, and *tsipoura*. It is where you can buy *basterma*, dried beef with a hot crust, and the spicy coriander-laden sausages called *sojouk*.

There is dried sage, or *fascomelos*, to make a tea that is said to be good for one's stomach; unsalted *mizithra*, which is like cottage cheese; *feta* cheeses from Thessaly and Bulgaria, and Attiki honey from Athens.

Greek food is far from subtle; its tastes are hearty and sharp, and from Little Greece's best restaurants, Kalyva, Roumeli Taverna, Taygetos, Taverna Vraka, and Athena, come the smells of *avgolemono*, that pungent egg-lemon soup; of *moussaka;* of octopus grilled whole over charcoal, and squid deeply fried in olive oil, of lamb baked with ricelike pasta called *orzo;* of *pastitsio*, a casserole of ground lamb and cheese, and of *saganaki*, which is sharply salted *kefalotiri* cheese that is served fried or grilled.

Thus surrounded, it becomes not at all difficult to imagine that you have been dropped into an Athenian byway, perhaps in the streets of Plaka, and like that lively and aromatic enclave of traditional Athens, Little Greece never closes.

According to Robert Nicolaides, a director and board member of the Hellenic-American Neighborhood Action Committee, a government-funded community group charged with helping immigrants become assimilated, there are approximately eighty thousand Greeks and Greek-Americans living in Astoria, many of whom in recent years have come from Cyprus as well.

Scattered through the area bounded roughly by Ditmars Boulevard to the north, 31st Street to the west, Steinway Street to the east, and Broadway to the south are eleven Greek Orthodox churches, from the starkly modern poured-concrete church of SS. Catherine and George Church to the high-domed orange brick Byzantine church of St. Demetrios, which is more than fifty years old and boasts the largest Greek Orthodox congregation outside Greece, according to its pastor, the Reverend Demetrios Frangos.

Most days—and nights—in Little Greece, it seems virtually everybody in that spreading neighborhood is out on the streets, walking, shopping, talking, or reading one of the thirteen daily newspapers in Greek for sale in its shops. Dozens of folding chairs are set out in front of the huge Continental Souvlaki Meat Center at 31st Street and 23rd Avenue, and even the roar of the trains on the elevated tracks above them seems not to disturb the men sitting around talking about their home villages in Macedonia and the Peloponnesus, on Corfu and Samos, and trying earnestly to solve the world's problems.

On warm nights in Bohemian Hall, an outdoor beer hall at

29-19 24th Avenue, not only can the sounds of Greek music be heard but those of Thrace and Crete as well, as lambs roast and imported beer from Greece is poured along with the red and white wines of Greece, many touched with *retsina*, and the Cypriot brandy called *agglias*. The traditional music and dancing are pervasively joyous in places like the Oyster Bay, the Crystal Palace, and the Grecian Cave, once three Greek nightclubs, now all melded into a vast entertainment center at Broadway and 31st Street.

In Taverna Vraka, 23-15 31st Street, Lambis Krokydas sings the sad songs that Aristotle Onassis once liked, and around the corner in the Athena Restaurant, 31-17 23rd Avenue, Demetri Stavridis sits in a stone alcove quietly playing his pearl-inlaid bouzouki and singing songs of Mykonos in a whisper.

Many of Little Greece's food shops are open at least until midnight and most tavernas and restaurants, including those inexpensive places the Greeks call *psistarias*, serve until four A.M. Every night the area's two *kaffenion*, the traditional Lefkos Pyrgos, at 31-25 Ditmars Boulevard, and the new, glossy two-story Hilton Pastry Shop at 22-06 31st Street, are filled with people drinking thick Greek coffee and doing what Greeks seem to like to do most, talking. And if they decide to talk through the night, the coffee shops obligingly stay open and keep the sweet cookies known as *koulourakia* and *kourabiedes* and the sweet custard-filled pastries called *flogheres* coming nonstop.

"In Astoria I feel like I am in my village in Greece," says Helen Stavropoulou, who has worked in Lefkos Pyrgos since coming to Astoria from her home in central Greece two years ago. And so do most of the people who live, work, and shop there.

Kiryakos Moutaphopoulos, the proprietor of Kiryakos Grocery, 29–29 23rd Avenue, a slight man of fifty-five who came to America eleven years ago by way of Istanbul, is as proud of his black kalamata olives and his vast selection of Greek dried peas and beans as he is of the United States citizenship he acquired just a month ago. "But 'Americans' don't come to my store," he says, adding that hardly anybody who isn't Greek and isn't from Astoria buys his jars of lemon, orange, almond, cherry, rose, and tamarind essences used in Greek cooking.

Little Greece was once an Italian immigrant enclave, and the two peoples still intermingle in its streets. Around the corner from Kiryakos is Europa Delicacies, 22–42 31st Street, which is owned jointly by the Greek immigrant Nick Haniotis and the Italian immigrant Salvatore Davi. The clerk, Andrea Damianou, is a Cypriot. It is a shop where you can buy *basterma* and pepperoni, salted Greek sardines and Italian bonito packed in olive oil, Greek bean salad called *fasolada* and Italian eggplant salad called *caponata*, and the cheeses *mizithra* and ricotta.

But their business union is a rarity. Most of the wonderfully aromatic shops in Little Greece are owned by native Greeks: places like John's Fruit Market, 31–27 Ditmars Boulevard, where Evangelos Barous from the island of Andros sells Cypriot sheep's-milk cheeses and thick, dense, hot *basterma*; Kalamata, 38–01 Ditmars Boulevard, where Constantine Rodas, from Volos in central Greece, sells thick cheeses from Metsova in northern Greece and *loukoumi*, gummy Greek candies flavored with roses and dusted with powdered sugar, and the K & T Meat Market, where Mr. Haritos, from the island of Ithaca, sells his lambs to customers from as far away as Connecticut and Riverhead, Long Island.

There is a sameness to the menus of the restaurants of Little Greece, but area residents know that certain dishes are best at certain restaurants. John Nikas, an assistant for ethnic affairs to Governor Cuomo, is a familiar figure in Greek Astoria. He goes to Taverna Vraka for its *sheftalies*, highly spiced sausages of lamb. Haroula Spilios, owner of Roumeli Taverna, 33–04 Broadway, is proudest of her selection of *mezadakia*, a traditional predinner selection of hors d'oeuvres that includes *taramasalata* (salad of carp roe), a garlic potato spread called *skordalia*, *tzatziki* (salad of cucumbers in yogurt), stuffed grape leaves, grilled lamb liver, and sweetbreads.

Many who live in Little Greece go to Mike Moraitis's Kalyva Restaurant, 36–15 Ditmars Boulevard, for his roast lamb and his broiled fish, and to Taygetos for the thick stews and peasant cooking of the Greek countryside practiced by the chef, Andreas Menegos, whose repertory includes thick slabs of fried eggplant and huge whole roasted peppers, stewed veal and lamb, and charcoal-grilled octopus.

Wherever you go in Little Greece, you are surrounded by food. It is perhaps the neighborhood's most unifying aspect. "Here in Astoria," says Matthew Vrasidas, "we have everything we need, everything."

A Sampler

These recipes, from restaurants in Astoria's "Little Greece," have been adapted for the home kitchen by Eileen Yin-Fei Lo.

SKORDALIA
(Taygetos Restaurant)

2 medium-size potatoes
3 ¼ cups water
3 cloves garlic

½ teaspoon salt
2 tablespoons olive oil
2 ½ tablespoons white vinegar

1. Boil potatoes in 3 cups of water for about 30 minutes or until tender. Peel and cut into quarters.

2. Place ¼ cup of water in blender with garlic and pulverize for 20 seconds.

3. Add 1 potato, salt, 1 tablespoon olive oil, 1 tablespoon vinegar, and blend for 30 seconds.

4. Add remaining potato, oil, and vinegar, and blend evenly for 30 to 45 seconds until all ingredients are smooth (the consistency will resemble that of pancake batter). Place in a bowl, cover with plastic wrap, and refrigerate at least 8 hours or overnight. It will thicken to a spreadlike consistency for serving.

Yield: 4 servings.

Note: Can be served as an appetizer, alone, as an accompaniment to vegetables or boiled fish, or with thick brown bread.

SHRIMPS TOURKOLIMANO
(Roumeli Taverna)

4½ tablespoons corn oil
1 pound large shrimp (about 24), shelled, deveined, washed, and dried thoroughly with paper towels
8 scallions, chopped

1¼ cups fresh tomatoes, cut into ½-inch dice
1 cup sliced fresh mushrooms
¾ cup crumbled feta cheese (about 2 generous slices)
2 tablespoons dry white wine

In a skillet, heat oil. Add shrimp and cook for about 1 minute until shrimp curl and turn pink. Add scallions, tomatoes, and mushrooms, and stir until well mixed with shrimp. Add crumbled cheese and mix well. Cook for about 1½ minutes. Add wine and simmer for 1 more minute. Remove from heat, place in a heated dish, and serve immediately over boiled rice.

Yield: 4 servings.

RED SNAPPER MYKONOS
(Kalyva Restaurant)

1 red snapper, 2 pounds
1 ⅛ teaspoons salt
3 ½ tablespoons olive oil
1 cup chopped onions
1 ½ cups chopped fresh
tomatoes

¼ teaspoon garlic salt
⅛ teaspoon dried oregano
Pinch black pepper
Juice of 1 lemon, about
¼ cup

1. Preheat broiler for 15 minutes to 425 degrees.

2. Clean and wash fish, and remove the membrane. Dry thoroughly with paper towels. Line a roasting pan with heavy-duty foil and place fish on it.

3. Sprinkle fish with 1 teaspoon salt, both sides and cavity, then rub both sides with 1 tablespoon olive oil.

4. Place fish in broiler. After 2 minutes, the fish skin will begin to puff and bubble and become brown-spotted. Reduce heat to 400 degrees. Broil for 8 minutes more.

5. Turn fish over, pour another tablespoon of oil on it, and allow to broil an additional 8 minutes. Raise heat to 425 degrees, and broil for 2 more minutes. Fish flesh should be firm.

6. As fish cooks, sauté onions in 1½ tablespoons of oil until softened. Add tomatoes and stir; add remaining ingredients and combine thoroughly. Allow to cook for 3 to 4 minutes until tomatoes soften.

7. Remove fish from broiler, place in a heated serving dish, pour sauce over it, and serve immediately.

Yield: 4 servings.

ROAST LEG OF LAMB
(Kalyva Restaurant)

1 leg of lamb, fresh, 8 to 10 pounds
Juice of ½ lemon
3 ½ teaspoons salt
½ teaspoon ground black pepper
½ teaspoon dried oregano
2 tablespoons chopped onion
½ teaspoon chopped fresh parsley
6 cloves garlic
2 cups water
1 cup good dry red wine
⅓ cup olive oil

1. Preheat oven for 15 minutes to 350 degrees.

2. Trim fat from leg of lamb. Rub it with lemon juice, then with 3 tablespoons of salt, on all sides.

3. In a bowl, mix remaining salt with the pepper, oregano, onion, and parsley. Peel and slice garlic.

4. With a knife make slits on both sides of the leg of lamb and stuff garlic slices and portions of the seasoning mixture into them.

5. Combine the water, wine, and oil in a roasting pan, and place the leg in pan. Roast for about 2 hours and 45 minutes. Every half hour, turn the meat over. Its surface will become crisp and acquire a reddish color. When cooked, remove from oven, slice, and serve on a heated platter, accompanied by its pan juices.

6. After skimming the oil from the surface of the pan juices, there should be about 1½ cups of gravy remaining.

Yield: 8 to 10 servings.

Note: Greeks serve this with rice or with peas and other vegetables, over which the gravy is poured.

A Glossary of Greek Gastronomy

Avgolemono—A sauce of egg and lemon, occasionally poured over other foods, more often used in a soup.

Basterma—Spicy dried beef coated with a peppered layer, somewhat like pastrami. In Greece it is often made from goat meat, in Turkey of camel meat.

Dolmades—Stuffed vine leaves, usually with rice, occasionally with bits of meat.

Feta—Mild, salty cheese, usually of goat's milk, though occasionally it is made from sheep's milk.

Graviera—A Gruyère-like firm cheese.

Haloumi—Soft sheep's-milk cheese from Cyprus. Served either fresh or fried.

Kalamari—Squid.

Kefalotiri—Salted sheep's-milk cheese that is often fried, and when fried is called **saganaki.**

Kokoretsi—A preparation of lamb liver, heart, and sweetbreads, wrapped in lamb intestines, and grilled over a fire. A traditional Easter season dish.

Moussaka—Casserole of baked eggplant with meat and/or vegetables, topped with a béchamel sauce.

Nea Fytini—A traditional Greek vegetable shortening. It is largely cottonseed oil, but contains a small amount of sheep's-milk fat.

Orzo—Rice-shaped pasta.

Pastitsio—Casserole of pasta with ground lamb, cheese, and béchamel sauce.

Pulpo—Octopus.

Skordalia—Appetizer usually made of potatoes and garlic, though occasionally based on soaked, stale bread and garlic.

Sojouk—Spicy sausage based on dried meat preparation, **basterma** (see above).

Taramasalata—A spread made of salted fish roe, olive oil, and lemon juice.

Tzatziki—A salad of cucumbers and garlic in yogurt.

Vakalaos—Salted codfish.

Pastries:

Baklava—A sweet, flaky pastry made with phyllo dough, filled with honey and nuts, and soaked in honey.

Dipla—Thin, fried wheat flour dough dipped in honey.

Kourabiedes—A soft, crescent-shaped cookie with bits of almond inside, dusted with powdered sugar.

Koulourakia—A semihard, breadlike, braid-shaped cookie brushed with egg yolk that is traditional at Easter.

Melomakarona—An oval, soft cookie filled with chopped nuts and soaked in honey.

Rizogalo—Greek rice pudding.

CHAPTER 44

....

Flushing: A New Asian Center

BY FRED FERRETTI

The signs and sights and smells of the "new" Flushing poke out unexpectedly from among the small haberdashers, hardware and dry-goods stores, and gift shops. Bharat, Ku Hwa, Mi-Mi, Shamiana, Sam Bok, Se-Ho Trading Company read the names of the food shops along Main, Union, and Prince streets, and on the smaller side streets that cut through them. The word "Seoul" has been carefully lettered in front of the name of the Little Angels Department Store on Main Street, bestowing upon it a new Asian identity like that of many Flushing stores.

More and more, the shopkeepers are Asian in what was once one of many suburblike, homogeneously white commercial centers in the city's "borough of homes." For them, and for many non-Asians as well, this area in Queens has become an exciting and exotic gastronomic mecca.

You can smell the paprika, fennel, sesame oil, and mango chutney, and the pungency of the spicy, hot Korean salad called *kimchee* brings water to the eyes. The fruit and vegetable stands have stacks of lotus and taro roots, bok choy and choy sum, dried black mushrooms, and cuttlefish alongside the fresh fruits and vegetables, and in the Sam Bok market on Main Street, Hono Pak will sell you five-foot-long sheets of dried seaweed and bottles of Mackoly, one brand of natural Korean rice wine.

Just a block away in the Indian Supermarket, Harris Khan, formerly of Bangladesh, sells packages of curries, fennel and mustard seeds, and *chapati* flour for those Indian breads *paratha, poori,* and *roti.*

In large markets like Ku Hwa and Kam Sen, and a dozen or so tiny groceries and vegetable stores, the produce is picked over by Flushing's Asians in such traditional costumes as cheongsams and saris, and by many longtime residents as well.

Berthold Flick, a seventy-year-old native of Germany's Black Forest region who has lived in the Main Street area since 1939, calls the metamorphosis "a fine thing, because the people have come to work." He said: "They bought up the dilapidated houses, fixed them up, and the neighborhood gets better and better. And now I can get the beef in the brown sauce that I like so much in the restaurants."

As she rummaged through piles of bok choy, spinach, and parsley in the Sam Bok market on Main Street, Marilyn Carroll, a local resident, said, "The stores have been making me eat healthier. I cook more vegetables now. That's good. We have the biggest ethnic mix in the country here in Flushing."

The Flushing area, in particular Main Street, its commercial spine, and such adjacent streets as Northern and Kissena boulevards and Union and Prince streets, has become an Asian microcosm. It is still another of the city's neighborhoods in transition, with a recognizable and sizable Korean-Chinese-Japanese-Indian profile.

Such Korean restaurants as Flushing Palace and New Kalubi House flourish, along with tiny curry restaurants, Chinese establishments like the China House restaurant on Main Street, and the Larmen Dosanko, the combination Japanese noodle parlor, sushi bar, and market on Union Street.

The growing importance of Main Street in Flushing as an Asian food center now brings weekend shoppers by car from Long Island and Westchester for their miso, brown rice, salted codfish roe, fresh octopus, dried red dates, seaweed, bamboo shoots and dried mussels, abalone and ginseng root. And the food stores, as is true in Manhattan's Chinatown, count Sundays as their busiest days.

The shoppers come, among other places, to the Ku Hwa Oriental Food Market on Union Street to buy the spicy and unsubtle *kimchee* that the family of Illkyum Kim concocts from either cabbage, radishes, or cucumbers, and which Mr. Kim sells in quart, half-gallon, and gallon jars.

Mr. Kim says that his *kimchee* is as traditional as that often cured in ceramic jars buried in the earth. "But we don't bury it," he adds with a grin. When his market opened, the *kimchee* was made in its basement, but the demand grew, and Mr. Kim needed more storage space. Now the *kimchee* is made by his family on Long Island, and Mr. Kim brings the jars in by car.

At the New Kalubi restaurant, there are *bulgogi* (marinated beef); *saengsun jun* (fried fish in egg batter), and *yook hae* (raw beef marinated in sesame) prepared by the chef

Han Ku Suk in Kyung Ok Kim's restaurant, which many consider the most authentically Korean in Flushing.

Terry Huang brings in bright green piles of bok choy, choy sum, Tianjin cabbage, taro, lotus roots, and other Chinese vegetables from New Jersey's truck farms to his market, Kam Sen on Main Street.

Shoppers also come to the Japanese market called Daido on Union Street at Northern Boulevard for fresh, bright red raw tuna (sashimi) and fresh fillets of tilefish, fluke, cuttlefish, and octopus for sushi feasts. Jentai Tsai, the owner who matter-of-factly calls himself "King of the Fish," says he buys all of his raw fish himself for his market and his sushi bar, and he insists that his tuna, "the best of sashimi," must be bright red in color. For that color he selects tuna flown in from Taiwan, Japan, Brazil, or Los Angeles, "wherever it is reddest," Mr. Tsai says. Daido, once a Chevrolet dealership, now has shelves piled high with dried soba noodles, various brands of soy, brown rice, tea, and at least nine different brands of horseradish to be consumed with Mr. Tsai's sushi. Alongside his cash register are stacks of day-old *Yomiuri Shimbun* newspapers. Just across the street a former bank has become a Korean church.

Mr. Tsai, a Chinese who grew up as a Japanese citizen when Taiwan was Japanese-controlled, opened Daido as the first Asian food market in Flushing, on Main Street, in 1969. He remained there until a fire gutted the building his market was in. He moved to Union Street and reopened the Daido, a sushi-shopper's paradise that is also a meeting place for the transient Japanese population of Flushing that waxes and wanes with the demands of Japanese businesses in the area.

"Flushing is the new Chinatown," says Mr. Huang of

Kam Sen, a former A. & P. that is now the biggest and new-est Chinese food market on Main Street. It is part of a chain of large Chinese food and dry-goods stores that include the city's two largest Chinese markets, Kam Kuo and Kam Kan in Manhattan's Chinatown. Mr. Huang notes that the esti-mated number of Chinese immigrants and Chinese-Amer-icans in the Flushing area has grown from a handful to about twenty thousand in about four years.

"There are more Koreans here than in any other single place in America," says Sam Rhee, owner of S. R. Jewelers on Main Street and vice-president of the Flushing Chamber of Commerce. S. R. Jewelers (for Sam Rhee) used to be S. L. Jewelers (for Sol Lieberman), and both sets of letters are displayed on his store, "for the old customers," Mr. Rhee says. He is also vice-president of the 150-member Flushing Korean Merchants Association, which estimates that there are 30,000 Koreans now living in the Main Street area.

As pleased as anybody about the ethnic change in Flush-ing are Gene Lebauer and Jack Rozanski, co-owners of Your Kosher Meats and Poultry, which is wedged between the Kam Sen market and Mr. Rhee's jewelry shop. Once each of the men had his own kosher butcher shop on Main Street. Then, says Mr. Lebauer, "It became a neighborhood not so good for a kosher butcher, we thought, so we got together, one shop."

"All of a sudden it's the new Chinatown," says Mr. Rozanski. "But I have to tell you, these people are the nicest neighbors we ever had. Do I buy there? Of course. Vegeta-bles, fish, they have wonderful fish. We don't buy meat there, of course."

Mr. Rozanski says that a good portion of his business comes from Asians who buy kosher meats, "particularly Indians who buy our chopped meat and our liver.'' He pointed to Mr. Huang's market. ''The finest people there, the finest. I don't go to his church; he doesn't go to my shul. But we get along fine.''

Recipes

Following are recipes, adapted for home kitchens by Eileen Yin-Fei Lo, from the food markets and restaurants of Flushing:

PAN-FRIED NOODLES WITH PORK AND SCALLIONS (Yuk See Chow Mein)

THE NOODLES AND MEAT:

½ pound thin fresh egg noodles (vermicelli)

1 teaspoon salt

1 ¼ cups thinly sliced scallions (use white portions and tender parts of green)

6 ounces fresh, lean pork, shredded

1 ¼ teaspoons minced garlic

4 ½ tablespoons or more peanut oil

THE MARINADE:

½ teaspoon ginger juice mixed with ½ teaspoon white wine

¼ teaspoon salt

½ teaspoon sugar

½ teaspoon light soy sauce

½ teaspoon sesame oil

1 ½ teaspoons oyster sauce

Pinch white pepper

1 teaspoon cornstarch

THE SAUCE:

¾ teaspoon sugar	1 teaspoon sesame oil
½ teaspoon dark soy sauce	1 tablespoon cornstarch
2 teaspoons oyster sauce	1 cup chicken broth

1. In separate bowls, combine all ingredients for the marinade and sauce.

2. Cook noodles for 10 seconds in a large pot of boiling water (6 cups) with 1 teaspoon salt. Add cold water to noodles, and then drain. Refill pot with cold water and drain again. Repeat twice more. Place noodles in a strainer to drain thoroughly for 1 to 1½ hours.

3. Place shredded pork in marinade. Set aside for 30 minutes.

4. Wash and dry scallions, and cut into 1½-inch lengths. Set aside.

5. In a large frying pan (preferably cast iron), heat 3 tablespoons of oil over high heat. When a wisp of white smoke appears, add noodles to pan. Spread evenly. Cook 1 minute over high heat, then lower heat and move pan over the burner to allow edges of noodles to cook evenly. Cook about 10 minutes or until noodles are light brown. If noodles stick to pan, add more oil. Turn noodles and repeat.

6. Heat wok over high heat. Add 1½ tablespoons of peanut oil. Using a spatula, coat the wok with the oil, and add garlic. When garlic turns brown, add pork. Spread pork in a thin layer, and cook 2 to 3 minutes. Turn the pork, and repeat until it turns white. Add scallions and mix thoroughly. Stir the sauce, make a well in the center of the pork mixture, and pour into the well. Stir and mix. When the mixture thickens and turns brown, turn off heat.

7. Spread noodles on serving dish, place the pork and scallion mixture on top, and serve.

Yield: 6 servings.

PAN-FRIED FISH FILLETS IN EGG BATTER (Saengsun Jun)
New Kalubi House

2 2-pound codfish, gutted, cleaned outside and in (leave heads and tails intact), washed thoroughly and dried on paper towels

Salt and pepper to taste
5 tablespoons peanut oil
Flour to coat fillets
2 eggs, beaten
½ cup light soy sauce

1. Preheat oven to 375 degrees.
2. Make 3 diagonal cuts on both sides of each fish, and then butterfly each fish. Cover heads and tails with foil so they will not burn. Place each fish on an ovenproof dish, each dish coated lightly with about 1 tablespoon oil to prevent sticking.
3. Bake fish for several minutes, until flesh becomes firm. Then remove from the oven, peel off skin, gently pull the flesh from the bones, and divide each fish into four fillets. Flatten each fillet gently.
4. Season to taste, dredge in flour, dip in beaten egg, and fry over moderate heat in a skillet, preferably cast iron, in 3 remaining tablespoons of oil until lightly browned. Remove from skillet, drain, and serve immediately with light soy sauce.

Yield: 4 servings.

KIMCHEE
Ku Hwa Oriental Food Market

1½ pounds Tianjin (Napa)
cabbage
2 tablespoons or more salt
2 ounces fresh hot red chili
peppers, thinly sliced

½ bunch scallions
4 cloves garlic, minced
½ tablespoon ginger, minced
2 ounces tiny boiled shrimp,
shelled and deveined

1. Cut cabbage into 1½-inch lengths, sprinkle with salt, and allow to stand, pressed down with a plate, for about 4 hours until cabbage is wilted.

2. Drain off excess water, and add chili peppers, scallions, garlic, ginger, and shrimp. Fill a ½-gallon glass jar to within 2 inches of the top, and add cold water. Cover lightly, but do not seal.

3. Allow the jar to sit at room temperature 2 or 3 days until bubbling and fermentation begins. Check for saltiness. Add salt if needed. When bubbles rise, the *kimchee* is ready. Cover the jar tightly and refrigerate. *Kimchee* can be served as a salad or as a relish for fish or meat dishes. It will keep indefinitely.

Yield: ½ gallon.

Note: Tianjin cabbage is available at Oriental markets.

CHAPTER 45

···

The Many Faces of Riverdale

BY PAUL GOLDBERGER

The years since World War II have brought vast amounts of development to Riverdale, so much so that travelers passing through on the Henry Hudson Parkway could well mistake this northwest corner of the Bronx for a community containing nothing but high-rise apartment blocks. But concealed behind those towers on both sides of the parkway are two of the city's most prized enclaves, with not only single-family houses but also great mansions, sprawling lawns, twisting lanes, and dense woodlands. While there are some plans for new construction, most sites on which large-scale development can take place are already built up—so the rustic illusion that the hidden Riverdale offers is not likely to disappear, and that alone makes this part of New York special.

Riverdale is three places, really—what might be called *haute* Riverdale, the community of large houses and narrow country roads that fills most of the land between the Henry

Hudson Parkway and the river; commercial Riverdale, the quarter of stores and high-rise apartments that is west of the Henry Hudson and south of Manhattan College Parkway, and Fieldston, a gracious, serene development of large and formal houses, mostly from the 1920s, that is west of the Henry Hudson Parkway and north of Manhattan College Parkway.

None of these places could be in Manhattan, or anywhere else in New York City for that matter. They still retain the sense of self-containment, the sense that they are communities unto themselves, in New York City, even of New York City, but certainly not typical of it. The Hudson River is only a part of this—it is the controlling visual presence on the Riverdale side of the parkway—but it is by no means the whole story, for it tells us nothing about why Fieldston, from which it cannot be seen at all, is still so remarkable, or about why those little hidden lanes on the river side have such charm.

Those who know Riverdale and Fieldston well frequently talk about how they represent an escape from the city—they talk of tranquility, of nature, of restful quiet. All true, obviously. But it is not true that Riverdale feels like a little New Canaan, or Fieldston like a little Bronxville. Those places are suburbs. But Riverdale is not; its physical appearance belies its true nature. The presence of the city so close energizes Riverdale and Fieldston in the same way that the tiny glimpse of the skyline through the trees energizes Central Park without taking away from its essence. Riverdale and Fieldston have that same intangible feeling of urbanity that, say, distinguishes the arbored residential quarters of the northwest section of Washington from the duller but physically similar suburbs outside the district line.

And the city is close by—midtown Manhattan less than twenty minutes down the Henry Hudson Parkway when traffic is light, and the rest of the Bronx just across Broadway, which runs north-south along the eastern edge of the neighborhood. In a sense, Riverdale and Fieldston are New York's equivalent of the neighborhoods of large, detached houses in which the well-to-do live in many cities—not just Washington, but also Atlanta and Denver and Minneapolis. But as nothing in New York precisely fits the pattern it takes elsewhere, neither do these places.

EXPLORATIONS BY CAR

Riverdale and Fieldston are best explored by car—public transportation can take you there, but moving around in the area can be too cumbersome. Coming from Manhattan, the simplest approach is the best—up the Henry Hudson Parkway (past the Cloisters, a visit to which can combine well with a tour of Riverdale) and across the Henry Hudson Bridge. Robert Moses placed the bridge at the highest point of the ridge overlooking Spuyten Duyvil, the point at which the Harlem River joins the Hudson; both engineers and estheticians argued in favor of lower sites that would have had less environmental impact. But Moses prevailed, and though Inwood Hill Park in Manhattan is the worse for it, the high prospect means that there is a spectacular view as you proceed north across the bridge.

From that vantage point, Riverdale looks as if it had been built entirely in the last decade—immense, blocky apartment towers seem to cover all the land both east and west of the parkway, jostling for space and air. Since the northernmost tip of Manhattan is the forested wilderness of Inwood

Hill Park, the motorist is confronted with a curious initial impression upon moving from Manhattan into Riverdale: It seems at first like a transition from serenity into dense over-building, not the other way around.

For this twisted image to change, one must plunge into the heart of Riverdale. It will take a moment: First, exit just after the bridge at Kappock Street, which at this end contains many of the undistinguished apartment blocks that were seen from the bridge. (Here, you are skirting the edge of commercial Riverdale, the area's least interesting section.) Follow Kappock Street around to the right past Knolls Crescent; keep to the right as you move down the hill and you will eventually come to be on Palisade Avenue. There are a few more apartment towers that block the view of the Harlem River; then, as Palisade Avenue descends further, it moves into a phase that seems not like the rest of Riverdale—or like anyplace else in New York—at all.

DOWN BY THE RIVER

Suddenly, the Harlem River comes into view, along with the great metal arch of the Henry Hudson Bridge, from this angle not a mere highway but a high, prancing span. The apartment blocks are gone, and down by the riverside are clusters of small frame houses, huddling together as if for protection. They are modest buildings, well kept but of note more for their setting than for anything else—they sit at the edge of the river as if they were cottages overlooking a stream in a tiny village, not houses stranded alone in a vast city.

You can, if you wish, turn left on Edsall Avenue and pass this cluster more closely. Edsall Avenue circles down to the water and the Spuyten Duyvil railroad station; you can return up the road and continue in your original direction by turning left when Edsall Avenue comes back to Palisade.

Stop at the corner of Palisade Avenue and Independence Avenue, and walk a half block up the hill to the Edgehill Church, one of Riverdale's several notable houses of worship. (Independence Avenue is one-way in this section, which is why driving up the hill is not the best idea.) The church, which dates from 1889, was designed by Francis H. Kimball, originally as a chapel for the Johnson Iron Foundry, which was once Spuyten Duyvil's major industry. Kimball was later the architect for a number of large office buildings in lower Manhattan; Edgehill, however, is a pure country church, made of fieldstone and shingle and half-timbering. It is now hemmed in by large apartment buildings, but its fitting relationship to the hilly landscape is easy to see—this is a church built to its land.

Continue on Palisade Avenue as it turns around to the right; here Riverdale's real grandeur begins. The Victoria apartments at 2475 Palisade Avenue is a solid château of deep, rich red brick perched over the Hudson; its architecture loosely uses Tudor motifs in the way that many New York apartment houses employed eclecticism in the early decades of this century. The Victoria was a true pioneer—the first riverfront apartment house in the area, and it remains the finest.

THE VIRGIN PALISADES

Part of the Victoria's appeal comes from the perfection of its view—at this point, opposite Riverdale, the Palisades have been preserved as a virgin landscape. The warm hills and the wide river combine to create a sight that would be majestic anywhere—but the notion that it can be seen by looking out a window in the city of New York seems to stretch credibility. This same remarkable view is shared by an exceptionally amiable group of town houses next door, which jointly hold the address of 2501 Palisade Avenue; their architecture is a pleasant mixture of gingerbread and Spanish and 1930s moderne, which somehow comes off.

Kappock Street returns into Palisade Avenue here; you can detour up it to have a look at Henry Hudson Park on the bluff at the corner of Kappock and Independence, and the hundred-foot-tall Doric column erected in 1912 as a memorial to Hudson. The column was designed by Babb, Cook & Welch; the bronze statue of Hudson atop it was by Karl Bitter and Karl Gruppe.

Return to Palisade Avenue and continue. Here, Riverdale's fine mansions begin; in this stretch, fairly formal houses line the river side, many Georgian or Spanish colonial in design and most coming from the great years of American eclecticism, the decades after World War I. The road runs rather close to the river here, though there is plenty of room for generous sites between Palisade Avenue and the Hudson. But most of the land bordering Palisade along here is wooded, and in this section more than anywhere the illusion of being in the country is maintained— there are some tiny stretches where no building at all can be seen.

Up high on the right are a number of high-rise apartment houses, most undistinguished, but one, the swooping Hayden House, greets the river with a curving facade that calls to mind the well-known building at 200 Central Park South in Manhattan. Hayden House also has a group of "matching'' town houses with windows in high arcs, presumably an attempt to echo the curve of the larger building.

RURAL 247TH STREET

Next, the visitor can detour to the right, onto 247th Street—the kind of street name one might associate with tenements and traffic, but in this case signifies a true country lane. Just up the hill on the right is Greyston, a mansion completed in 1864 to the designs of James Renwick, Jr., the architect of St. Patrick's Cathedral and Grace Church. Greyston is not Renwick's finest work—it seems bulbous rather than graceful—but it stands as an important reminder of Riverdale's early days as a community of immense riverfront estates.

Greyston is surrounded by a number of small lanes, and the contrast between the great mansion and the smaller, informal houses scattered casually about the landscape is typical of this section of Riverdale. The roads here can be confusing; the easiest route is to return back down 247th Street and turn right to continue north on Palisade Avenue.

Palisade will turn right itself on 248th Street, past the river campus of the Riverdale Country School, a portion of the estate of George W. Perkins, a partner of J. P. Morgan. The road will turn again to the left, becoming Independence Avenue; just after that turn, one of Riverdale's most grandiose houses, the red-tile-roofed Count Anthony Campagna residence, will come into view high on the hill to the right. Designed by Dwight James Baum, Riverdale's most active and talented eclectic architect, this Italian–Spanish house (it is really best thought of as American Mediterranean Hollywood Eclectic) was completed in 1922. Its approach up a driveway from 249th Street is a noble, if theatrical, processional.

Continue on Independence Avenue just past 249th Street to the entrance to Wave Hill, the main section of the Perkins estate, on the left. Wave Hill's full name today is the Wave Hill Center for Environmental Studies. It contains a pair of mansions and a splendid piece of land overlooking the river that now functions as a public park. The original house, which gave its name to the entire estate, was built in stages beginning in 1844; Dwight James Baum added a section to display an armor collection in 1928. It has housed a number of notable tenants over the years, including Mark Twain and Theodore Roosevelt. The other house, the neo-Georgian mansion Glyndor, was built in the early twentieth century by Perkins to replace an earlier house destroyed by fire. Wave Hill is the site of a number of public events, including frequent concerts.

Continue along Independence Avenue to the end of the Wave Hill property at West 252nd Street and turn left. There is a bizarre and rather nervous new house just ahead on Independence Avenue, its anxious angles a rather desperate case of architectural overeagerness. To return to some semblance of tranquillity, turn right onto Sycamore Avenue, a lovely street of somewhat smaller houses, many of which hug the road in the manner of houses in an English country village. Behind them open up generous yards to the river.

At West 254th Street, Sycamore ends at one of the more ambitious pieces of modern architecture in Riverdale, the Salanter Akiba Riverdale Academy of 1974, by the firm of Caudill Rowlatt Scott. A religious school, the building is stepped back to echo the profile of the land; it is not a subtle gesture, and it yields a building that does not fit in particularly well with the houses around it, but it does yield good teaching spaces inside.

Turn right on 254th Street, and right again on Independence Avenue to see not only a group of fine houses, these much older than the 1920s eclectics and at least as gracious, but Riverdale's best views as well. Here the river can be seen by everyone, and from this high vantage point the vista is powerful indeed.

Turn left on 252nd Street and continue to the service road just at the edge of the Henry Hudson Parkway. Turn right before crossing the parkway; on the right just ahead at 249th Street will be James Renwick's other major effort in Riverdale, the delightful Riverdale Presbyterian Church of 1863, with its cottagelike parsonage next door. This is another real country church, and it is smaller than Greyston, despite its status as a public building.

VIEWS OF FIELDSTON

Continue to 246th Street and turn right, bearing right to stay on 246th Street as you pass high-rise apartments, for a look at the old Riverdale turning into the new—one of Riverdale's great estates, the eleven-acre Delafield property, now in the process of being divided into new housing units. The centerpiece of the estate is a mid-nineteenth-century house of fieldstone with a splendid classical portico that was altered in 1916 by Dwight James Baum; long owned by Columbia University, the house will now contain three residential units, and the rest of the property will have twenty-two attached houses and eight single-family residences, all designed by James Stewart Polshek in an attempt to straddle modernism and traditional domestic architecture.

Double back along 246th Street and cross over the Henry Hudson Parkway, and turn left again onto the east service road. At 250th Street is another religious building, Congregation Adath Israel, completed in 1962 to the designs of Percival Goodman—a determined, self-assured composition of warm brick and cool concrete. Turn right at 250th Street, and move up the hill, bearing left and then curving left into Iselin Avenue to the Ittleson Center for Child Research at Number 5050. To this old estate, now a center for the treatment of disturbed children, were added a series of pavilions in 1967; they were designed by Abraham W. Geller with Michael Rubenstein, and they show the influence of Louis Kahn. The pavilions, which are set back somewhat from the street, cannot be visited, but their modest and strong general outlines can be seen—they surely rank among this neighborhood's more thoughtful works of contemporary architecture.

The road will curve back down the hill to the parkway's service road; you will be turning right, but churchophiles may want to detour to another significant church back to the left, Christ Church of 1866 by Richard Upjohn, architect of lower Manhattan's Trinity. Christ Church is quieter than the other Riverdale country churches; the chief pleasure it offers, aside from the serenity of its overall form, is the striping of the red tiles and gray slate sections of its roof.

Turn around again, and continue north; the service road will curve around and hook into the north end of Fieldston Road at the Fieldston campus of Riverdale Country School. Turn right onto Fieldston Road; not long after passing the school, you will enter the heart of Fieldston itself—

announced rather triumphantly by the splendid field-stone Tudor house on the left at Number 5000 (you will see its back before you see its front) and the Georgian house of fieldstone at Number 4730.

What follows as you move down Fieldston Road is an array of houses, mostly Georgian and Spanish colonial, as fine as any suburban grouping from the 1920s. Many were Dwight James Baum's designs, and though not all are distinguished, few are disappointing. Fieldston Road here is one of the city's great residential streets—wide, serene, self-possessed, a kind of Park Avenue of single-family residences. It points up the differences between Riverdale and Fieldston—this is no country village manque but a planned development, formal where Riverdale is casual, ordered where Riverdale is random.

Continue down Fieldston Road past the wildly overbuilt mansion at Number 4650, a Georgian pile that looks more like the headquarters of a corporation than a residence, past the exquisite tiny yellow stucco house across from it, to the circle at the intersection of Fieldston Road and West 246th Street. Here you can turn right and bring your visit to an end by returning to Henry Hudson Parkway, or turn left and explore further—left on 246th and left on Livingston Avenue to glimpse the private treasure of Fieldston property owners, the hidden Indian Pond in its own little park, or further down Fieldston Road, Waldo Avenue and 246th Street for a look at some more of New York City's finest free-standing houses.

CHAPTER 46

....

Touring the North Shore of Staten Island

BY DOUGLAS C. McGILL

It is fitting that the shining white steeple of the Reformed Church in Brighton Heights, Staten Island, is visible from the Staten Island ferry the minute it pulls away from Manhattan. The church, built in 1861, has served for decades as a navigational landmark for ships approaching Staten Island, and even today, spotting the steeple is a fine way to begin a tour of the island's North Shore.

The church also serves as a reminder of how the landmarks of Staten Island—its churches, homes, restaurants, winding streets, and panoramic views of New York Harbor— tell the maritime history of the region: Here, a church was built by the heir to a shipping fortune; there, a cultural center was once a home for old sailors; over there, a bridge is named after the Italian-born explorer and discoverer of Staten Island, Giovanni da Verrazano.

In the buildings of the North Shore the island's maritime past merges with the present—sometimes in contrast, sometimes smoothly. The Bay Street Landing, a good example of the contrast, is a housing development and pleasure-boat marina just east of the St. George ferry terminal. The Landing's monolithic white buildings, which were once used as storehouses for ship-delivered molasses, grains, and coffee, are now being converted into cooperative apartments costing up to $225,000.

As seen from the sea, however, the terraced hills of the North Shore present a view of historic continuity. Starting at the waterfront and moving up the hill, the residential homes remain basically as they were at the turn of the century: small, sometimes ramshackle houses near the piers (originally the houses of dockworkers and deckhands) turn into middle-size, middle-class Victorian homes at the middle of the hill, with stately mansions (often the former estates of shipping magnates) perching on the hillcrests.

As a modern seafaring visitor to the North Shore, notice when your ferry pulls into the terminal that the steeple has disappeared behind a large brick building that looks transplanted from the Loire Valley. This is the Borough Hall. It was built in 1904 by Carrère and Hastings, the architects that also designed the main New York Public Library building in Manhattan. A series of murals on the first floor of Borough Hall provides a history of Staten Island, from its discovery in 1524 by Verrazano to the building of the island's first steam railroad in 1860.

Walk two blocks up Hyatt Street, and take a left at the Reformed Church. Walk down St. Marks Place to Victory Boulevard (noting the spectacular view of the Verrazano Bridge), turn back up Victory Boulevard one block, and continue walking south on St. Paul's Avenue. The avenue was called Mud Lane in the nineteenth century because it forms a terrace that caught mud sliding down from the steep hill above it.

The old Mud Lane is dotted with architecturally interesting buildings. One is the fortresslike Board of Education's Bureau of Maintenance building, at the corner of St. Paul's Avenue and Grant Street. The delicate wood mullions in the windows, tracing complex designs, bring the hulk to life. Two blocks up, to the left on St. Paul's Avenue, is St. Paul's Episcopal Church, which was built in 1866 with a donation from Judge Albert Ward, who was heir to the Ward Steamship Lines fortune. This landmark church is considered one of the finest examples of High Victorian Gothic architecture in the United States. It is notable for its strong, simple architectural design, free of the elaborate stone tracery and rococo decorations of many Victorian Gothic Revival churches. The boarded-up windows are the result of a fire at the church in October 1983; renovation should be completed by 1986.

Two houses south of St. Paul's Church is a restored Queen Anne revival building, a residential home at 239 St. Paul's Avenue. The owners, Merle Hairston-Branch and Addison Branch, have restored the building to closely resemble its original appearance in 1890: They exposed the original shingles, painted the house in a maroon, green, and earth-tone Victorian color scheme, and also exposed a stained glass window over the front door.

Continue along St. Paul's Avenue, past the gargoyled Trinity Lutheran Church to Occident Avenue. Take a right, and climb up the steep and winding road to Sunrise Terrace, where you might think that you were in San Francisco instead of Staten Island. A few feet up Sunrise Terrace, turn around and see a spectacular, almost aerial view of the Bay and Brooklyn.

Follow Sunrise Terrace, which turns into Louis Street, and continue until Victory Boulevard, where the view of Manhattan and New York Harbor is equally breathtaking. From here you can see virtually everything between New Jersey and the Verrazano Bridge, looking straight over the Statue of Liberty to the twin towers of the World Trade Center, the Empire State Building, and the new American Express building, which huddle like four giants at center stage.

On Victory Boulevard, take a Number 6 or a Number 107 bus (each runs every twenty minutes, including Saturdays and Sundays) back down to Bay Street. If you want to keep walking, head north on Bay Street toward the ferry terminal, but if you're hungry you might want to try brunch at the Landing Café, at the Bay Street Landing. Take the entrance to the Landing next to the Buick dealership and walk across the railroad tracks, all the way to the Landing Café at Pier 4 on the water. The café serves a Sunday brunch from noon to 3:30 P.M.

After you have eaten, you might want to head south on Bay Street to browse in the island's four-block-long antiques district in downtown Stapleton. The intersection of Bay Street and Broad Street (about a mile south of Victory Boulevard on Bay) is at the heart of an area that includes more than a half-dozen antique stores, offering everything from the truly trivial to good bargains in quilts, prints, and furniture.

A good place to start is Corner Copia, 680 Bay Street, which carries mostly Art Deco items: jewelry, lampshades, radios, ashtrays, sugar bowls, cigarette lighters, clocks, and more than a few sculptures of nymphs holding up such things as candy trays and globes of light.

Silver Sixpence, at 694 Bay Street, specializes in "country kitchen" items—chocolate molds, porcelain spice boxes, cast-iron trivets—as well as antique furniture. Next door, at Susan's Corner, also at 694 Bay Street, odd collectibles are the main stock—anything from an old telegraph key, to a photograph from World War I, to a still filled bottle of Grove's Chill Tonic might be found.

Other antique shops in the area include Print Exclusively, at 25 Broad Street (which specializes in antique prints, illustrated books, and original signed prints); Red Rooster, at 646 Bay Street (offering a variety of antiques); Sands of Times Antiques, at 669 Bay Street (antique furniture exclusively); and Yesteryear's, at 665 Bay Street (bric-a-brac from floor to ceiling).

When you have finished antiquing, take a bus back to the ferry stop, and from there walk north on Richmond Terrace to Nicholas Street, continue two blocks to St. Mark's Place. On this block, the past and the present merge colorfully in many Victorian homes. The recently restored house at 125 St. Mark's Place, for example, was once owned by the silent-screen comedienne Mabel Normand. Down the street, past St. Peter's Church, is the Second Empire–style house of a nineteenth-century physician named Walser, at 17 St. Mark's Place, whose offices were at 1–5 St. Mark's Place, at the end of the block.

Turn right at Dr. Walser's former medical office, follow Westervelt Avenue, which is itself lined with handsome Victorian homes, back to Richmond Terrace. Walk a block

west to York Avenue, then north on York a block to
Fillmore Street (look for the garden at the corner), and west
on Fillmore to Franklin Avenue. At the corner of Fillmore
and Franklin, find the Christ Episcopal Church, which was
formed in the late 1840s. The present Christ Church building, dedicated in 1905, is distinguished by its five stained-
glass windows made by Louis Comfort Tiffany. Another
window, by the renowned stained-glass craftsman Frederick
Lamb, is also not to be missed. The nave window depicts the
Annunciation; it is best seen at dusk, when the sun shines
directly behind Christ's head and forms a halo of deep, rich
golden hues that fill the whole church.

Finally, follow Fillmore Road west for four blocks, to the
East Gate of Snug Harbor, the eighty-acre, twenty-six-
building complex that was built in 1831 as a home for retired
sailors. It is now a rapidly growing cultural center operated
by the city, where concerts, plays, art exhibitions, and other
activities are frequently held. The grounds are a mixture of
woods, meadows, and trails. Call (718) 448-2500 for information about activities.

The five main buildings of Snug Harbor are among the
finest examples of Greek Revival architecture in the United
States. While the buildings are presently half-hidden behind
scaffolding erected for major renovations, their pediments,
Ionic columns, and broad steps are still visible and stand
testimony to that time, in the late eighteenth and early
nineteenth centuries, when American architects believed
that the Greek style best embodied the ideals of their new
republic.

Before catching the Number 1 bus on Richmond Terrace
back to the ferry terminal (the buses go by at about ten min-

utes before the hour and the half hour), stop by Snug Harbor's Main Hall, whose doorways are painted with slogans that captured the essence of the old sailors' home: Port After Stormy Seas, and Rest after Dangerous Toil. Not a bad place, historically speaking, to end a tour of the North Shore of Staten Island.

Calendar of Events

Most events listed below recur annually. Specific dates can be obtained from the Visitors Information Center of the New York Convention and Visitors Bureau at 2 Columbus Circle (212-397-8222). The bureau is the source of this listing.

JANUARY

Postholiday sales in stores, all boroughs.

Thoroughbred racing at Aqueduct Racetrack, Queens (through mid-May).

New York Philharmonic, Avery Fisher Hall, Lincoln Center (through mid-June).

Sunday jazz vespers, St. Peter's Church, Citicorp Center (all year).

New York City Ballet, New York State Theater, Lincoln Center (January–February).

463

Collegiate basketball season opens, Madison Square Garden.

Volvo Grand Prix Masters Tennis, Madison Square Garden.

National Boat Show, Coliseum.

Winter Antiques Show, Seventh Regiment Armory.

Wanamaker Millrose Games, Madison Square Garden.

Greater New York Auto Show, Coliseum.

FEBRUARY

Black History Month, programs in all boroughs.

Ice Capades, Madison Square Garden.

Chinese New Year.

Annual Exhibition, National Academy of Design.

Lincoln's and Washington's Birthday sales, all boroughs.

Westminster Kennel Club Dog Show, Madison Square Garden.

Washington's Birthday Parade, Fifth Avenue.

Empire Cat Club Show.

Virginia Slims Women's Tennis, Madison Square Garden.

MARCH

Big East Basketball Tournament, Madison Square Garden.

American Cup Gymnastics, Madison Square Garden.

St. Patrick's Day Parade, Fifth Avenue.

Flower Show of the Horticultural Society of New York, Hudson Exhibition Pier near 53rd Street.

Golden Gloves Finals, Madison Square Garden.

Greek Independence Day Parade, Fifth Avenue.

National Invitation Basketball Tournament (NIT), Madison Square Garden.

Circle Line cruise operates, foot of West 43rd Street.

APRIL

Mets baseball season opens, Shea Stadium, Queens.

Yankee season begins, Yankee Stadium, the Bronx.

Children's Zoo opens for season, the Bronx Zoo.

Ringling Bros. and Barnum and Bailey Circus, Madison Square Garden.

International Art Exposition, Coliseum.

Easter lilies display, Channel Gardens, Rockefeller Center.

Great Easter Egg Event, the Bronx Zoo.

Easter Parade, Fifth Avenue.

Stuyvesant Park Festival, Second Avenue, 15th to 17th streets.

Annual Spring Flower Show, Macy's.

City Ballet, spring season, Lincoln Center (April–June).

Five Boro Bike Tour, starts and ends at Battery Park.

Public School Art Show, Lever House.

MAY

Sakura Matsuri (Japanese cherry blossom festival), Brooklyn Botanic Garden.

SoHo Festival, Prince Street, West Broadway, Avenue of the Americas.

Contemporary American Crafts Festival, Columbus Avenue, 55th to 81st streets.

Park Avenue Fair, 23rd to 34th streets.

Solidarity Day Parade, Fifth Avenue.

Armed Forces Day Parade, Fifth Avenue.

Annual Brooklyn Heights Promenade Art Show.

Ukrainian Festival, East 7th Street between Second and Third avenues.

Ninth Avenue International Festival, 35th to 57th streets.

Thoroughbred racing at Belmont Park, Queens.

Bronx Week: dance, concerts, theater, and athletics throughout the borough.

Bronx Day Parade, Grand Concourse.

Norwegian Constitution Day Parade, Brooklyn.

Martin Luther King, Jr., Parade, Fifth Avenue.

Hudson River Day Line operates, foot of West 41st Street (late May–mid-September).

Washington Square Outdoor Art Show, Greenwich Village (late May–early June).

City Beaches open.

Memorial Day Parade.

Outdoor dolphin shows begin, Aquarium, Coney Island.

JUNE

Free Metropolitan Opera parks concerts, all boroughs.

Children's Day Fair, Staten Island Museum.

Salute to Israel Parade, Fifth Avenue.

Museum Mile Celebration, Fifth Avenue, 82nd to 105th streets.

Feast of St. Anthony, 187th Street, the Bronx.

Festival of St. Anthony, Sullivan Street, Greenwich Village.

Belmont Stakes, Belmont Park, Queens.

New York Women's Jazz Festival, various sites.

Puerto Rican Day Parade, Fifth Avenue.

Seventh Heaven Street Festival, Park Slope, Brooklyn.

Flag Day Parade, Fulton and Water streets to Fraunces Tavern Museum.

Lower East Side Jewish Festival, East Broadway, Rutgers to Grand streets.

"Celebrate Brooklyn '85," including two weeks of Shakespeare in Prospect Park (June–September).

Guggenheim Concerts, Damrosch Park in Lincoln Center and Seaside Park in Brooklyn (late June–early August).

Jazz Festival, citywide concerts (late June–early July).

Lexington Avenue Festival, 23rd to 34th streets.

Feast of St. Paulinus, Williamsburg, Brooklyn.

JULY

Free Shakespeare in Central Park, Tuesday–Sunday, Delacorte Theater (July–August).

"Music for a City Evening," Wednesdays, Rockefeller Center (all July).

Free outdoor entertainment, Wednesdays, World Trade Center Plaza (July–August).

Summerpier jazz concerts, South Street Seaport (July–August).

Harbor Festival, July 4th parade, Bowling Green to City Hall, entertainment at Battery Park and World Trade Center Plaza, international lifeboat races off Battery, 10-kilometer race over George Washington Bridge; parade of power and sail boats, Macy's fireworks (July 4).

City Opera opening night, Lincoln Center.

Annual American Crafts Festival, Lincoln Center.

Feast of Our Lady of Mt. Carmel, Belmont, the Bronx.

"Mostly Mozart," Avery Fisher Hall, Lincoln Center (mid-July–August).

Festa Italiana, Our Lady of Pompeii, Greenwich Village.

AUGUST

Philharmonic parks concerts, all boroughs.

Harlem Week, culminating in Harlem Day.

Lincoln Center Out-of-Doors Festival (mid-August–September).

Greenwich Village Jazz Festival: concerts, films, lectures (late August).

Festival of the Americas, Avenue of the Americas, 35th to 50th streets.

Brighton Jubilee, Brighton Beach Avenue at Coney Island Avenue, Brooklyn.

Governor's Cup Race, Pier A, Bay.

Thoroughbed racing, Belmont Park, Queens (late August–mid-October).

United States Open Tennis Championships, USTA National Tennis Center, Flushing Meadow, Queens (late August–early September).

SEPTEMBER

Jets football season opens, Giants Stadium, Meadowlands.

Giants football season opens, Giants Stadium, Meadowlands.

County Fair, Richmondtown Restoration, Staten Island.

Washington Square Outdoor Art Show, Greenwich Village.

Bread and Roses Festival, 42nd Street, Ninth and Tenth avenues.

West Indian–American Day Parade, Eastern Parkway, Brooklyn.

Labor Day Parade, Fifth Avenue.

One World Festival Street Fair, St. Vartan's Armenian Cathedral, Second Avenue at 35th Street.

Judson Book Fair and Street Festival, Washington Square South, Greenwich Village.

TAMA County Fair, Third Avenue, 14th to 34th streets.

African-American Day Parade, Adam Clayton Powell Boulevard and 111th Street.

Feast of San Gennaro, Mulberry Street, Little Italy.

New York Is Book Country fair, Fifth Avenue, 48th to 57th streets.

Steuben Day Parade, Fifth Avenue.

United Nations General Assembly opens.

Autumn Splendor, New York Botanical Garden, the Bronx.

Columbus Avenue Festival, 66th to 79th streets.

Flatbush Frolic, Cortelyou Road, Brooklyn.

Schooner Week, South Street Seaport Museum.

Philharmonic opening night, Avery Fisher Hall, Lincoln Center.

New York Film Festival, Lincoln Center.

Annual Fifth Avenue Mile footrace, 82nd Street to 62nd Street.

Atlantic Antic 10, Atlantic Avenue, Brooklyn.

Metropolitan Opera opening night, Lincoln Center.

OCTOBER

Rangers hockey season opens, Madison Square Garden.

Mayor's Cup Schooner Race, South Street Seaport.

Video Expo, piers 88 and 89.

Brownstone Fair, Brooklyn Heights.

Pulaski Day Parade, Fifth Avenue.

Rockefeller Center ice-skating pond opens.

Irving Place Festival, Irving Place, 14th to 20th streets, Gramercy Park.

Columbus Day Parade, Fifth Avenue.

Annual Harvest Festival, Jacques Marchais Tibetan Museum, Staten Island.

Massing of the Colors Parade, Fifth Avenue.

New York City Marathon, five-borough run.

Knicks basketball season opens, Madison Square Garden.

National Horse Show, Madison Square Garden.

Halloween Parade, Greenwich Village.

NOVEMBER

"Ghosts of Christmas Past" tour, South Street Seaport Museum (November to December).

National College Fair, Coliseum.

Kiku-ka Ten (Japanese chrysanthemums), New York Botanical Garden, the Bronx.

Veterans' Day Parade, Fifth Avenue.

City Ballet opening night, fall season, Lincoln Center.

"The Magnificent Christmas Spectacular," featuring the Rockettes, Radio City Music Hall.

Macy's Thanksgiving Day Parade.

DECEMBER

Annual Christmas Tree and Baroque Crèche exhibition, Metropolitan Museum.

Origami Christmas tree, American Museum of Natural History.

Christmas in Richmondtown, Richmondtown Restoration, Staten Island.

Christmas tree lighting, Rockefeller Center.

Choral groups sing carols, Fifth Avenue lobby of Empire State Building.

"Traditions of the Holiday Season," New York Botanical Garden, the Bronx (December–January).

"The Spirit of Christmas," Hayden Planetarium.

Chanukah candle lightings at City Hall.

ECAC Holiday Basketball Festival, Madison Square Garden.

New Year's Eve public celebrations throughout city, including Times Square, fireworks and midnight run in Central Park.

Index

Acknowledgments

Grateful acknowledgment is made to the following for permission to reprint previously published material:

New Directions Publishing Corporation: Excerpt from *Quite Early One Morning*, by Dylan Thomas. Copyright 1954 by New Directions Publishing Corporation. Rights in the world excluding the United States administered by David Higham Associates Limited (London). Reprinted by permission of New Directions Publishing Corporation and David Higham Associates Limited.

New York Public Library, Astor, Lenox and Tilden Foundations: From the Henry W. and Albert A. Berg Collection: Letter from John C. Peters to Oliver Wendell Holmes (1859); newspaper accounts of Washington Irving's death from the collection of John C. Peters (1859); letter from Sara Teasdale Filsinger to Edmund Wilson (1928); letter from Lord Dunsany to Clayton Meeker Hamilton (1919), copy-

497

right Lord Dunsany (reprinted by permission also of Curtis Brown Ltd. as agent for John Child Villiers and Valentine Lamb, literary executors of Lord Dunsany); letter from Carlotta O'Neill to Carl Van Vechten (1941) (reprinted by permission also of the Collection of American Literature, the Beinecke Rare Book and Manuscript Library, Yale University); letters from Robert Smythe Hichens to Carl Van Vechten (reprinted by permission also of A. P. Watt Ltd. as agent for the Estate of R. S. Hichens). From the General Research Division: Excerpt from Henri Pène du Bois, *Four Private Libraries of New York* (Duprat & Co., 1892). From the Science and Technology Research Center: Excerpt from Catherine E. Beecher and Harriet Beecher Stowe, *Principles of Domestic Science* (J. B. Ford, 1870).

Putnam Publishing Group: Recipe for "Marzipan Potatoes." Reprinted by permission of the Putnam Publishing Group from *The Russian Tea Room Cookbook* by Faith Stewart-Gordon and Nika Hazelton. Copyright © 1981 by Faith Stewart-Gordon and Nika Hazelton.

T. B. Harms Company: "All in Fun," written by Jerome Kern and Oscar Hammerstein II. Copyright © 1939 T. B. Harms Company. Copyright renewed (c/o The Welk Music Group, Santa Monica, California 90401). International copyright secured. All rights reserved. Used by permission.

The New York Times: From *The World of New York Magazine*, November 4, 1985, and from *The New York Times* (dates as indicated). Copyright © 1976, 1980, 1981, 1982, 1983, 1984, 1985 by The New York Times Company. Reprinted by permission. All rights reserved.